DATE DUE

PITT SERIES IN POLICY AND INSTITUTIONAL STUDIES

RICHARD W. COTTAM

# Iran and the United States

## A COLD WAR CASE STUDY

University of Pittsburgh Press

Published by the University of Pittsburgh Press, Pittsburgh, Pa. 15260
Copyright © 1988, University of Pittsburgh Press
Feffer and Simons, Inc., London
Manufactured in the United States of America


Library of Congress Cataloging in Publication Data

Cottam, Richard W.
    Iran and the United States.

    (Pitt series in policy and institutional studies)
    Bibliography: p. 275.
    Includes index.
    1. United States—Relations—Iran.   2. Iran—
Relations—United States.   I. Title.   II. Series.
E183.8.I7C68   1988         303.4'8273'055        88-1340
ISBN 0-8229-3588-0
ISBN 0-8229-5407-9 (pbk.)

# CONTENTS

*Iran and the United States*

# 1

## *INTRODUCTION*

In the last days before the culmination of the Iranian revolution, electricity workers who had joined the revolution turned off the lights in Tehran each evening. Then from rooftops throughout the city came the chant "God is great." But there was as well another chant, a counter theme, "Death to America." The same slogan could be read on virtually every wall in every city in Iran. The Iranian revolution was quite possibly the most popular revolution in human history. Why should such a revolution in Iran, a country many thousands of miles from the United States, erupt in a spirit of hatred for America? And why should that hatred be so enduring that years after revolutionary victory Iranian crowds continued to chant "Death to America"? The question is particularly perplexing because as recently as the early 1950s the United States was viewed broadly in Iran as the one Western state whose government and people really were sincere advocates of the rights of freedom, independence, and dignity for Iran. Indeed, in 1951 when another Iranian government insisting on full sovereign independence for Iran came into power, it looked to the United States as its protector against an almost inevitable British and/or Russian effort to overthrow it.

Somehow in a little more than one generation, American policy toward Iran had succeeded in replacing what was probably unreasonably strong good will toward the United States with unreasonably strong resentment. The American moment in Iran was of short duration, but it evoked an intensity of feeling that for most Americans is simply mystifying. What was the nature of the Iranian-American relationship and how could that relationship generate feelings of such extraordinary intensity? And now that the American moment in Iran has ended, what conclusions can be drawn regarding the impact on Iranian history of that brief but intense encounter? These are the major questions this study addresses.

3

*The Nature of the Relationship*

Anyone seeking perspective on the historical relations of two peoples would be well advised to look carefully at the terminology the two peoples have used to describe each other and their purposes in the relationship. Particularly revealing are the metaphors used. Metaphors are likely to capture the essence of the relationships as seen by contemporaries. Terminology suggests image of self and the other, and it is this image that defines the situation. For Americans concerned with Iran and other "Third World" countries in the post–World War II era, the descriptors that easily occurred were "developing" and "emerging." The task of the United States was to help Iranians in the process of "modernizing" and "nation-building." The impression is of a youthful, even childlike, people moving inexorably toward an adulthood quite similar to our own. We are the model, the end state of the progression. In rapidly increasing numbers, Iranians were "awakening" and becoming "politically aware," that is, aware of our "advanced" culture and of the world as we see it. They were emerging from a "traditional" society of which we, for our part, need not be aware.

One description of the U.S. task in the Third World that was never used by Americans is "civilizing mission." That was the terminology of the era of Rudyard Kipling, an era in which the term "imperial" evoked pride. It was an era in which the term "lower race" could be used without embarrassment. Few Americans saw any resemblance between their government's policy and that of the British empire. But Iranians looking at the past two centuries of their long history have difficulty distinguishing between the policies of nineteenth-century Russia and Britain and those of the late twentieth-century Soviet Union and the United States. In both centuries there were Iranians who did indeed see an imperial power as a model and who welcomed and even solicited the imperial involvement. Other Iranians in both centuries bitterly resented this external involvement in their affairs and firmly rejected the model as gratuitously and, in their view, arrogantly advanced. For these Iranians, "nation-building" is a transparent euphemism for "civilizing mission" and the twentieth-century American, like the nineteenth-century Briton, has assumed a paternal role toward an Iranian society that both described as "immature."

Regardless of U.S. and European imagery, Iranians, like the Chinese, Egyptians, and Greeks, have a very long recorded history. And that history includes extended periods of external domination. There were centuries of domination by Greeks, Arabs, and Turco-Mongols, each with their own peculiar characteristics. Seen in this perspective, the Khomeini period may well mark the end of a fourth extended period of external domination—a period that reasonably can be described as European. Just as in the previous eras of external domination, strong domestic forces have been developing in this period seeking to regain for Iranians control over their own destiny. The Tobacco Rebellion of 1891–1892, the 1906 revolution, and the two and a half years of Musaddiq's premiership, 1951–1953, were of this genre, as was the revolution of 1979. The two periods of the Pahlavi dictatorship, in contrast, were more like efforts at accommodation. This too is a common historical pattern in Iran: some substantial sovereignty exercised within the context of an imperial overlay. The Iranians who supported the revolution of 1979 saw the United States as simply the last in a long succession of external powers that had exercised imperial control over Iran. There was extreme disappointment and bitterness in that judgment because Americans, through much of the period of European domination in Iran, had seemed to sympathize with the Iranian yearning for real independence and dignity. Yet by 1979 the United States had become the preeminent imperial presence in Iran and the primary external target of the revolution.

It could hardly be expected that the American public and those Americans intimately involved in policy toward Iran could see their involvement in such perspective. U.S. policy toward Iran in the few years of intense involvement was derivative. It was first the product of the effort to defeat Nazi Germany and then of the effort to contain a Soviet Union perceived to have historical and ideological interests in controlling Iran. Americans saw in Iran a weak and backward state that must somehow be persuaded to make the effort to defend itself. Seeing the American role in Iran as "modernizing" and "nation-building," Americans projected a benevolent paternalism in their self-image. However, because of a historical rejection of imperialism, they could not admit this even to themselves. Thus when anger and hatred toward the United States on the part of the Iranian mass public became undeniable during the hostage crisis, the American response was one of bewilderment and indignation. "After all we have done for them" was a common lament.

## The European-American Period in Iran

The period of European influence in Iran was by most standards a prolonged one, spanning as it did two centuries. But Iranian recorded history is one of the world's longest[1] and it embraces eras of great imperial adventures by Iran and four eras of prolonged external domination. Each of the four had a unique motivation and the historical impact on Iran varied accordingly. The Hellenic era, which began with the conquest of Iran by Alexander the Great around 330 B.C., was driven to a remarkable degree by cultural messianism.[2] The Hellenes had their own civilizing mission many centuries before the British appeared on the scene. There are, in fact, strong resemblances between the European and Hellenic imperial eras in Iran. The Europeans shared with the Hellenes a contempt for traditional Iranian culture—a contempt the Europeanized Iranian shared, as the Hellenized Iranian probably did many centuries earlier. European motives rested far less on a desire to spread what they saw as a superior culture than the Hellenes; still, the parallels are close. The Iranians' cultural rejection of Hellenized Parthia parallels the Khomeini regime's fierce condemnation of the secular materialism that it sees as the European cultural legacy in Iran.[3]

Neither the Arabs, whose conquest of Iran for Islam was completed in A.D. 650, nor the Turco-Mongols whose invasions occurred over a period of six centuries beginning with the tenth century, viewed Iranian culture with such contempt.[4] The Arabs were motivated by religious messianism and the Turco-Mongols by the pressures of overpopulation.[5] Each produced a profound and lasting impact on Iran, the Arabs bringing their religion and the Turco-Mongols altering significantly the demographic composition of the country. But both became integrated comfortably into the Iranian culture. The largest Turki-speaking minority in Iran, the Azerbaijanis, indeed have become, along with Farsi-speaking elements, part of the ethnic core of the Iranian nation. Because of this history of cultural acceptance and integration, there has been little tendency among Iranians to equate these early eras of external influence of domination with the European era.

The Europeans concerned themselves with Iran for three important reasons. There was first an interest in trade. Before the discovery of oil, commercial elements were concerned with Iran primarily because of its geographical position: the land route from West to East crossed Iran. Second their presence in Iran became a matter of national prestige. Trade and other economic objectives were surely the most important initial determinants of European involvement in the non-European world. But no pattern is more clear than that of a rapid association of prestige and economic interests. Similarly, the third primary determinant of European expansionism in this era was the natural association of the first two: to defend one's expanding interests from one's European competitors. The three determinants were hence mutually reinforcing.[6]

There were other motives, to be sure. But they were of lesser importance. The "civilizing mission," for example, was a manifestation of cultural messianism that was surely a primary determinant of Hellenic expansion. And indeed there were individual Europeans who were dedicated to the "civilizing" task in Iran. But their policy impact was relatively minor. Cultural messianism in the European period, unlike the Hellenic, was confined largely to the level of symbolic expression, more the wrappings in which imperialism was clothed than as an important determinant of that imperialism. Similarly, the interest in bringing Christianity to the infidels was of intense concern to a few missionaries, but never seems to have given much definition to state motivation. Religious messianism, so important to the Arabs, was of little real interest to the Europeans. And no point can be made with more assurance in this study of Iran than that U.S. and European interest in bringing their ideology to this area was at the level of rationalization only.

The European period for Iran and for much of what we now call the Third World, therefore, began as a consequence of perceived opportunities for commercial gain on the part of Europeans, who were a few generations ahead of Asians in technological advances, and in developing the economic and governmental base for taking advantage of these opportunities. But it evolved quickly into prestige rivalry and a need to defend economic interests. It was made possible because of technological developments in Europe and the United States and because of the multigenerational lead of the Europeans in mass participation in politics. But this historic imbalance is disappearing today and with it the advantage of the Europeans. Yet the memory of European domination is so strong, both in Europe and the non-European world, that relational patterns that are no longer valid, given changed circumstances, still persist.

The period of intense U.S. involvement in Iran extends from 1941 to 1979, with American influence at a level that was not far removed from the colonial during the 1953–1963 decade. Indeed, many Iranians saw their position as fully colonial. This view could not have been in sharper contrast with the American view. U.S. awareness of American intervention in the domestic affairs of Iran was really limited to a tiny group of officials whose policy concerns were with Iran. Even the most attentive elements of the U.S. public were unaware of that role.

The asymmetry between the Iranian and U.S. public views was most dramatically apparent at the time of the hostage crisis. Americans could not comprehend the display of rage and hatred directed at them for no apparent reason. It seemed to be a form of madness, a lunatic interval. Iranians, for their part, saw the brief U.S. involvement in their nation's affairs as another chapter in the long history of European domination in Iran. It was exceptional only in that Iranians had once had high hopes that the United States, alone among the Western powers, might be a disinterested protector of Iranian freedom and dignity. These hopes were dashed in 1953. By 1978, the Iranian view was that America was the number one imperial power in the world. The revolution, climaxing in early 1979, was directed against imperial control of Iran and hence necessarily was against the United States.

Americans, of course, were as unaware of the exceptional benevolence of the Iranian view of their country over the first half of the twentieth century as they were of the exceptional malevolence of that view during the third quarter of the century. Indeed, prior to the taking of hostages, Americans were essentially unconcerned with Iranian attitudes toward the United States and with the genesis of those attitudes. In self-image, Americans, whose nation was born out of a struggle with imperial Britain, believed that they remained true to the principles of national self-determination. Occasionally, divergences from those principles have been too blatant to deny, but still the anti-imperial self-image persists.

Iranian judgments of America, on the other hand, varied with the course of U.S. interaction with European imperialism in Iran. The early popularity of the United States in Iran was a consequence of American support—in part inadvertent and in part fully conscious—for Iranian efforts to throw off the European imperial yoke. Not surprisingly, American actions in this direction associate with an era, pre–World War II, when official U.S. interest in Iran was low and American public interest entirely lacking. When, after World War II, the United States began to assume the role of protector of the West, American policy began to follow patterns that closely resembled the patterns of imperialism with which Iranians were only too familiar.

## A Cold War Case Study

Intense U.S. involvement in Iranian affairs occurred at the height of the cold war in which Iran was a major battleground. A history of American-Iranian relations in these years must be therefore a case study of cold war behavior.

U.S. and European discussions of strategy in the cold war era are overwhelmingly concerned with nuclear weapons as a factor in deterring perceived Soviet aggression.[7] Some attention is paid to subnuclear violence, limited warfare, and even insurgency and counterinsurgency.[8] But only a tiny proportion of the literature is concerned with what future historians may well conclude was the central battlefield of the cold war, the battle for preeminent influence in the political affairs of strategically important Third World states.[9] As one of the most strategically vital of these states, if not the most vital, Iran could not avoid being the focus of intense interest on the part of both the United States and the Soviet Union.

The explanation for the competitive involvement of the superpowers in the domestic affairs of Third World states is rooted in the weapons system revolution. The nineteenth century and first half of the twentieth can be described as the era of total war. In this era governments were able to mobilize popular support and an unprecedented proportion of resources to confront violently a comparably mobilized adversary. With the development of nuclear weapons, however, the era of total war, at least for nuclear states, had come to an end. Now, it was understood, total war involving the use of nuclear weaponry would destroy all belligerents and much of the rest of the world as well. Nuclear warfare as conscious policy became an unacceptable option, as did any kind of conventional warfare that had a serious potential of escalating to the nuclear level.

The distrust and hostility that characterize Soviet-U.S. relations in this nuclear era is sufficiently high that in the prenuclear era it likely would have led to "total war." Denied the outlet of resolution of this intense conflict by resorting to direct violent confrontation, however, the battle between the two camps has been conducted at levels that do not involve the danger of uncontrolled escalation. Much academic and public attention has focused on a level of violent confrontation referred to as "proxy wars" in which the two competitors give assistance to client states involved in violent confrontation.[10] In such encounters, the hidden rule of the game is that the superpower mentor will accept the defeat of a client rather than to indulge in dangerous escalation of conflict. But encounters such as those in Korea, in Vietnam, and between India and Pakistan, the Arab states and Israel, were exceptional. For the most part, the Soviet-American battle took the form of gaining preeminent influence in third states and denying influence to the other. Europe being quickly polarized, the United States and the Soviet Union turned their attention to the Third World, in particular the part of the Third World adjacent to or near the Soviet Union. Since this was an area in which Western influence had been preeminent before World War II, the Americans quickly found themselves in the position of defending a status quo that reflected the success of Western European states in the imperial era. The Soviets meanwhile found themselves the natural ally of those forces seeking to overturn that status quo. For American policymakers, the danger was seen as Soviet subversion. The beneficiaries of the status quo, usually traditional authoritarian regimes, were described as "pro-West." Opponents of the status quo, often liberal and almost always militantly anti-imperialist, were described as "anti-West." The presumption of this terminology was that the pro-Western elements accepted the values of the "free world" and that the anti-Western elements were Marxists. But only on rare occasions was this actually the case. If any generalizable pattern developed, the Americans allied themselves with local leaders who favored slow, tightly controlled change and the Soviets with those who favored rapid change.

It is within this context that the asymmetry between U.S. and Iranian public attitudes developed. For Americans, involvement in Iran was only a small aspect of a sudden worldwide involvement. The history of Iran, like the history of almost the entire non-European world, was unknown to Americans except for those brief episodes such as the war between Persia and Athens, when Iran was in conflict with people of interest to Europeans. In the cold war era, Iran was one of many obscure states whose security interests Americans believed coincided with those of the United States. The common objective was to contain the Soviet Union and in so doing to permit states such as Iran to remain part of the free world.

For Iranians the post–World War II era was a continuation of a losing struggle against European imperialism. U.S. influence rose as British influence declined and the Russians were still present now in the form of the Soviet Union. But these were surface changes. Iran was, as it had been for a century and a half, the battleground of two imperial powers. To be sure, there was some shifting of roles. Now, in contrast to a half-century earlier, the Russians were the mentors of the more progressive forces. The Anglo-Americans were mentors of conservative forces. However, for the most part the imperial powers behaved in patterns that were entirely familiar to Iranians. U.S. predominance in the imperial conflict paralleled British predominance of previous generations. And for those Iranians who could not reconcile themselves to the fate of imperial domination, it was the United States that was the primary target, no longer the British. As Iranians had learned long before, the ideology of the Western democracies was not for export. The Russians took their ideology more seriously, but Iranian observers noted that the Soviet Marxists had no difficulty cooperating closely with Iranians, including the shah, who evinced no attraction to Marxism.

The Iranian view is especially understandable because of the style of imperial involvement in Iran throughout the European period of dominance. Like Thailand, Iran was never formally incorporated into someone's empire in this period. This anomaly was a product of the peculiarities of Iran's strategic position at the meeting point of the British and Russian empires. Neither imperial government could bring Iran into its empire without risking a major conflict. For both governments, the potential price was too high. Yet, at the same time, each government feared its rival would attempt to gain indirect control of Iran. Thus, just as in the cold war, there developed a struggle for preeminent influence both in Iran's economy and its politics. Patterns of intervention developed that were repeated in all their essentials during the later Soviet-American cold war rivalry. Iranian leaders quickly saw the potential in playing with the competing ambitions of the two governments, for profit and for maintaining a tenuous independence from both. Furthermore, each government wrapped its interventionist policy in attractive symbols and indeed appeared to see its policy as entirely benign and in Iran's interest. Thus for generations Iran had to deal with the fact of external involvement in its internal affairs.

### Rapid Change in Iran

But if the interventionist patterns of the primary external power remained essentially unchanged, internal conditions in Iran did not. The tempo of change along a number of dimensions increased unevenly but dramatically. European economic penetration of Iran was a major catalyst for rapid change, though this was surely never the Europeans' conscious intent. On the contrary, European political intervention, in retrospect, appears to have been designed to counter the force of change they had helped to generate in other ways.

Contact with an industrializing Europe that wished to import raw materials from Iran and export finished goods to Iran was highly disruptive of Iran's traditional economy. Iranian merchants sought to adapt to European trading practices and bitterly resented the concessions granted to Europeans. Iranian landowners and entrepreneurs began to see the opportunities in making agriculture and the production of raw materials more commercially lucrative. They were joined in their rejection of Iran's traditional system by religious intellectuals who sought to bring new vitality to Islam so that it could withstand the inroads of the Christian imperialists. Secular intellectuals looked to the political values incorporated in European regimes with both envy and resentment for the European's contempt for the Iranian nation.

Once initiated, this process of change gained momentum. As later events would demonstrate, the process of change could be temporarily slowed in one or several areas, but over time it proceeded in geometric progression. However, internal and external forces did influence the direction of change in at least some respects. Indeed, external interventions in Iran—European and then American—have had a profound impact on the direction of Iranian development.

Among the elements of change, three are of central sociopolitical importance. The first has been described, particularly in discussions of American developmental politics, as a "political awakening" or the coming of "political awareness."[11] This terminology tells at least as much about those who coined and used it as it does about their subjects. What it refers to is an observed growing comprehension on the part of "developing" peoples of world society as seen by observers in Europe and the United States. Implicit in the terminology is an assumption that such awareness would be coupled with acceptance—that the newly aware would awaken to the desirability and attainability of Western political culture.

Of course, many Iranians were already aware of Western political culture, but rejected it. U.S. observers assumed them to be individuals who either stood to lose by the passing of traditional society or were so conservative or reactionary as to oppose change or to favor a return to a previous period. Thus the Khomeini phenomenon was explained as a consequence of the shah's having moved too quickly for the ignorant, barely aware Iranian to be able to follow his lead. In fact, however, even though Khomeini was a master manipulator of traditional religious symbols and was able to convince many of his countrymen that he was returning them to a previous era when God's laws were the basis of society, he changed Iranian political and social norms at a pace that can only be described as revolutionary.

Those who looked at this dimension of change had assumed a unidirectional movement toward the Western model.[12] The Khomeini phenomenon is strong evidence that this assumption was wrong. But if this manifestation of change is described not in terms of seeing a new model and moving inexorably to embrace it, but rather in terms of a growing willingness to play an active role in the political process, it may be one of the most important aspects of political change in Iran. Mass politics exists when the level of participation approaches the universal. Iran and the entire Third World have moved in this direction; it is unlikely that any external power could reverse the momentum.

A second kind of change concerns the largest politically relevant community with which an individual identifies intensely. In the early stages of the change process in the Third World, this community is likely to be a parochial one—the extended family or clan. Soon, however, a strong trend develops toward intense identification with a larger community that may be at base ethnic, territorial, racial, or religious—or any combination of these four. A similar trend developed in Europe in the nineteenth century and gave rise to behavior that came to be described as nationalism. Western analysts assumed that a parallel kind of nationalism would appear in Iran and other Third World states and that this nationalism was an inevitable aspect of the development process. Indeed, Americans and Europeans often described the policy of assisting Third World peoples as one of "nation-building." Nationalism, ethnic-based and closely associated with secularism on the European model, did become a major factor in the change occurring in Iran. But the Khomeini phenomenon suggests there is no inevitability here either. Khomeini saw secular nationalists in Iran as acculturated individuals seeking pathetically to become Europeanized. The large community focus for him was the *ummah,* the Islamic community, which is multiethnic, multinational, and multiracial.

It is the third dimension of change that is most affected by external forces. As change occurs in the first and second stages, change in the governing elite is certain to follow. But there is no inevitability here either as to the rate or direction of change. The story that will unfold in the following chapters will describe change in the Iranian governing elite that is an accommodation to both internal and external forces. It was the fate of Iran that the European era of Iranian history coincided with a period of profound internal change. And the United States' moment of intense concern with Iran was associated with the period of most rapid change. Since external involvement in the Iranian political process characterized this period from beginning to end, the external influence on Iranian change patterns has been on many occasions decisively important.

The importance of the external factor in determining the direction of change in Iran is consistently underestimated by Western observers. But it is overestimated, often wildly so, by Iranians. Many exiles from the Khomeini regime, for example, believed that Khomeini's coming into power in Iran was a consequence of American actions. In one sense they were not entirely wrong. U.S. policy in Iran in the 1953–1978 period helped set the stage for Khomeini's movement. But these Iranian exiles believed Khomeini's coming to power was part of an explicit and very clever U.S. strategy designed to contain the Soviet Union. Here they clearly were wrong. The case will be made in this study that neither the United States, the Soviet Union, nor the concerned European states have ever had an explicit strategy for dealing with Iran, only ad hoc tactical schemes. But these ad hoc schemes have tended to follow a consistent pattern, and it is therefore a fairly easy task to describe their overall impact on Iranian sociopolitical development. Seen from this perspective, external interventions in the cold war resembled closely those of the late nineteenth and early twentieth centuries. The logic of the situation, in other words, apparently differed very little for the avowedly imperialistic British and the Americans who took great pains to dissociate themselves from earlier imperialism. The reasons for this parallelism should become clear as the case unfolds.

However, the process of rapid change in Iran along the three dimensions outlined above is approaching its conclusion. The Iranian revolution of 1979 gave clear evidence that Iran has now entered the era of mass politics. In the course of a century, participation in politics has broadened from that of a tiny traditional elite to that of nearly the entire population. External intervention in the form it took before the mass politics period is no longer possible. Although many Iranians have yet to recognize the fact, Iran is as capable of controlling its own destiny as are so-called developed states of comparable capability. Furthermore, this is true of much of the Third World, and its implications for international politics are profound. Competitive interference in the affairs of Third World countries can no longer be the central characteristic of the Soviet-American cold war.

## Evaluating the American Impact on Iran

The purpose of this book is to describe and to evaluate the impact of U.S. policy on Iran. Given Iran's long history, the few decades of preeminent American influence, one would think, should appear momentary and of quickly passing importance. In fact, however, those few decades coincided with the most critical moment in a period of profound change in Iran. The case will be made that the impact of U.S. policy was to alter in major ways the direction of this change. In other words, U.S. policy has changed in important respects the course of Iranian history.

In contrasting Western and Iranian analyses of the internal politics of Iran, nothing is more apparent than the differing emphases placed on the external factor. Western analysts, as noted above, are inclined to pay little attention to that factor. Iranian analysts, particularly those not trained in Western institutions, are apt to see the role of external powers as approximating a conspiratorial orchestration of Iranian political developments. My argument will be close to that of the Iranian analysts in terms of the importance of the external factor, but I do not accept the assumption of external manipulation of Iranian politics. I will argue that U.S. policy has been largely uninformed and almost totally lacking in long-term strategy. The impact on Iran, therefore, has been inadvertent. To be sure, Europeans and Americans in Iran have indeed on many occasions resorted to conspiratorial acts that have influenced critical political developments. However, in every case, these conspiratorial interventions were accompanied by a profound innocence manifested in a lack of awareness of the hidden impact of the interventions. This lack of awareness in turn was rooted in an essentially contemptuous view of Iranian political culture as persistently "immature." Presumably, any intervention by the representatives of "mature" societies would assist in the "growth" process.

Judgments of the motives underlying American involvement in Iranian affairs in the post–World War II period also vary sharply. Most common among Iranians is a conclusion that the United States, as the leader of the capitalist world, sees its interests largely in terms of the multinational corporations. Others see U.S. concern as more narrowly focused on oil and, through the 1960s, on a rivalry with the British regarding oil. The conclusion here is that although American motives regarding Iran is a mix of several interests, including certainly economic interests, a primary motivation has been to defend the West against a perceived threat from the Soviet Union. The accompanying situational view is that the Soviets seek to gain control of strategically vital Iran and are most likely to make the effort to do so through subversion. From the time American policy in Iran crystallized in the early 1950s, the goal has been to encourage and to strengthen an Iranian regime that is aware of and capable of resisting this alleged Soviet purpose. Much of this study will consist of fleshing out and developing this point.

In the view of successive U.S. administrations, Iran was the great "strategic prize" of the region and U.S. policy was directed toward keeping Iran on the American side and to avoid losing it. Identifying patterns of U.S. policy and of the impact of that policy on Iran is a central objective of this book. Iran of course is a unique case in many respects. But the patterns that will be identified are cold war–associated patterns and can be seen in U.S. policy toward much of the Third World. The fact that U.S. policymakers inadvertently altered the course of Iranian history is likewise characteristic of the impact of U.S. policy throughout the Third World. Developments inside Iran were seen in terms of a world view that was instructed by the supposed all-consuming need to defeat Soviet aggression. Iranian politicians who appeared to be allies in this purpose were viewed in strongly benevolent terms. Those who appeared to threaten this purpose, it follows, were viewed as serving Soviet objectives. I will flesh out this stereotypical cold-war view of reality as it has been applied to Iran. Here too the resemblance to the U.S. view of other Third World peoples is striking.

The social and political patterns inside Iran that were influenced by U.S. policy will be described in terms of the three foci of rapid change in Iran outlined above. My development of the case, both with regard to American foreign policy and Iranian sociopolitical change, will necessarily be parsimonious. The treatment of American policy toward Iran and of social, political, and economic change in Iran cannot be comprehensive. Still, I will attempt to provide an analytic base for explaining both the genesis and the course of the Iranian revolution and to make some preliminary assessment of the extent to which the course of that revolution was a consequence of U.S. policy.

The virtual elimination of the American presence in Iran after the revolution does not signify the elimination of U.S. influence in Iranian internal developments and external policies. A central and easily identified pattern in Iran continues to be a view of reality in which a hidden American hand is exceptionally able to dictate developments inside the country. That view is gradually losing credibility, but it is doing so differentially. Iranians in exile and a surprising proportion of Iranians involved in the affairs of the Islamic Republic persist in seeing a U.S. capability that is only slightly diminished by the United States' expulsion from Iran. Exiles appeal daily to U.S. officials to overturn a despised regime which, they argue, is highly inimical to American interests in the region. Iranian officials fear that a restoration of formal relations between the two governments will lead to a new and quite possibly successful effort to execute a coup d'état. Furthermore, they believe with apparent sincerity that U.S. capability is sufficient to inaugurate and orchestrate the Iraqi invasion of Iran, to orchestrate OPEC economic policies designed to deprive Iran of the revenues needed for defense, to sponsor the Kurdish rebellion in Iran, and to carry out acts of terror inside Iran. U.S. policy, or rather the persistent illusion of U.S. policy, thus strangely continues to have a major impact on Iranian affairs. Only now that impact is entirely inadvertent.

However, this continuing U.S. influence in Iran is certain to dissipate over time as expectations based on it fail to be realized. The old basis of U.S. influence in Iran was destroyed along with the regime of the late shah. Future influence, one can be sure, will rest on very different foundations. It is likely to resemble structurally the influence of American policy in dealing with middle-level European states.

The chapters that follow will first describe in chronological order the sociopolitical picture inside Iran and the trends associated with it of concern to the United States and other external actors. Then American policy toward Iran will be outlined. Finally, I will analyze the impact of that policy and that of other external powers on sociopolitical trends within Iran.

# 2

## THE ILLUSION OF SYMPATHY: POLICY BEFORE WORLD WAR II

The Iran the Europeans encountered in the eighteenth and nineteenth centuries was, in today's terminology, a traditional system. A traditional system is by definition stable and resistant to change. It rests on a habitual acceptance of rules and customs by the mass of the population; for those who accept their station in life and who live in accordance with a long and well-established routine, confrontations with authority are likely to be infrequent and minor. Of course, conflict — even serious conflict — occurs in such a system, but it is likely to center on the efforts of individuals and groups to achieve greater influence and material rewards within the established elite structure. Even if these efforts are successful, they are likely to follow well-established conflict patterns that will not affect seriously the overall functioning of the system. The system is threatened only when the rules and customs that give definition to it are seriously challenged.

The irony of the European period of Iran's history is that the Europeans by their actions and by their example induced forces that would challenge and ultimately overturn the traditional system. Yet throughout the period, the strategy of the Europeans was to attempt to control and slow down the process of change and to preserve as much as possible of the traditional system.

Traditional nineteenth-century Iran was pre–mass politics and pre-national. It is fairly described as authoritarian. But its authoritarianism maintained control with remarkably little reliance on coercion. Given Iran's geography and ethnic mix, the system tended to be decentralized, and administrative control from Tehran gave the appearance of a casual simplicity that was highly misleading. In fact, successful administrative control of Iran required an intimate understanding of a web of competing group and personal interests and the ability to manipulate these competing interests with finesse. Ad-

19

ministrative incompetence at the center was quickly reflected in loss of control in provincial and tribal areas. As a consequence, individual authority was always fragile at base, and social mobility, upward and downward, was far greater than traditional Europe had experienced.

The basis for individual power in this system was primarily landholding. Most of Iran was arid, and agricultural production depended on elaborate and difficult-to-maintain irrigation systems. Commonly this consisted of underground canals in which water flowed to villages, often for many miles, from water tables in nearby mountains. Because maintaining such a system required cooperation and organization, landownership in Iran reflected this requirement. Landowners typically owned the villages and provided the organization for maintaining the irrigation system and the livestock needed for cultivation. A few landowners owned hundreds of villages, while others at the opposite end of the power spectrum shared in the ownership of a single village. But the landowners did not constitute a class comparable to the feudal nobility of Western Europe. Landholding families, even the greatest of them, rarely had held that status for more than a few generations. The difficulty of exercising control over so large, so diverse, and so lightly populated an area was reflected in frequent reversals of authority, particularly in provincial sections. Landowners typically acquired their holdings through the beneficence of a shah or provincial leader whom they had helped to achieve or to retain power. As a consequence, the landowners did not develop the cohesion of a long-established feudal class and proved far less of an obstacle to rapid change than might have been expected.

For the fifth or so of the population that was nomadic, the basis for power was authority within the tribes. The tribe in traditional Iran was generally not an identity unit. Rather, the tribe was a complex of extended families and clans, and authority rested on an elaborate alliance system.[1] The organization of nomadic tribes necessary for the great semiannual migrations made for natural paramilitary units. These could constitute a threat to a central authority, but also provided an opportunity for them. Tribal units were the most natural and least costly coercive instruments available to the central government and, until radical change gained momentum, were largely sufficient for the government's coercive control purposes. Thus the central government developed a generally satisfactory, but always somewhat dangerous, modus vivendi with the tribes. It contracted for the services of warrior contingents from tribes with which it had good relations. But in order to maintain control over these tribes, it had to have an accurate understanding of the operating tribal alliance systems and had to be able to intervene in that system to prevent the development of dangerously strong tribal authority. Weakness or incompetence at the center commonly meant a loss of control over the tribes.

A third concentration of power in traditional Iran was found within the clergy. But the clergy, even less than the landowners and tribal leaders, did not constitute a unified force. They were highly diverse in both role and philosophy. Thanks to the institution of the *waqf* (the endowment of property as a religious duty), the church amassed great landholdings. But the clerical administrators of these estates tended to share the views of the landowners. Other clerics were closely associated with the guild leadership of the town and city bazaars and helped legitimize and perpetuate the guild system — a mainstay of traditional Iran. But religious scholars were the politically most significant element of the intelligentsia in traditional Iran and the one group that frequently challenged the normative base of the system. When the change process began that was ultimately to bring down the old system, religious intellectuals were major contributors. Many religious intellectuals believed that the Qoran required of them an activist role in furnishing guidance and even direction in political as well as social and legal affairs.[2]

At the apex of the traditional elite structure stood the royal court, including the shah, his family, leading government officials, and the bureaucracy.[3] The administration of central power appeared at the same time casual and inefficient, capricious, corrupt, and on occasion shockingly brutal. Aspirants to high position — for example, the governorship of a province — saw the position as a sure path to personal wealth and influence. But, even though some were most successful in these regards, their task was difficult. Lacking a strong coercive arm, they had to rely for success on skillful manipulation of the provincial elite power structure. This meant contending with individuals who had access to and influence in the power structure of the court in Tehran. On occasion, when an official's position was particularly secure, a dangerous and obstreperous subject could be dealt with brutally. But most commonly the mode of control was to play competing interests against one another. A heavy price could be paid for any serious miscalculation.

## The Appearance of a Counter Elite

That the traditional system in Iran worked, that it was able to resist major change, is best demonstrated by the size and quality of the coercive force the authorities relied on. It consisted mainly of barely controlled tribal contingents and a Russian-officered military force of low quality. Convulsions within the elite structure occurred rather frequently, but these affected individual fortunes, not the structure of the system. However, as the nineteenth century progressed, elements of fundamental change developed; by the end of the century, the signs were strong that the traditional system itself would be challenged. A counter elite was appearing that wanted far more than simply to replace the old elite. Its demands were for a change in the roles and the customs that gave definition to the old system.

The change can be viewed easily along the three dimensions outlined in the introduction. There were first of all three groups that were beginning to insist on an active role in the political process of Iran. In each case, the example of the new political structure of Western Europe and the policy of European powers in Iran were the primary stimulants for the group activity.

The group most attracted to the emerging liberalism in Western Europe, particularly in France and England, was a developing secular intelligentsia. With a long intellectual history, Iranians have been, by any standard of measurement, among the most creative peoples in human history. Artistic, literary, scientific, and mathematical achievements are highly valued in Iran and intellectuality is a quality that attracts respect. Yet the intelligentsia, even though always strongly attracted to philosophy, had not played a significant role in politics in the traditional system. But in the nineteenth century many secular intellectuals were strongly attracted to the values that had taken root in Europe during the Enlightenment and were increasingly willing to adopt an activist role in bringing those values to Iran. Others, although they were few in these early days, were attracted to the ideas of Marx and other strands of socialist thought. Since direct contact with Europe was largely limited to those Iranians who had the means to travel, the activist secular intelligentsia included a disproportionate number of sons and daughters of the social elite.

The policies of the European powers toward Iran, particularly those of Russia and England, had a strongly negative impact on this intelligentsia. British and Russian involvement in Iranian internal affairs by the late nineteenth century was so extensive as to become an important force in the Iranian political process. Much of the intelligentsia was deeply resentful of this involvement and the implicitly contemptuous attitude of the Europeans toward Iran. By the end of the century this response was clearly nationalistic and indicated that this section of the intelligentsia now were intensely identified with the nation of Iran. Identity change, the second dimension of change, was now taking place; and nationalism in Iran was developing into a major determinant of Iranian behavior.[4]

This same pattern of positive attraction toward nationhood and negative resentment against Europe was seen in a second group that was moving toward political activism: the commercial community. On the positive side, progressive elements of this community saw in the European example a model for broadening their commercial horizons. Opportunities were presenting themselves for a much expanded trade with Europe, and the hold of the guilds, a mainstay of conservatism, was weakening. But Iranian merchants were troubled by and resentful of the economic concessions being extracted by the British and Russian ministers in Iran. It appeared increasingly that the Europeans could gain control of Iran's basic raw materials and its communication and transportation system. The commercial community thus was attracted to the economic liberalism they saw exemplified in British commercial attitudes, but repelled by the economic imperialism of the British and Russian governments. Hence their reaction was also increasingly nationalistic.

The third group to develop activist attitudes was the most progressive group of religious scholars. Activism on the part of religious leaders can be found throughout the history of Islam in Iran. But by the end of the nineteenth century, the number of proponents of activism among religious scholars was large and growing. An extraordinary individual who appeared in this period was Jamal ad-Din al Afghani, who played a major catalytic role in generating activist attitudes among religious scholars and leaders in Egypt and throughout the Ottoman Empire, Iran, and the Indian subcontinent.[5] Religious activists also saw both positive and negative features in European civilization. The changes occurring in Europe in technology, improved life styles, and mass political participation were looked on with favor. But the domination of Islam and the contemptuous attitudes of Christian imperialist governments was deeply resented. Identity change was occurring here too, but it was far less clear-cut than that seen in the other two groups. There was an unambiguous shift toward an intensified identity with the larger community of Moslems. Jamal ad-Din on occasion—there was much inconsistency to his thought—advocated a political pan-Islamic movement. But also much of the progressive leadership felt an intensifying attachment to the Iranian national community. Since both the Islamic and nationalist groups were victims of external imperialism, the responses dictated by both attachments were virtually identical in the prerevolutionary period; hence no real awareness developed of the differing patterns of identity change occurring among progressive religious leaders as compared with the other two groups. The beginnings of such an awareness did develop, however, shortly after the revolution.

### Revolution in Iran

The process of rapid change had begun. By the late nineteenth century there were already indications that the traditional system would be unable to adapt to its challenge. In 1891, protesting the grant of monopoly control of the tobacco trade to British commercial interests, religious leaders organized a boycott of tobacco that was astonishingly effective.[6] It led to a cancellation of the concession by the government and to a sudden realization that the government would have difficulty controlling a popular movement. The elements of the population that were preparing to challenge basic government policies and the normative elements of the social order— the secular intelligentsia, progressive merchants, and activist clerics— were well situated in the power structure. But in terms of numbers they were surely, even including uncomprehending followers, no more than 1 or 2 percent of the population. Yet in 1906 they launched a revolution that was initially successful and survived until 1912. How was it possible for a system that had survived so many serious shocks to succumb so easily to so minor a challenge?

The answer is not difficult. In the first place, the coercive forces available to the regime, tribal contingents and the Cossack unit, were well suited to the task of dealing with challenges to the authority from traditional rivals. But they were of little use in controlling urban crowds, especially when those crowds were led by sons or nephews of the ruling elite. Second, the regime could not buy off the challengers by granting them a share of power. This might work with a traditional challenger whose primary interest was increased material rewards and influence. But the revolutionaries were insisting on replacing the governing elite with individuals who rejected the old reward system. Third, the old order had no legitimacy with these challengers. Traditional leaders could not pose as defenders of the nation or of Islam, symbols the revolutionaries responded to, because they were viewed as having betrayed both communities. In short, the old regime could not come up with an effective strategy for controlling the revolutionary forces. When those forces succeeded in paralyzing the commerce and governance of Tehran, the government capitulated.

At almost no cost in blood, the revolutionaries succeeded in forcing the acceptance of a new regime, a constitutional democracy. The new constitution, modeled on the Belgian, retained the monarchy on a limited basis. It granted Iranians basic freedoms, including the right freely to elect a parliament. And there was suddenly a flourishing free press and a government responsive to the parliament. The constitution, reflecting the vital importance of religious leaders in the revolution, included a provision for a board of religious scholars who would have the task of assuring that legislation was in accord with the holy law.

But the new regime had its own control problems. Its appeal was limited to the three supporting elements described above plus their followers. And from the beginning it was the religious leaders who were best able to bring the beginnings of mass support for the regime. Outside Tehran and Tabriz, support for the revolution was thin. Since the new authorities were unable to satisfy the demands of tribal and provincial leaders, still thoroughly attached to the traditional order, rural areas passed out of their control. Tribal and provincial powerholders acted as they always had when control from Tehran was weak. But now they could not—as they could have done in the traditional era—move into Tehran and replace the ineffective leaders. Support for the regime in Tehran was much too strong for that. An impasse developed, and much of Iran could be described as in anarchy.

Yet in the next five years (1906–1911), a process of adaptation did develop. Political leadership passed into the hands of men who were able to live in both worlds. Anticonstitutional traditionalists, such as Mohammad Ali Shah, were rejected, as were intransigent revolutionaries. Progress was made in constructing internal security forces capable of maintaining order both in the cities and in the provinces. The support base of the regime was broadened by what amounted to an evangelical educational campaign. Both nationalism and enthusiasm for a reviving Islam deepened, and the proportion of the urban population that was politically active began to multiply.

Conceivably, a new stability could have developed and the change process could have resulted in an evolutionary transformation of the system. But there were serious problems. Traditional opponents were both numerous and capable of insisting on virtual autonomy in their areas of influence. Tensions also developed among revolutionaries. One particularly ominous and — as events ultimately would demonstrate — potentially fatal threat to the new order appeared in the challenge of Sheikh Fazlullah Nuri to the revolution. A respected scholar and early supporter of the revolution, Fazlullah Nuri saw in the secular nationalism and liberalism of the revolutionary regime a fundamental challenge to the kind of Islamic society he saw ordained in the Qoran. Executed as a traitor to the revolution in 1909, Fazlullah Nuri nevertheless personified the fundamental rejection by a religious leader of the secular implications of the revolutionary ideology.

## The External Response

But the 1906 revolution did not fail because of its serious problems in establishing control, or because of the narrowness of its support base, or because of its internal contradictions — although any one of those factors might have sufficed. It failed because of intervention by Russia and England. This act inaugurated a pattern that was to persist until the Iranian revolution of 1979. Having by example and by their policies played a major role in stimulating basic change in Iran, the external powers intervened directly to alter the direction and to slow the pace of change. In so doing, they played a primary determining role in twentieth-century Iran's history.

European interest in Iran began to develop as the period of exploration and trade in the non-European world took shape. Private and official contacts became increasingly numerous in the sixteenth, seventeenth, eighteenth, and early nineteenth centuries. In these years intra-European imperial conflicts had expanded geographically to the point where Iran was perceived as of strategic importance. Russian expansion to the east and southeast took the form of a Russian manifest destiny to incorporate the territories along its oriental frontiers in a great land empire. That Iranians were in the path of this manifest destiny was made clear in 1722 and 1733 when Peter the Great incorporated temporarily the Caspian Sea and its littoral, including the Iranian provinces of Gilan and Mazanderan, in his empire.

British expansion had focused particularly on the great Indian subcontinent. British control of this territory was such that a so-called forward policy to the northwest seemed to its advocates essential if British interests in India were to be preserved. To the northwest of India lay the territories of Iran and Afghanistan. Thus the dynamics of two great imperialist forces led toward confrontation in Iran and Afghanistan.

Napoleon saw opportunities in the Anglo-Russian imperial rivalry in southern Asia. He played first with a scheme of cooperation with the Russians to invade British India. Then, having turned on the Russians, he explored an alliance with Iran against Russia. In both these endeavors, the British took energetic measures to keep the Iranians out of Napoleon's sphere and then to fortify the Iranian determination to resist Russia's expansion southward. However, by 1828 and the Treaty of Turkomanchai, the Russians established the borders of their empire in the Caucasus at the Aras River. Iran by this treaty gave up its ancient claims to Georgia and was compelled as well to accept extraterritoriality. By the 1880s the Russians had established control over the Turkish *khannate*s that were Iran's neighbors to the northeast. Any further movement of the Russians to the south now must be at the direct expense of Iran.

The British for their part were fearful of Russian designs on India and were determined to resist any Russian effort to establish control over Iran or Afghanistan. They saw Iran's plans in the nineteenth century to incorporate the Herat area of Afghanistan in Iran as Russian-instigated and actively and successfully opposed the Iranian design.

By the late nineteenth century a pattern had developed to Anglo-Russian rivalry in Iran.[7] Interest in incorporating Iran in either empire was not sufficiently intense for either imperial power to be willing to risk violent confrontation to achieve it. But neither was either power willing to see the other gain political or economic preeminence in Iran. Consequently, both governments entered a period of intense competition for political influence. The battle was primarily fought over commercial concessions, financing Iran's foreign debt, and constructing and maintaining Iran's transportation and communication infrastructure. To gain a competitive advantage, the Russians and British had to become adept at playing the game of traditional politics in Iran. They each made alliances with influential Iranians who came to be known as pro-Russian or pro-British. This offered to Iran's shahs and their ministers a major opportunity. They were in a position of playing the two powers against one another for personal profit and advantage—a strategy that came to be known as negative balance. This strategy gave the shah and his entourage optimal returns for granting concessions or favorable refinancing of the debt, but its long-term consequence was to generate an ever deeper involvement of the Russians and the British in Iran's economic, social, and political life. And as this involvement intensified, so did mutual Russian and British suspicions.

At the turn of the century, the British in particular were becoming aware of a threat from imperial Germany to the European balance of power. Rivalry with Russia over competing imperial interests in Iran, Afghanistan, and Tibet stood as an obstacle to what the British began to see as essential for their dealing with the German threat: an alliance with Russia. Therefore, as Iran moved toward revolution, Britain's number one interest in Iran was to bring stability to Anglo-Russian relations in Iran.[8]

But Iranians had become habituated to Anglo-Russian rivalry in Iran's internal affairs and, as the revolution approached, expectations were that the rivals would take opposed sides in this great affair. Not unreasonably, those advocating change, especially the secular intellectuals, believed the British would side with them and that the authoritarian Russians would oppose them. To be sure, the British had been the primary target of the tobacco boycott, but overall the pro-British Iranians were considered more progressive than the pro-Russians.

In fact, because British diplomatic correspondence for the period is published, the evidence is conclusive that Iranian expectations were far off in several respects. First, neither the British nor the Russians were aware of the strong social forces that were moving Iran toward revolution.[9] Second, when the revolution occurred, both the British and Russians saw some real hope in it. Both legations viewed the Iranian government as corrupt, indifferent to Iranian national interests, and hopelessly incompetent.[10] The revolutionaries seemed at first to be a substantial improvement on each of these counts. The Iranians, since they expected British support, made strong overtures to the British. Most spectacular evidence of their belief in British sympathy was to be seen in the 14,000 merchants camped out on the grounds of the British summer legation north of Tehran. The British in fact did advise the Iranian government to agree to the terms of the revolutionaries. But, completely counter to Iranian expectations, so did the Russians.[11]

## American Policy and Revolution in Iran

U.S. interests in nineteenth-century Iran were confined to two areas: the activities of American missionaries in Iran and the beginnings of Iranian-U.S. commercial relations. The Iranian foreign office was always alert to the possibility of enticing third countries into diplomatic and commercial activity in Iran that could be used to counter the British and Russians. But the U.S. envoys in their dispatches to Washington indicated a full understanding of this game. Both they and the Department of State agreed that the American role should remain minor and noninvolved.[12]

Still, American missionary activity in Iran was sufficiently extensive that incidents were certain to occur that would demand some serious U.S. diplomatic responses. Prior to the revolution, there were two incidents of a serious nature. The U.S. response tells much about how the American staff in Iran viewed that country. In 1890 the Nestorian Christian wife of an American missionary was murdered by an Armenian. The American legation was convinced that the murderer should be executed if the missionary community was to be safe from hostile native Christians. When the murderer was sentenced to life imprisonment instead, the suggestion was made to the American minister, Mr. Pratt, that he ask the British minister, Sir Henry Drummond Wolff, to intercede with the Iranian government. Pratt acknowledged that such an intercession would be successful, but he stated, "Still, from long and careful study of the situation, I am forced to conclude that when the representative of a disinterested power here applies to the envoy of one of the powers directly concerned in Persia's politics to officially support in forcing any particular measure upon the Shah's Government, he incurs the risk of placing himself in the very embarrassing position of being called upon to reciprocate in some future occasion in a manner which may not accord with the policy of neutrality his own government would desire him to preserve."[13]

In 1904 an American missionary, Benjamin Labaree, was murdered by four Kurds in the Azerbaijan city of Urumia. The U.S. legation took this episode much more seriously and, since a British subject was also killed, coordinated its activities with the British. The governor of the area, who had no security forces available to him and who no doubt retained some influence by participating in the complex local alliance system, did nothing. This outraged the American minister, who found it intolerable that the government had no security forces in the region. Indeed, his many dispatches to Washington on the subject made clear his total lack of understanding of how the traditional system in Iran functioned. He joined with his British counterpart to insist on the government's sending a large force to the area.[14] The case consumed American diplomacy for over two years and was clearly of greater interest to the United States than was the revolution in Iran. Ultimately there was success. The governor was dismissed and the culprits were extradited from Turkey and placed on trial. Just as Minister Pratt had predicted, American policy looked less like that of a disinterested neutral and more like that of a British ally.

Official U.S. interpretation of events in Iran also paralleled that of the British. There was a very low regard for establishment political activity. As one official noted in May 1904, "There is evidently in Persia at the present time a progressive and a reactionary party, but neither appears as yet to have inhaled the genuine spirit of patriotism, but on the contrary the ideas of both, I am afraid, are sadly adulterated with selfishness."[15] But there is also no sign that the Americans had any direct contact with the pro-change elements that were becoming assertive. Concerning the 1891 tobacco boycott, an event that was a major portent of things to come, there was surprise and mystification. "This affair has brought forth a power in the country that the oldest Orientalist and even the Persians themselves did not dream of, to wit, the extent of the power of the mullahs."[16]

As the 1906 revolution unfolded, the U.S. legation summarized its view of the situation.

In a despotism more like that of Cyrus and Xerxes than that of any government existing elsewhere today, a parliament seems to have risen from the ground.[17]

The impression is general among my colleagues and in the best informed circles that nothing substantial and permanent will grow out of this sudden movement for reform. Among the many reasons advanced in support of this opinion I may cite the following:

1. The great body of the Shah's subjects have no idea of the meaning of "constitutional government". . . .
2. The mass of the people are illiterate. . . .
3. There is no middle class. . . .
4. Outside the cities not one person in a thousand is a freeholder. . . .
5. History does not record a single instance of a successful constitutional government in a country where the Mussulman religion is the state religion: Islam seems to imply autocracy.
6. It is generally believed that the mullahs, or Mohammedan priests, who sided with the reformers or revolutionists in the recent agitation and whose influence gained the victory for that party, will soon return to their traditional support of autocratic ideas.

But then the minister concludes incongruously, "The further development of the struggle will naturally attract the interests and sympathy of the friends of liberty throughout the world."[18]

The U.S. response differed in no substantial degree from that of the British. Contempt for Islam, an inability to recognize the beginnings of a real public opinion, and—despite the role of the merchants in the revolution—an inability to see an assertive commercial middle class seemed to characterize the entire European diplomatic community. Individuals did know and understand the revolutionary elite. Edward Browne, the British Iranist, did his best to bring an awareness of the situation to his countrymen.[19] And some American missionaries understood and had some sympathy for the movement.[20] But official sympathy was momentary and without depth.

## External Intervention in the Revolution

That an early approval of the revolution by official Britons and Russians would soon be replaced by antagonism and cynical dismissal was, given Anglo-Russian relations in Iran, probably inevitable. The revolution quickly resulted in a loss of central control in provincial Iran. Chaos and turmoil followed. In 1906 both governments wanted to regularize Anglo-Russian relations, and internal chaos made maintaining a delicate balance difficult.

Both the British and the Russians looked for a formula that could restore some degree of stability to Iran. The Iranian revolutionaries were sure they knew what that formula would be. The notion was widely accepted that in prerevolutionary Iran there were progressive and reactionary parties—that Anglophile Iranians were likely to be progressive and those favoring Russia would be reactionary. This is much too neat a picture, but there was truth in it. Muzaffar ad-din Shah, who agreed to the revolutionary demands, died in 1906 and was succeeded by the virulently anticonstitutional Mohammad Ali Shah. A significant number of the new shah's entourage were considered friends of Russia and the view that Russia favored the overturn of the constitutional government was natural. Several of the best-known Anglophiles, by contrast, were willing to accommodate themselves to the new government and cooperate with it. Therefore, the conclusion was only to be expected that in Iran's internal struggle the revolutionaries would have British support and Russian antagonism.

However, the British diplomatic correspondence makes clear that this was never the case. There were deep mutual suspicions, but both ministers obviously favored close coordination of the policies of the two governments. The objective of minimizing distrust and optimizing cooperation was primary for both. No doubt both governments were under pressure from their Iranian friends. Yet the fact remains that the official policies were parallel.[21]

Iranians became aware of the real Anglo-Russian formula when the announcement was made of the Anglo-Russian Agreement of 1907 dividing Iran into spheres of influence. The north of Iran was the Russian sphere, the southeast bordering on British India the British sphere, and in the remainder of the country, presumably, the rivalry would continue along old lines. The agreement shattered the illusion that somehow England would protect the revolution and, even more, that the British placed a high value on the development of liberal democracy in Iran.

Maintaining the appearance and reality of Anglo-Russian cooperation became increasingly difficult in the following two years. Mohammad Ali Shah and his entourage were determined to destroy the constitutional movement. In 1909 the reactionary forces came close to total victory, but resistance in the city of Tabriz kept the movement alive. Mohammad Ali finally was defeated and forced into exile. Russian sympathy for him was obvious; on occasion Russian policy seemed to tilt in the direction of restoring him to the throne. His opponents, many of whom were friendly with the British, pressured the British to oppose the Russians. But regardless of these opposing pressures and tendencies, a difficult compromise was achieved and at critical moments the British and Russians acted in concert. The two powers acquiesced in Mohammad Ali's defeat, both agreeing that the constitutionalists were both more patriotic and less venal than the shah's entourage.[22]

The event that pushed Russia toward overt opposition to the constitutionalists was indicative of the degree of Russian paranoia. Iranian governments, pre- and postrevolution, were always looking for technical assistance from foreigners who were citizens of disinterested powers. Belgians, for example, were chosen to be customs officials. But, unfortunately from the Iranian point of view, the Belgians quickly associated themselves with British and Russian interests. In 1911, with parliamentary approval, the government appointed one W. Morgan Shuster, an American financier, as treasurer-general of Iran. Both the Russians and the British agreed to the appointment. The U.S. government's role in Shuster's selection and appointment was scrupulously correct. Shuster was to be an employee of the Iranian government and the Americans did no more than submit his name among others as a man of suitable competence for the post. But Morgan Shuster was no ordinary technician. He saw himself as an employee of the Iranian constitutional government and was determined to do his creative best to serve that government. He refused to recognize any right of a European government to infringe upon the sovereign independence of Iran. Since the Iranian government had refused to acquiesce in the terms of the Anglo-Russian Agreement of 1907, Shuster saw no reason to concern himself with those terms.[23]

Trouble developed almost immediately after Shuster's arrival. He was advised to pay his respects to the European legations, particularly the British and Russian, but he refused on the grounds that, as an employee of the Iranian government, he had no diplomatic function. The British in particular found this attitude annoying. But the really serious objections came from the Russians. Shuster appointed an Englishman, Major C. B. Stokes, as his assistant in the province of Azerbaijan, the most important area in the Russian sphere of influence. The Russians immediately saw in this action a British conspiracy. In their eyes Shuster was a British agent engaged in a blatant and brazen assault on the Anglo-Russian Agreement. To reduce these suspicions, the British refused to allow Stokes to accept the position. But Shuster did much more. He made the gendarmerie into an effective internal security force, with Swedish officers who were as willing as Shuster to offend traditional interests. Prominent Iranians had properties confiscated for nonpayment of taxes and one of them in particular, a Qajar prince living in exile in Russia, was a major figure among pro-Russian Iranians. Furthermore, Shuster was making progress in bringing order to Iran's finances and played a significant role in helping the Iranian government resist an effort by Mohammad Ali, arriving from Russia on the Caspian seacoast, to return to power. As an added measure, he wrote an article for the London *Times* castigating the British and the Russians.[24]

The British saw the entire episode as reflecting bizarre ineptitude and innocence on Shuster's part. But they also understood the seriousness of the potential complications for Anglo-Russian relations. Both governments sent troops into Iran in their spheres of influence. But the Russians sent an ultimatum as well demanding Shuster's dismissal. The Iranians rejected the ultimatum but capitulated when a Russian military force began to approach Tehran.

The official U.S. response to this major crisis revolving around an American citizen was to dissociate themselves from it. The Iranian government urgently solicited Washington's assistance, but the most the Department of State was willing to do was to insist on the safety of Shuster and his American associates.[25] However, the Shuster episode was a major determinant of Iranian attitudes for a half-century and, more than anything else, was responsible for pro-American feelings in Iran.

The 1906–1911 period was one in which basic Iranian foreign policy attitudes were shaped. Pro-change elements who were associated with the constitutional movement came to see European imperialism as ineluctable in its determination to keep Iran a raw material–

producing colonial area to be exploited according to the needs of the capitalist system. In this view, the British and Russians differed not at all. The British were no more concerned with the fortunes of liberal democracy in Iran than were the despotic Russians. Both were extraordinarily, almost irresistibly, powerful; they could and would control Iran primarily by operating with a "hidden hand," manipulating Iran's politics by virtue of their ability to recruit and control Iranian officials. Virtually the entire traditional elite was susceptible to this manipulation.

The only real hope for Iran, therefore, was to solicit a counterforce relatively equal to that of the Russians and the British. The ideal candidate for this role was the United States. But distance and lack of direct interest made American involvement unlikely. This left only one real option: an alliance with an enemy of the enemies of Iran's aspirations. In 1912 that meant an alliance with Germany and Germany's ally, the Ottoman Empire.

Political leaders of the constitutional period of Iran gravitated toward one of two political groupings that began to crystallize. The Democrats were generally more in favor of rapid change and less willing to yield to the influence of the British and the Russians. The Moderates were more accepting of the external influence and accommodating toward the traditional elite. Indeed, they could be viewed as the progressive wing of that elite. Thus when Anglo-Russian intervention forced the regime to capitulate, Moderate leaders were willing to accept the new reality and even to play a major policy role in successor governments. The Democrats were not. When World War I broke out, many of them worked actively with the Germans and Ottomans. But most of Iran spent the next seven years under a restored traditional rule for which the Russians and British provided the coercive instrument of control. The period was a difficult one for Iran. Many battles were fought on Iranian soil by opposing forces, the economy deteriorated, and terrible distress — even starvation — was common. Iran was in effect under foreign occupation. However, the occupation force was small and the exercise of control over the country loose and only partially effective. American concern for Iran diminished almost to the vanishing point.[26] It was a period of arrested development. But the forces of change, having been inaugurated, persisted, and post–World War I Iran was to witness some major manifestations of this process.

*External Rivalry in Iran After the Bolshevik Revolution*

Given the fact that the role of tsarist Russia in Iran was interventionist and given the profound importance of the Bolshevik Revolution for Russian history, one might well expect that Iranian history too would be changed fundamentally by that event. In the short run, there were important consequences. The social beneficiaries in Iran of interventions by the Soviet Union would be very different from those favored before. But the patterns of intervention and control established in the late nineteenth and early twentieth centuries would persist in general outline. The Iranian Revolution of 1979, not the Bolshevik Revolution of 1917, marks the end of the era of European intervention.

Still, the impact of the Bolshevik Revolution on Iran's relations with European imperialism is instructive. In the complex of motives that underlay European imperialism in Iran, defense against the perceived aggressive intent of a primary rival was most important. But suddenly, if temporarily, Britain's imperial rival in Iran—Russia—withdrew from the game. Indeed, by 1919, a critical year in Anglo-Iranian relations, the British perceived the French, not the Russians, as their primary European rival in Iran.[27] Thus defense as a motive was downgraded, and overall British willingness to make major material sacrifices to maintain a strong presence in Iran diminished. Yet motives of imperial grandeur and concern with imperial communications and economic interest—now particularly focused on oil—remained. At this point the British developed a new and imaginative policy that tells much, both of how they perceived Iran and of the intensity of their concern to remain a major force in Iran.

The British foreign minister, Lord Curzon, had a deep and long-standing interest in Iran and Central Asia. Opposing Russian infiltration in the area, real and imagined, had been a major preoccupation of his. Now with Russia consumed by a momentous internal convulsion, Curzon felt, as his biographer Harold Nicolson puts it, "that in general we should assume toward Persia the role of a determined although liberal protector."[28] The vehicle for accomplishing this would be the Anglo-Persian Agreement of 1919. The Iranian government would pay for and the British would provide experts who would build an Iranian security force capable of providing the essential coercive control for an Anglophilic and traditional-based government. Technicians who could train Iranians to manage and develop the economy, to provide essential social services and to staff the judiciary and other departments, would also be provided. Curzon, Nicolson remarked, saw the agreement as in the interests of the Iranians. "It seemed incredible to him that Persians could fail to recognize in him their constant, their lordly, their disinterested and their inspired friend."[29] Yet of twenty-six journals published in Tehran, all but one, *Ra'd,* edited by Sayyid Zia ad-din Tabatabai (who was assumed to be in the pay of the British), denounced the agreement. They described it as a transparent effort to establish a wonderfully inexpensive colonial control of Iran.

British diplomats and the correspondent of the proimperial journal, the *Near East,* reported a favorable public response.[30] They saw Iranian protests as French-engineered. In fact, the agreement was an accurate reflection of the official British view of Iran. There was a recognition of a need for a coercive force very different from that of the prerevolutionary period. There was also an acceptance of the necessity to accommodate to basic change. But there was implicit in the formula a belief that the rate and direction of change could be controlled with relative ease. The British did not accept the existence of a developing public opinion with which an Iranian government must somehow come to terms, whether through accommodation or suppression. Instead, they gave to the Iranian government a rather considerable sum of money through which, presumably, support could be purchased from various traditional interests, including the clergy.[31] The formula would be followed many times in the next half-century by the British and then by the Americans.

In 1919, however, American policy in Iran was assertively ideological. Woodrow Wilson's representative at Versailles, Colonel House, had argued the case for an Iranian delegation's being allowed to present its case. Lord Curzon responded that the matter of Iran's demands was being dealt with through negotiations with the Iranians. When the fruits of these negotiations were published, President Wilson and Secretary of State Lansing expressed their annoyance.[32] This was compounded by an article in *Ra'd,* called by the American minister in Tehran "the official cabinet organ," which stated flatly, "America, the only Government able to assist Persia abandoned her." Given the perception that *Ra'd* spoke for a British-dominated government, this statement was broadly assumed to be part of a British

campaign to destroy any illusion Iranians might have of being able
to counter British control. Lansing instructed Minister Caldwell to
do what he could to counter this impression, and what followed
electrified the proconstitution Iranian public. The local staff of the
U.S. legation were instructed to distribute strongly phrased denials
of an American approval of the agreement.[33] The Iranian minister
in Washington was told, "We would feel very sorry to see an arrangement made by the terms of which Persia would lose part or
the whole of its sovereignty."[34] Official British representations of the
matter were firmly rejected by Washington.

This episode ranks with the Morgan Shuster case in terms of its
impact on Iranian perceptions and attitudes. The difference was that
this time, as did not occur in the earlier period, Iranian interpretations of the American government's interest in a free and independent Iran were supported by documentary evidence. Still, the United
States was a far distant country and the intensity of interest in Iran
was low. The incident was a brief one and did not forecast heightened U.S. concern with Iran's sovereign independence or with its constitutional movement.

The British were soon denied the luxury of Russian unconcern
with Iran. As part of the allied campaign against the Bolsheviks,
British troops occupied the city of Baku in Russian Azerbaijan. But
in 1920 the Bolsheviks recaptured Baku and then pursued the British forces across the Caspian Sea to the Iranian port of Enzeli and
established a considerable presence in the Iranian Caspian province
of Gilan.

The men now in command of a Russian force in Iranian territory resembled very little their predecessors in the years before the
Bolshevik Revolution. But the structural dynamics were not dissimi-
lar. Anglo-Russian rivalry for influence in Iran persisted as a major
determinant not only of Iran's foreign relations but also of her internal developments. The new Russian leaders discovered quickly
the resentment and anger in Iran at British efforts to establish what
at best could be called a tutorial control of Iran. In the province of
Gilan there was a paramilitary force led by one Kuchek Khan that
was in rebellion against what the rebels saw as the British-controlled
government of Tehran. Similarly, in the neighboring province of
Azerbaijan, Sheikh Mohammed Khiabani was leading a rebellion.
Whatever their understanding of Iran—and presumably it was

slight — the Soviet officials could hardly fail to see the potential opportunity in these two movements. Their overtures to Kuchek Khan were successful. Strong elements in Kuchek Khan's entourage, including his second in command, Ehsanollah Khan, viewed the Bolshevik Revolution with favor, and a working relationship quickly developed. Khiabani, however, rejected any suggestion of a similar cooperative relationship.[35]

The British withdrew from northern Iran, and the British minister in Tehran indicated to his American counterpart, Caldwell, that British interests in Iran, except in the extreme south, surely would be sacrificed. He indicated, though, that protection would be given Tehran in the event of a Bolshevik invasion. Caldwell saw in the British policy a major opportunity. He wrote Washington suggesting that in view of the United States' "lively interest in the possibilities of certain natural resources of Persia" Washington should consider playing a strongly activist role in Iran. Caldwell asserted that in his view thirty experienced American officers could reorganize the Iranian "forces" and could prevent Iran's "being driven into the arms of Soviet Russia." Financial and other technical experts would also be needed. Caldwell reported that "Persians of all classes still have unbounded confidence in America" and argued that Washington's decision could "determine the fate of this part of the world for a generation." Caldwell's case was presented in terms of security needs, containing the Soviets, and economic opportunities, that is, oil. The earlier ideological stance apparently came from Washington, not the U.S. minister in Tehran.[36]

The State Department largely ignored this suggestion. It was one generation too early. But Caldwell would not be the only American diplomat in Iran to find the Iranian desire for American involvement irresistible.

In any event, Britain's supposed indifference to Iran's fate, which led Caldwell to see his opportunity, was surely illusory. British reporting of the atmosphere in Iran in 1921 resembled Caldwell's picture very little. The British saw a favorable public response to the agreement, but external agitation — French, Soviet, and a strangely innocent U.S. opposition — against it. But Britain's policy was not to capitulate. The British looked instead for another formula that would achieve similar results to those expected from the agreement. By late 1921 that formula suddenly crystallized. It was to look with favor on efforts by Anglophile Iranians to carry out a coup d'état and establish a strong authoritarian regime. As is typically true in such situations, the British became in effect the allies of a group of Iranians with whom they had a commonality of objectives. Their lack of concern with how Iranians would view the coup is indicated by their approval of Sayyid Zia as leader of the coup and as the prospective prime minister. Since Sayyid Zia was regarded as a major British agent in Iran, especially by constitutionalists, it was inevitable that the coup would be perceived as a British operation. The ranking military officer of the coup forces, Colonel Reza Khan, therefore would be perceived as another important individual instrument of British policy.[37]

### The Political Emergence of Reza Khan

The coup was successful. Briefly it appeared that the British had accomplished their objective—a stable Iranian regime able to resist popular agitation, entirely friendly to Great Britain, protective of British interests, and able and willing to stand up to the Russian threat. Sayyid Zia did declare the Anglo-Persian Agreement null and void and signed the 1921 Treaty of Friendship with the Soviet Union. But these acts were simply an acceptance of a geopolitical reality. The new regime would need a strong internal security force to provide the essential coercive control; it was soon apparent that Colonel Reza Khan would develop the necessary coercive arm and that it would be both effective and independent of external control. The emerging Iranian regime differed sharply from Britain's preferred model, in which control was exercised by individuals who would look to the British for direction. Reza Khan was not such an individual. True, he was indebted to Britain for his rise to power, but his loyalties clearly were to Iran. But even though Reza Khan was showing signs of being an Iranian nationalist who would work to reduce external intervention in Iran, Britain's perceived role in his first appearance on the political scene denied him legitimacy with the secular nationalists. Reza Khan's role in Iranian history was in important respects comparable to that of Ataturk in Turkish history. His inability to convince intellectuals favorable to change of his devotion to the nation, however, is the most important area in which the parallel breaks down. Furthermore, there was circularity here. Confronted with hostility and suspicion from the progressive, secular element, Reza Khan dealt with them brutally; in so doing, he further confirmed their view of him.

Ahmad Shah, the last of the Qajar dynasty, is a much-maligned historical figure. The mention of his name conjures up adjectives such as "weak," "fat," and "slothful." But the converse of this picture is that he probably would have been a good, constitutional monarch. Was there any real potential in 1921 for another constitutional government? The negative case is easy to make. The problem of establishing control over a still overwhelmingly traditional Iran was difficult. The support base was narrow, divided, and largely confined to Tehran, Tabriz, and a few other cities. No political figure had appeared with a charismatic appeal and—given the narrow base of the population predisposed to participate in politics—none was likely to appear. Furthermore, probably the politician with the broadest popular appeal was Sayyid Hassan Modaress, a religious leader who was only slightly less skeptical of secularists than was Fazlullah Nuri and later Khomeini.[38]

But there is a positive case to be made as well. The Tehran press favored the constitution and the constitutionalists had demonstrated significant strength in defeating the Anglo-Persian Agreement. A number of leaders now with a good deal of experience were available to lead the movement and to mobilize ever larger numbers of people into active participation in the political process. In any event, the constitutionalists, having administered a shocking defeat to the British and Iranian supporters, believed they could provide a strong and stable leadership; yet they were being denied that possibility by the British. Their resentment was intense, and there was no real possibility of their ever granting those perceived as personal instruments of British policy, like Reza Khan, any real support.

What is incontrovertible is that Reza Khan began his climb toward absolute power in Iran with British approval.[39] Iranian constitutionalists were inclined to believe that British assistance persisted and that the strategy Reza Khan followed was in fact British-orchestrated. So convinced were they of the validity of this surmise that they regarded anyone who disagreed as either innocent or disingenuous. And indeed this frame of mind was (and is) a major factor in explaining Iranian external policy even to this day. Having observed or imagined the subtlety of British policy, the intricate understanding of the personalities involved, and the ability to manipulate the process without ever revealing their controlling role, the Iranians concluded that the British modus operandi could best be described as that of the "hidden hand." No conspiracy was too elaborate, too intricate, and too demanding in terms of orchestration to be impossible for the British. Reza Khan's rise to power was often rocky, and on more than one occasion he appeared to falter. But in the conspiratorial view, even the faltering was planned.[40]

In fact, Reza Khan's rise to power was through an open and obvious strategy. He needed first of all to gain control of and to strengthen drastically an internal security force. He did this by centralizing authority over all the various security organizations, by removing foreign officers and replacing them with his men, and by disciplining and ultimately eliminating tribal contingents. The process was slow, but by 1925, when he was proclaimed shah and the founder of the Pahlavi dynasty, it was equal to the task of dealing with any probable combination of domestic rivals. Furthermore, the officer corps became a mainstay of the regime. Handsomely rewarded, not only in salary but also in terms of prestige and perquisites, the officers viewed their own and the regime's fortunes as inseparable.[41]

Even though he began his rise to power in alliance with members of the traditional elite, Reza Khan quickly demonstrated that he favored rapid and accelerating change in Iran. This meant conflict with former allies and a forging of alliances with forces favoring favoring change. Of the three groups that came together to produce the revolution in 1906, the one with which Reza Khan had the greatest success was the commercial middle class. The interests of this group called for internal stability, a strong communications and transportation infrastructure, and a fiscal and commercial policy that encouraged trade and industrial development. Reza Khan/Reza Shah made considerable progress in all these areas. There were grounds for serious complaint. Corruption, caprice, and gross favoritism made for bad feelings. But rapid progress was undeniable, and since ideology was of small concern to mercantile elements, Reza Shah's mode of coming to power and his authoritarian qualities were small impediments to their support.

Ideology was important, however, for many of the secular intelligentsia. It was within this element that hostility to Reza Shah was deepest and most persistent. Those whose opposition was intransigent were dealt with brutally, and oppositionists realized that their ability to overthrow the regime was virtually nonexistent. With little or no hope of a regime change, professional and technocratic elements moved toward accommodation. The regime welcomed their services and rewarded them well materially. However, this cooptation process did not result in enthusiasm for the regime. Reza Shah was never really able to convince them that he was indeed an Iranian nationalist whose early collaboration with the British was no more than a recognition of power realities of that period. In any event, Reza Shah's policies in education and technological change, especially, led to major growth of the professional and technocratic population.

The third element involved in the 1906 revolution was the clergy. Yet Reza Khan, like his son a quarter of a century later, seriously underestimated the strength of this group. Secular opponents of Khomeini, both pro- and antiroyalist, commonly accept the proposition today that Khomeini is a product of British policy in Iran. This perception, with dual and deep roots, is still a major factor in the persisting underestimation of clerical strength. It helps explain Reza Khan's attitude toward the clergy and that of most Iranian secularists since his time.

A central part of the explanation for the underestimation of the clergy lies in the role of the clerical element in the traditional control of Iran. The relationship of clerics, the court, the social elite, and the bureaucracy was close and interactive. As the element with the most intimate relationship with the mass of the people, the clergy received some monetary rewards, but more important, autonomy in dealing with their estates. When the British and Russians began intervening in Iran's internal politics, they came to understand this process. They cultivated clerical leaders and on occasion rewarded them financially for their cooperation.

Another part of the explanation is the sharply different aspiration of secularists and religious leaders who favored change. Whereas secularists tended to see Western Europe as their model, religious leaders looked to an idealized image of early Islam. In fact, both sets of aspirations were radical. But secularists failed to differentiate among religious leaders. Evidence that clerical leaders seeking radical social and political change were able to mobilize popular support, even in traditional Iran, is strong. Both the tobacco boycott and the revolution of 1906 provide evidence of this. Yet the image of the clergy as a conservative force anxious to collaborate with external intervention persisted, and persists today.

Reza Khan's underestimation of Islamic radicalism was particularly dramatic. Identifying with the militant secularism of Ataturk in Turkey, Reza Khan let it be known that he would like to be president of a republican Iran. Much of the clerical leadership, especially those associated with Modaress, opposed this plan. Reza Khan suddenly was confronted with large, hostile crowds opposed to the creation of a secular state. For the first time since 1921, the momentum of Reza Khan's drive for absolute power suffered a major reversal. His response was to move quickly to allay clerical hostility. Reza Khan abandoned his advocacy of a republic and made a number of gestures indicating his personal devotion to Islam. But there was no real reversal in his attitudes. Later, as Reza Shah Pahlavi, he curbed clerical influence in a number of ways—the most important of which was in the realm of law. The Napoleonic code was adopted and the judicial system effectively secularized, and the politically most effective of the radical religious leaders were exiled. As he continued to consolidate his near-absolute control, Reza Shah moved steadily to reduce the influence of the clergy in the daily life of the people. Codes of dress, nonreligious state holidays, secular social organizations—all reflected a diminished clerical presence. The shah even went so far as to regulate the procedures by which an individual gained the right to wear a turban.

Most clerics, whatever their private views, accepted publicly their loss of influence. But as later events would demonstrate, the percentage of the population that had beceome secular was still small (though growing rapidly), and the clergy were still very able to reach the mass public. Reza Shah and Ataturk were contemporaries, and their aspirations for their countries were similar, but Turkey was more than a generation ahead of Iran in the change process. As a result the impact of Ataturk on Turkey was far more profound and enduring than the shah's influence in Iran. In no area is this difference more apparent than in the relationship between the state and religion.

Still, Reza Shah's reign as absolute monarch of Iran was characterized by exceptionally rapid change. The percentage of the population predisposed to participate in political life multiplied several times, and this newly participant group identified strongly with the nation of Iran. The economy, thanks to rapid development of the transportation and communications infrastructures, became truly national. Education, health, and social services were developed, and Iranian dependence on foreign powers declined.

## The External Influences: The British

The nationalist intelligentsia continued to see the Pahlavi dictatorship as manifesting a British plan. Given the Iranians' long experience with Anglo-Russian intervention, this view was understandable. But there is no documentary support for it. Reza Khan may well have been given an early assist in his drive for power by the British, but he quickly demonstrated his independence. The dilemma that emerged for the British was that they were losing control of developments in Iran, but to a government that was providing the stability and protection for British interests that they desired. Reza Shah, although personally obstreperous, really did serve central British purposes. Cognizant of this fact, they did not seriously consider opposing his role. Since Reza Shah suppressed tribal and provincial forces that sought autonomy, and since many of these groups had a long history of collaboration with the British and/or the Russians, Britain could not favor him without being accused of betraying friends and long-term allies. Occasionally the British did help old friends. Sayyid Zia, for example, went to the British mandate of Palestine and lived comfortably in exile after he lost his battle with Reza Khan. Many others were not so lucky; not a few perished.

The common Iranian view—one held, ironically, most intensely today by supporters of the Pahlavis—that the British hoped to keep Iran in a semicolonial condition as a supplier of raw materials and a market for finished goods, is difficult to defend, given Britain's clear satisfaction with Reza Khan/Reza Shah's role as leader. Events suggest that Britain was not opposed to change in Iran that would lead to economic transformation. What the British seem to have feared was uncontrolled change which could damage their economic interests and could lead to advantages for Britain's imperial rivals. An authoritarian tutelary rule that guarded against both of these dangers was fully acceptable.

Reza Khan and his strengthened internal security force steadily broadened and intensified central control in Iran. Abandoned by his Soviet allies, Kuchek Khan was easily disposed of. So were rebellions in Azerbaijan and Khorassan. Tribal autonomy was curtailed and migrations restricted. With these changes, the British modus operandi in Iran changed as well. There was no longer a need to subsidize and cultivate tribal and provincial leaders. The all important oil fields and refinery complex of the Anglo-Persian Oil Company were fully secured. Because urban opposition elements were suppressed or intimidated, there was no need for the British to subsidize forces capable of competing with the opposition in its access to the urban mass or to brutalize opposition leaders; the British previously had worked with religious and mob leaders for these purposes. Furthermore, the government's strengthened control reduced the ability of imperial competitors to deal with these same traditional elements. British diplomatic correspondence in the decade 1921–1931 indicated little interest in events in Iran.

Surely much of the explanation for Britain's attitude is to be found in the behavior of the Soviet Union in South Asia, which reflects a low level of perceived threat to British interests from the USSR. The Treaty of Friendship signed by Iran and the Soviet Union in 1921 was on the surface an act of self-abnegation rarely seen in international politics. The Soviet government agreed to cancel all concessions made to Russia except the fishery agreement and to the abrogation of capitulatory rights. Article Six, claiming a continuing right to intervene to counter any foreign presence in Iran, ominous though it has come to seem later, was understood to be essentially defensive. Furthermore, early Soviet behavior toward Iran was in harmony with the spirit of the treaty.

The treaty presented the British with an opportunity, but also with a dilemma. The opportunity was to expand the scope of British oil concessions to include northern Iran. They moved quickly to gain control of the Khoshtaria concession, which had served as the basis for much of tsarist Russia's claims to develop northern Iranian oil. Much of Britain's diplomatic activity in the ensuing decade would revolve around this claim and the Iranians' insistence that it had no validity.

The British were not pleased with the precedent set regarding capitulatory rights. Having a low regard for Iranian administration of justice, the British saw extraterritoriality as essential for the preservation of British interests in Iran. With the consolidation of Reza Khan's control and especially after his becoming shah, the Iranians' sensitivity to any sign of European arrogance heightened. Consequently, a second major focus of British diplomatic activity in the 1920s was to construct a formula that would protect British and other foreign commercial interests and at the same time would satisfy Iranian sensibilities. Reza Shah's talented foreign minister, Abdol Hossein Teymurtash, forced a steady European retreat in this area, so that by the end of the decade the British were not far from the Soviets in their acceptance of Iranian legal sovereignty.[42]

The second decade of Reza Shah's dictatorship witnessed a further erosion of external influence in Iran. The pattern is demonstrated well by the oil crisis of 1932. Reza Shah challenged the British regarding the terms under which the Anglo-Persian Oil Company operated. But he also demonstrated a sense of exactly how far he felt the British could be pushed. Britain's ability to intervene in Iranian internal affairs was by this time fairly low. But oil interests were important enough that military intervention could not be ruled out. Reza Shah obviously was not looking for a test of British resolve. The result was an altered agreement improving the financial terms for Iran and a slow movement toward Iranification of the enterprise. So modest were the gains for Iran that Reza Shah's nationalist opponents could depict it as a British-orchestrated charade designed to give Reza Shah some badly needed claims to legitimacy.[43]

But the real challenge to the British in Iran came later. Reza Shah saw in the rise of Adolf Hitler a possibility of increasing his bargaining strength with both the British and Russians. No pattern is better established in Iranian diplomatic history of the past century. Iranians had come to expect and to believe that as serious as Anglo-Russian rivalry appeared, cooperation between Britain and the USSR at Iran's expense was always a possibility.[44] Thus a third power able to threaten both seemed an ideal potential collaborator. This was by now an intuitively understood point. Hitler was more than willing to cooperate. Increased trade with Germany, technical assistance, and diplomatic support were all quickly forthcoming. There is, however, no compelling evidence of ideological attraction. Hitler played on the name *Iran* to suggest that Iranians were fellow Aryans. But this was never a significant theme in the editorial line of Iran's controlled press. Furthermore, Iranians were little attracted by Reza Shah's spectacular show of independence from the British and the Russians. As would be true of his son as well, Reza Shah was never able to project the image of an Iranian hero standing up to Iran's historic enemies.

Even with the shah's movement toward Nazi Germany, the British did not show much concern with the direction of developments in Iran. They were generally slow to recognize the threat to British interests in the Nazi movement. Reza Shah's relations with Nazi Germany were a matter of note, but prior to the beginning of World War II the British showed no interest in regaining internal influence in Iran. Reza Shah at the end of the 1930s took little note of the developing world crisis. In foreign policy he was preoccupied with countering affronts to Iran and to himself. He was unwilling to accept even minor slights from foreigners, and appears to have developed an entirely unrealistic view of Iran's position in the international community. Not only did he establish close relations with the prospective enemy of the two external powers most capable of intervening in Iran, but also he allowed personal pique to lead to difficult relations with two other major world powers, France and the United States.[45] In 1939 he broke diplomatic relations with France because of what he saw as a rude article published in a French newspaper. Nazi Germany's and Soviet Russia's sudden cooperation in 1939 was a major shock. But Reza Shah did little to adapt Iranian policy to the resulting alteration in the Iranian bargaining position.

*External Influences: The Soviets*

Soviet policy toward Iran in the interwar period seems to have been an unsuccessful effort to reconcile a number of conflicting objectives. But probably the most telling observation one can make is that neither Great Britain nor the United States saw any compelling need to contain the Soviet Union in the Near East. At the beginning of the period, when Bolshevik forces pursued British troops from Baku into Iran, the British did see a serious threat from Bolshevik Russia. But this perception soon faded. Diplomatic correspondence between the United States and Great Britain evinced little concern with Soviet policy until the Nazi-Soviet pact in 1939. Even then expressions of concern were mild and bore no resemblance to the obsessive preoccupation with the Soviet threat that came to characterize the post–World War II era.[46]

The low level of Western concern with the Soviets in Iran is particularly interesting since Soviet policy, especially in its early days, had strong and explicit ideological overtones — a statement that cannot be made of Soviet policy since World War II. At the Baku Conference of 1920, Soviet leaders announced a policy that was, in terms of doctrine, highly defensible. Given the stage of development of Iran and other Asian peoples, the conference leaders argued, Soviet policy should support bourgeois elements seeking to oppose capitalist imperialists and proclaiming the right of national self-determination. Actual policy followed this line in important regards. A number of self-denying agreements were made or proposed. That concerning Iran was the Treaty of Friendship of 1921. In addition, the Soviets announced their intention to withdraw all Soviet troops from Iran when the British withdrew from the southern part of the country.

After the first years, the primary determinants of Soviet policy seemed to shift to a concern for the Soviet economy and for Soviet security. In 1922, with ideology still much in policymakers' minds, a trade agreement with Iran similar to that established with other Asian states granted Iranian merchants particularly favorable trade opportunities.[47] But because of the extreme economic distress in the Soviet Union in the 1920s, this generous policy could not be sustained. Between 1923 and 1926, Soviet policy vacillated wildly, no doubt reflecting policy battles in Moscow. At its worst moments, serious damage was done to Iranian commerce in north Iran, and an effective Iranian boycott of Soviet goods was organized in response. In 1927 a treaty stabilized relations on a most-favored-nation basis. For the remainder of the period, trade relations were generally good and improving.[48]

Possibly even more revealing of the USSR's interest in Iran was Soviet policy regarding Iran's northern oil fields, generally believed at the time to be extensive. In abandoning tsarist concessions gained from Iran, the Soviets made one exception: the Caspian fishery industry. No exception was made regarding oil and the Soviets appeared relatively unconcerned when U.S. companies, first Standard Oil of New Jersey and then Sinclair, explored with official Iranian encouragement the possibility of developing oil production in the north. The Soviets did, after much procrastination, refuse to grant Sinclair transit rights for oil extracted in Iran; this led to Sinclair's abandoning the project in the mid-1920s.[49]

As late as 1937 when the American company, Amiranian, was granted a small concession in northern Iran, the Soviets were generally agreeable. Their only complaint was that the Iranian government had not informed them of the negotiations with Amiranian. But they were willing to grant transit rights. Soviet representatives did inform U.S. officials that they would not have allowed a German concession in the area.[50]

Soviet academicians disagreed in analyzing the historic role of Reza Shah and the type of change he was bringing to Iran.[51] One view was that it was progressive in terms of the dialectical process, a liberal nationalist bourgeois phenomenon that should serve to advance the dialectic. A second view was less sanguine, seeing Reza Shah as the product of a British-sponsored coup and thus the ally of landlords, tribal chiefs, and the clergy. The liberal bourgeois appearance was, in this view, a false veneer. It followed from the first view that a policy of accommodation to Reza Shah would serve the ideological purpose. It followed from the second that any support for Reza Shah would retard the dialectical process.

Even the second view is a far cry from the conspiratorial picture that tsarist representatives of the previous generation held regarding Iran. A diabolically clever Great Britain was not part of Soviet imagery. Nor was there any serious effort to influence Iranian sociopolitical developments in the interwar period. There were efforts to cultivate and to influence Iranian officials—in particular, Foreign Minister Teymurtash. And the Soviets did encourage Marxist intellectuals in Iran. But the arrest of the communist leaders in Iran did not upset Soviet-Iranian relations.

The interwar period was, strangely, an interlude in the intense Anglo-Russian competition for preeminent influence in Iran. Reza Shah thus had the luxury denied his predecessors of freedom of action in Iranian internal affairs. Competition between the two powers had already influenced the direction of Iranian sociopolitical development. Moreover, Reza Shah was the unintended beneficiary both of early British aid and of British intervention against an assertive liberal nationalist elite. But the developmental patterns of the two decades of Reza Shah's dominance in Iran were the product of internal Iranian processes independent of external control.

## External Influences: The United States

U.S. policy in the 1920s and 1930s did nothing to support a generation-old view in Iran that the United States, alone among Western nations, cared for the Enlightenment values of national self-determination. The last clear evidence to support this view—perhaps the only example—came during the Wilson administration and has been outlined above. Wilson's minister to Iran, Caldwell, was the only U.S. diplomat in Iran during the interwar years to advocate a strongly activist American role.

U.S. diplomatic correspondence in this period is negatively revealing. There is no serious effort to present an analysis of Iranian sociopolitical developments. Caldwell's rationale for advocating an activist policy was, first, to exploit the great economic opportunities in the area and, second, to stand against any inroads into the area by the Bolsheviks. After Caldwell, evidence that the United States perceived a threat from the Soviet Union appears only after the Nazi-Soviet pact in 1939.

U.S. dispatches evinced four areas of concern. There was first a good deal of correspondence reporting on the efforts of U.S. oil companies to establish a claim in northern Iran. The Iranian government and the Majlis were anxious to attract the American companies to balance the widely resented British control of southern oil. The only condition was that the Americans not share the concession with another national group. Yet Standard of New Jersey did negotiate an agreement of cooperation with Anglo-Persian that led to a breakdown in negotiations with the Iranians. The U.S. legation expressed their sympathy with this cooperation and did not advise Standard of the seriousness of the Iranian position. Morgan Shuster, once again working for the Iranian government, did understand that the Iranians were adamant and communicated that view to officials of Sinclair. But the legation's reporting was still insensitive to this attitude.[52] In 1937 the U.S. minister did give a good analysis of British and Soviet attitudes about the Amiranian concession, but was little interested in the Iranian view.[53] In contrast to the previous cases involving Standard and Sinclair, however, the British now had no illusions about the possibility of their gaining control of northern Iranian oil. Furthermore, they were interested in seeking a deeper involvement of U.S. capital and policy in Iran to offset the influence of Germany. Thus there was briefly a commonality of interest among the Iranians, the Americans, the British, and the Soviets on the matter of a U.S. concession. But there was no indication in any of the negotiations of U.S. concern with helping Iran gain more economic independence.

A second focus of official U.S. interest was a trade relationship with Iran on a most-favored-nation basis. The Soviet surrender of capitulatory rights set a bothersome precedent for Western governments in their dealings with Iran. In this regard, U.S. diplomats followed the British lead. Far from sympathizing with Iranian aspirations, they, if anything, were more reluctant to give up privileges than any of the Western Europeans.[54]

A third focus concerned American Protestant missionaries in Iran and especially their educational activities. The exceptionally favorable image of the United States owed its genesis largely to three factors. There was first of all Morgan Shuster, who became for Iranian constitutionalists one of the heroes of the struggle against imperialism and for national self-determination. Second, in large part because of Shuster and the assumption that the U.S. Department of State was more responsible for his performance than it admitted, there was a conviction that true sovereign independence for Iran was an objective of American policy. This conviction was reinforced greatly by the United States' open opposition to the Anglo-Persian Agreement of 1919. But as should be clear, this view was illusory. More sympathy for Iranian sensibilities can be seen in British documents regarding Iran than in American ones during this period. Third, some of the missionary community in Iran were highly empathetic and understood the aspirations of constitutionalists for Iran. This was particularly true of Dr. Samuel Jordan and some of his staff at the Elburz College, a secondary school in Tehran. The impact of Jordan and his staff was great; the students of Elburz would later become a virtual who's who of Iranian opinion formulators of the 1940s and 1950s. Given the stage of Iran's development, this numerically small group was to play an exceptional role in mobilizing and giving form to Iranian attitudes in the post–World War II years.

However, both his nationalism and his conviction that Iranians need an authoritarian rule led Reza Shah to view the missionary educators with skepticism. But neither the Americans nor the Iranians were prepared for Reza Shah's sudden decision in August 1939 to nationalize all foreign education institutions within two weeks' time. This led to a flurry of diplomatic activity on the part of the U.S. legation. There was no suggestion that the directive be rescinded, but rather that it be amended to allow a year for an orderly transition.[55]

Reza Shah's behavior in the late 1930s was assertively and angrily nationalistic. But it was a strangely solitary response to external influences. Reza Shah understood well enough that he needed to create national institutions and to generate a public response to national symbols. But the confrontations he generated in the period were mainly reactions to personal affronts rather than affronts to the nation. A case in point, and a fourth cause for American diplomatic concern, was his decision to close the Iranian legation in Washington because of an article published in the *New York Mirror*. The offending article had unfairly referred to him as having been a stable boy in British employ. The article was published in 1936 and relations did not become normal until 1939. Iranian foreign policy officials had no choice but to carry out his orders, but they did so with obvious embarrassment. Far from exciting the Iranian public with a display of assertive independence, Reza Shah was seen as capricious and rude even by close lieutenants. His foreign minister, Baqer Kazemi, who later would be a charter member of the liberal Iran party and a deputy prime minister to Musaddiq, was in the unenviable position of having to suggest that the U.S. Constitution be amended to reduce freedom of the press.[56]

An episode that was apparently far less interesting to U.S. diplomats than the Iranians assumed involved the appointment of an American financial adviser to the Iranian government in 1922. The Iranians of course wanted Morgan Shuster, but were instead steered to a very different man, Arthur Millspaugh. There have been no suggestions from any quarter that Millspaugh lacked qualifications for his job. But in temperament he was in critical respects Shuster's opposite. Whereas Shuster had been highly empathetic with Iranians, Millspaugh tended to view them much as would a Tory British colonial officer: as an immature people in need of Western tutelage. Whereas Shuster carried to an extreme his refusal to deal with foreign diplomats because he saw himself as an Iranian government employee, Millspaugh quickly established close relations with the British, gaining their respect and confidence. Whereas Shuster was sympathetic with Iranian constitutionalism and correct in his dealings with Iranian officials, Millspaugh made clear his preference for authoritarian control and dealt with Iranian officials contemptuously. In 1927 his position was terminated, Reza Shah explaining to the American minister that Millspaugh lacked respect for Iranian dignity.[57] The Millspaugh episode tarnished slightly the luster of the

image of the United States derived from Shuster. But the U.S. legation expressed little concern either with his imperious style or with
the Iranian decision to terminate his contract.

After the Nazi-Soviet Pact was concluded, the American legation
began to send back somewhat alarmed reports concerning rumors
of Soviet activity in Iran.[58] But in general official reporting on Iranian attitudes toward the developing world conflict reflected bemusement. There was nothing to indicate serious apprehension. Iran's
requests for loans to purchase U.S. arms were reported, but the reports generated little interest. America remained essentially the disinterested observer of events in Iran well into the year 1941, even
after Hitler had invaded the Soviet Union.

On the eve of the American moment in Iran, the Iranians held
an idealized image of the United States. The expectation was that
the Americans would do what they could to allow Iranians to gain
control of their own destiny. This would entail standing up to the
British and the Russians and opposing their efforts to control Iran,
cooperatively if possible, or by dividing Iran if cooperation was too
difficult to achieve. On the U.S. side, the lack of awareness about
and understanding of Iran included an ignorance of this image. Only
the exceptional American had any real notion of the great expectations the Iranians had of U.S. policy. Iranian disillusionment was
inevitable. But before it occurred there was to be a surprising rein-
forcement of the Iranian image of the United States and, it follows,
even greater expectations after World War II.

# 3

## THE COLD WAR TAKES OVER

On April 6, 1941, Hitler invaded Yugoslavia and a few days later German spearheads were in Greece. The invasion coincided with a German offensive in North Africa that pushed toward Egypt. The possibility of a German invasion of western Asia began to look like a probability. Furthermore, within the Arab world, much of which viewed Britain as the Iranians did, there would be many who would welcome the Germans. In Iraq, Rashid Ali al Gaylani, a prominent nationalist politician, and his military allies broke with Britain and openly solicited German support. The French mandates of Lebanon and Syria were under the control of Vichy France and were thus available for German cooperation.

In Iran there were early signs that the Soviet Union intended to treat southern Asia as its natural sphere of influence, just as they had demanded in the Ribbentrop-Molotov conversations, and would insist on the use of Iranian airfields and ports.[1] The German presence in Iran was already substantial and, as long as the Nazi-Soviet Pact held, Reza Shah's ability to resist Soviet demands was limited. But if Reza Shah's position was difficult, the British situation in Iran and in the entire eastern Mediterranean–West Asian region was becoming untenable.

Then came dramatic changes. British troops forced Rashid Ali to flee Iraq and restored a pro-British government there. Allied forces invaded Syria, and by July 1941 the Vichy French had been forced to surrender. But the event that would most affect Iran's history was Hitler's invasion of the Soviet Union on June 22, 1941. On August 16 the British and Soviets sent an ultimatum to Iran demanding the expulsion of all Axis citizens. Reza Shah responded by insisting that Iran was a neutral country. On August 25 British and Soviet forces invaded Iran and quickly occupied the country.

Reza Shah, in a plea to Franklin Roosevelt, insisted he had no real indication of how seriously the British and Soviets regarded the

German presence in Iran. He concluded, therefore, that this was simply a pretext for what was in fact unprovoked aggression.[2] Reza Shah's bewilderment was understandable. The British and Soviets had been strangely acquiescent in the face of Reza Shah's audacious diplomacy in the late 1930s. That he would be permitted to establish with impunity good commercial and political relations with Nazi Germany, the potential mutual enemy of Britain and the Soviet Union, was surprising. Right up to 1941 he had received a relatively good press in Great Britain. The shah's image in serious British journals was that of a progressive leader who was playing a benevolent tutorial role in Iran.[3]

But this benign image was suddenly discarded in the summer of 1941. Now the shah was depicted as a vicious tyrant who brutalized his own people and who found in Adolf Hitler a natural ally. That Reza Shah and his regime would see this sudden change in attitude as reflecting a longstanding but usually hidden Anglo-Russian conspiracy was only to be expected. Indeed, many Iranians who despised the shah viewed it this way.

The benign image of Reza Shah that persisted almost to the moment of the Anglo-Soviet invasion strongly suggests a satisfaction in both countries with the status quo in Iran. Reza Shah was in absolute control of his country and neither the Soviet nor the British government saw his role as giving a competitive advantage to the other. His increasingly close relations with Germany obviously alarmed neither. A scenario by which Hitler could gain control of Iran was not apparent to either government until German armies were in the eastern Mediterranean and headed toward the Caucasus. After Hitler invaded the Soviet Union, however, both Britain and the USSR recognized an exceedingly serious German threat in Iran, the essential land bridge for the allies in getting supplies to the Soviet Union. Suddenly the shah who had maintained stability in Iran, who had been careful to establish a balanced policy toward the Soviets and the British, and who had protected the economic interests of both states was perceived as being in league with the deadly foe of both.

Reza Shah fared no better with his own public. The Iranian press, now suddenly free, rejoiced at the demise of the tyrant even while regretting and condemning the Anglo-Soviet invasion.[4] The lesson much of the press drew was in harmony with longstanding Iranian perceptions. The shah, according to this view, owed his rise to power to the British and for most of his reign was faithful to his mentors. So pleased were they with his rule, the British were willing to sacrifice longstanding agent relationships to help him consolidate control. Through the early 1930s, apparent confrontations with the British, such as the oil crisis of 1932, were really charades designed to deceive the Iranian people into accepting Reza Shah as a legitimate national leader.[5] But in the late 1930s Reza Shah began to take himself seriously and to forget the ties to Britain. When he moved toward Germany, the British had no choice but to remove him. To do so, they were forced to reveal the usually hidden and secret Anglo-Soviet alliance. So went a common Iranian interpretation.

But if basic foreign policy attitudes had changed little in two decades, Iranian society had changed dramatically. Reza Shah's policy of building a transportation and communications infrastructure had given his government easy access to the great mass of Iranians living in villages once reached only by camel or donkey. His policies in education and conscription had brought an awareness of the modern world to children of peasants, tribesmen, and urban laborers who had previously been aware of little beyond their own extended families. His policies of suppressing tribal autonomy, centralizing administration in Tehran, and encouraging commerce led to an increasingly centralized state and a disproportionate growth in importance and population for the capital city of Tehran. His secularization of the legal system and reduction of the influence of religious leaders sharpened the public focus on the national community. At the end of his reign, the percentage of the Iranian population that was now aware of the nation-state of Iran and was willing to grant a loyalty to it had expanded several times. The vast majority, surely 85 to 90 percent, could still be classified as traditional. But Reza Shah's rule had added certainly more than a million Iranians to the rolls of those predisposed to participate in political affairs.

By 1941 Iran had a mass base for political participation. The attraction of the national community for this newly aware element was strong, and nationalism was now a vital force in Iranian political life. And the old political elite that had dominated Iran through the nineteenth century, though still a major part of the elite structure, had suffered serious and irreversible blows to its ability to exercise political control in Iran.

Yet the paradox for Reza Shah, as for his son thirty-seven years later, was that although he had brought vast numbers of people into the political process, he had not succeeded in generating any deep attachments to himself. Reza Shah had sought to socialize Iranians entering the political process into a devotion to the nation of Iran of which the Pahlavi dynasty was an integral part. He wanted to produce an attachment to the values of order, authority, and modernization. For him the latter consisted of technological change, industrialization, urbanization, and a literate, technically and scientifically competent population. He displayed no interest in the values associated with liberalism and freedom and seemed to care very little for social justice. As long as he could coerce compliance and satisfy the material demands of the attentive section of his public, his regime was secure. But when the Anglo-Soviet invasion decimated his military force, the public response to his departure into exile was one of open relief and rejoicing.

## Post–Reza Shah Iran

Considering the massiveness of the change that had occurred over the two decades of Reza Shah's dominance in Iran, the emerging political elite in 1941 was something of an anomaly. The occupying powers wanted the Pahlavi dynasty to remain, but with Mohammad Reza, the shah's oldest son, as ruler.[6] This would provide, they assumed, continuity and some stability. But the young shah was far from being in absolute control. Rather, he shared power with men who represented primarily the traditional landowning elite, the group with which the British had been most comfortable in the years before Reza Shah's rise to power.

But this traditional domination could prevail only because the occupiers provided the security forces that guaranteed order. When they departed, as they promised to do once the war was over, there would be a challenge. At that point, the survival of the old oligarchy would be much in question. There was by now a numerically large and assertive element of the population demanding rapid change and an end to the old system. To be sure, this change-oriented element was deeply divided regarding the type of system they wished as a replacement, and these divisions would allow the old system a period of grace. But the only way the old elite could retain power would be for external forces to provide the necessary coercion to contain those calling for radical change. If the oligarchs created a security force sufficient to provide order, they would have great difficulty controlling it. A man on horseback would be a probability. The other alternative was to seek a compromise with the most moderate leaders of the new force. But any progress on that front would lead to a sharing of power with more radical groups and hence would risk losing control to them.

The British response to the situation was to return to old patterns of interference they had not employed since the early 1920s. Sayyid Zia left his exile in Palestine and returned to Iran. Not only did politically active Iranians see this as an open British maneuver, so did both the U.S. and Soviet representatives in Iran.[7] The National Will party that Sayyid Zia had set up and his newspaper *R'ad Emruz* were perceived universally as expressions of British strategy. Furthermore, in the Iranian view Sayyid Zia's activities were only the tip of the British iceberg. Men regarded in Iran as British agents were located in the court, the military, the Majlis, street gangs, the clergy, and all-important tribal groups. The Freemasons of Iran were considered in particular the locus of the MI-6's (British intelligence's) primary recruitment. The Anglo-Iranian Oil Company, the British Bank, and virtually all major British corporations were assumed to include among their staff members of the British intelligence service. A significant section of the press, especially low-circulation gossip sheets, were seen as British-subsidized. The pattern Iranians saw was clear. Britain had major assets in all the traditional institutions of Iran and was in a position to orchestrate the traditional political system in the country. In addition, since secret Anglo-Russian collaboration was assumed, there was no surprise in seeing the easy relations between Soviet occupation forces and traditional elite elements in north Iran. And likewise the Tudeh party, the Marxist party particularly strong in the oil fields, was widely seen as a joint Anglo-Soviet enterprise.

What part if any of this picture, so widely accepted in Iran then and now, was true? The question is naive. No large bureaucracy is capable of orchestrating a conspiracy so elaborate as that the Iranians attributed to the British. Great Britain was engaged in a struggle for national survival. Maintaining the flow of supplies to the Soviets as the war approached the climactic battle of Stalingrad was one of the most vital aspects of this great struggle. Concern for the internal

situation in Iran must be seen in this context. There had to be sufficient stability and tranquility to permit the flow of supplies to the
Soviet Union and the flow of oil to the British war economy. In this
crisis situation, problems would be dealt with even more on a day-
to-day basis than in less troubled periods. British documents that
have been released reflect exactly this—a preoccupation with the primary problems of the day. There is no evidence whatsoever of a
master plan such as the Iranians perceived.

Iran's view of events and its behavior parallels that of other peoples
who have been ruled indirectly. In all cases, the image of the mentor
approaches the stereotypical. But the image would atrophy were it
not reinforced by the behavior of the mentor. The British in Iran
certainly corroborated the Iranian view of them. They were aware
of how Sayyid Zia was perceived and knew that his actions would
be attributed to their direction. Yet they not only did nothing to
disabuse the Iranians of their view of Sayyid Zia, but also gave every
appearance of consciously verifying it. The conclusion that can be
drawn, therefore, is that the British did see Sayyid Zia as a man who
could provide the internal stability their interests required. The conclusion also follows that, as had been true one and two generations
earlier, they did not take seriously the new forces demanding a role
in Iranian politics. Nor did they appear to see any major difficulty
for a Sayyid Zia–type regime attempting to maintain control once
the external forces had withdrawn. There was no effort to seek out
a Reza Khan for Sayyid Zia this time, a man who could rebuild and
provide inspiring leadership for the security forces.

But the process of change was in fact strong. Most Iranian politicians showed by their behavior that they, unlike the British, recognized this fact. Political leaders who favored a sharp break from the
traditional system can be placed in three categories, although within
each category there was great variance. The first (and at that time
least capable of gaining control in Iran) were the Marxists. They
had been successful in attracting to their ranks some outstanding intellectuals, but their base of support outside the intelligentsia was
so small that only a serious assist from the Soviets could have brought
them to power. Yet they were growing in strength and appeal and
were a factor to contend with.[8]

The second were the democratic nationalists. This was a large
conglomerate group. Some were little more than reformists wishing

to move gradually in a controlled democracy toward a more liberal system. Others were laissez-faire liberals, Fabian socialists, or more orthodox Marxists opposed to any form of tutelage from the Soviet Union. Some were liberal and favored a functioning constitutional government. Others were populists, recognizing the appearance now of a mass base that would respond to nationalistic appeals and little interested in liberal institutions. For such a diverse group to act with any real coherence almost certainly necessitated the appearance of a leader with vast appeal. In the war years Mohammad Musaddiq had yet to achieve that status.[9] Nevertheless, the potential of this group was great, as events would soon show, but none of the occupying powers, and in 1942 that included the United States, saw that potential.

The third group was the progressive-to-radical wing of the clergy. Their differences, evident in 1906 and again in the early 1920s, were by now even more exaggerated. Ayatullah Abol Qasem Kashani, in the direct line of Modaress in wishing to see a preeminent role for the clergy in politics, was willing to engage in a political alliance with secular leaders. Ruhullah Khomeini shared most of Kashani's ultimate goals, but, like Sheikh Fazlullah Nuri, refused to sanction the leadership of secular nationalists—an element he saw as effectively acculturated. Already, even in the war years, the populist appeal of Kashani was apparent. Other "political mullahs," as they were referred to, had far more liberal views and were comfortable in an alliance with liberal secularists.[10]

The British did take note of these three elements. Not unexpectedly, they were most concerned with the first, the Marxists. As long as the USSR's ability to halt Hitler's forces was in question, Britain's worries focused on the Tudeh party and its power to complicate the operations of the Anglo-Iranian Oil Company. Iranians would find no evidence in British documents to support their belief that the Tudeh party was Anglo-Soviet inspired. On the contrary, there was from the beginning strongly expressed concern about Soviet infiltration. After the turn of the tide of battle at Stalingrad, the British expected the Soviets to make use of Iran's Marxists in an effort to establish control in Iran. With regard to the other groups, the British were inclined throughout the 1941–1951 decade to play down their importance.[11] Whenever the name of Musaddiq or his allies appears in British correspondence, one is likely to find two accompanying adjectives: "fanatic" and "extremist." Kashani is dismissed as a "demagogue." But nationalistic "fanatics" and religious "demagogues" are likely to have large, receptive publics to listen to their diatribes and therefore should be taken seriously — or so one might think. However, the British were not sufficiently interested in this possibility to make any extended analysis of the base of support for either group. Official British policy likewise ignored them.

## Wartime Occupation of Iran

When the Anglo-Soviet invasion of Iran began in 1941 and Reza Shah sent his urgent note to Franklin Roosevelt, he asked the United States to intervene with the British and the Soviets to halt the invasion. Reza Shah's request was forwarded by an American legation in Tehran that was not unsympathetic to the Iranians. Secretary of State Cordell Hull responded quickly and emphatically in the negative.[12] But the legation's attitude toward the British and Soviets in Iran remained skeptical and occasionally antagonistic for the next several years. After the United States became involved in World War II, the American role in Iran was suddenly an important one. A U.S. military force was sent to secure transportation and communications lines. But even more important, American technical missions were requested and provided in the areas of finance, the economy, and internal security.

Iran's preference for American advisers followed a pattern that by now was well established. The geopolitical purpose was obvious. But there was also an element of nostalgia, a yearning for a relationship with American advisers similar to a romanticized version of the Shuster relationship thirty years earlier. Two of the primary American advisers came close to meeting that standard. H. Norman Schwartzkopf headed an advisory mission for the gendarmerie. He was personally well liked and his dealing with Iranians reflected both sensitivity and an ability to empathize with them.[13] General Clarence C. Ridley, who headed a military advisory mission, also avoided the patronizing tendency that characterized so many Europeans dealing with Iranians.[14] But the opposite was the case with the director of the financial mission, Arthur Millspaugh. His behavior should have been predictable. He had revealed in his previous tenure in Iran an imperious quality to his personality that led to the termination of his employment. But in the 1920s he had advised a government headed by an absolute dictator. In the war years in Iran, the government was weak and depended on occupation forces for internal security. In this setting, Millspaugh's imperious nature pushed him toward insisting on near-dictatorial powers. The Iranian government, never really sure of the extent to which Millspaugh's policies were the policies of the occupying governments, acquiesced in these demands many times. But anger and resentment developed to the point that parliamentary speeches and most of the press were openly hostile. Significantly, *R'ad Emruz,* Sayyid Zia's newspaper, supported him, thus leading virtually all politically interested Iranians to conclude that he had British support.[15]

The American legation found itself in a contradictory position. It insisted that Millspaugh was an employee of the Iranian government and in no way represented U.S. policy, but it also did its best to smooth feathers that Millspaugh seemed to delight in ruffling. Finally the resentment was too great and Millspaugh's resignation was accepted. Millspaugh wrote a book, *Americans in Persia* (1946), that is almost a classical expression of the imperial view of the "lower races."[16] For him, Iranians were an immature people who, like children, were impetuous, often charming, selfish, and undisciplined. They needed a long period of tutelage by civilizing mentors. He concluded by recommending that Iran be divided into Soviet and Western spheres.

A reading of American documents from the war years reveals surprisingly parallel pictures of the British and the Soviets. In sum, the difference that appears is that American diplomats were sure of Soviet intentions but confused about those of the British. On occasion, the British were presented as desiring a sovereign and stable Iran.[17] But more frequently this purpose was questioned.[18] The Soviets were regularly depicted as seeking inordinate influence in Iran, an influence well above that necessary for winning the war.[19] However, there was nothing in the American dispatches that approximated the later cold war view of the Soviets. Rather, the picture of both was closer to that of a sluggish imperialism in Iran.

The British modus operandi was well understood. Secretary of State Hull went so far as to authorize his representatives in Tehran to tell their British and Soviet colleagues that a government of Sayyid Zia was undesirable.[20] Pro-British politicians identified by name were of the Freemason variety. The British were depicted as toying with tribal elements. Less clear was Soviet behavior. Soviet policy was seen as self-serving, but through 1944 the USSR was not accused of using the instrument of Iranian Marxists or of attempting to gain control of Iran's northern oil reserves.

U.S. reporting of Iranian internal politics focused almost exclusively on personalities. Such questions as what was the domestic support for the shah and for various contenders for the premiership were not asked. There was apparently little to no interest in the three groups described above (the Marxists, the democratic nationalists, and the progressive clergy) as ready to challenge the traditional oligarchy. Communists and religious leaders were occasionally mentioned. The nationalists were seen much as the British saw them, as extreme and irrational. Their opposition to Millspaugh was mentioned and one speech of Musaddiq was described as "absurd."[21] The Iranian nationalistic intelligentsia who placed such hopes on support from an ideologically sympathetic United States would have been shocked and disillusioned had they been able to read the American official correspondence.

In July 1944 the U.S. legation sent a long dispatch calling for some basic decisions in Washington regarding Iran. There were, this dispatch argued, two possible courses of action. One was to return to the "relatively unimportant position we occupied prior to the war." But the second and preferred policy proposal tells much about how official America saw Iran, the allies, and the kind of role the United States as an awakened world power could play:

The second course open to us would necessitate a stronger and broader implementation of policy than we have hitherto attempted. As I see it we could have to decide that our interests in Iran, political and economic, practical and idealistic, are sufficiently important to warrant continuing strong affirmative action regardless of whether or not such action could be directly related to the prosecution of the war; this is [the] true premise adopted by the British and Soviets who by no means restrict their activities in Iran to promotion of the war effort.

This Legation keenly aware of actual or potential Russian and British opposition and faced daily with adviser problems largely the result of proffered help to an ignorant people dominated by leaders who prefer not to be helped is nevertheless inclined to favor the second course.[22]

This important dispatch is in all respects similar to a January 23, 1943, memorandum to the State Department sent by John Jernegan.[23] In both, the British-Russian rivalry is treated almost in nineteenth-century terms, Jernegan stressing the notion of a "Russian" interest in warm-water ports, and never mentioning the "Soviet Union" or its desire to spread communism. Both imply a strong interest in making permanent the United States' scope of influence in Iran. Both have all the earmarks of a bureaucratic interest in a vastly expanded domain for foreign policy activity. In both, the tutorial role for the "ignorant" Iranian people and saving them from their venal leaders is stressed. The Jernegan memorandum does observe that the Russians could make Azerbaijan a separate Soviet state any time they wished, but does not wonder why they do not do so. There is in fact through 1944 no real sign of the cold war mindset that would so soon be the basis of the U.S. definition of the situation in Iran.

Soviet behavior through much of 1944 was straightforward. Engaged in a desperate struggle with Germany, the Soviets treated Iran as a supply lifeline to its allies. Order and stability were essential to maintain this lifeline, and the Soviets followed a pragmatic policy to achieve it. Soviet armed forces secured the transportation and communications lines and provided the essential bases for an effective internal security force. But interaction with Iranian politics was inescapable. Here the Soviets effectively followed a policy of working with Iranians who could best and most easily keep the situation under control. This led officials of the vanguard of the world communist movement, the Soviet Union, to deal primarily with traditional leaders. Where, as in Kurdish areas, local elements were inclined to follow disruptive policies, the Soviets through 1944 assisted in their suppression.[24]

However, Azerbaijan was a special case. Not only were the people of Iranian Azerbaijan ethnically close to those of Soviet Azerbaijan, but also there were many Iranian Azerbaijanis living in the Soviet Union who were prepared to return to Iran under Soviet auspices. After the Soviet invasion, many of these people did return and were in a position, just as Jernegan suggested, to establish a separate pro-Soviet regime in Azerbaijan. Mohammad Pishevari, the leader of this group, would be called on to become premier of the autonomous republic in 1945. Prior to that time, however, the Soviet occupation forces in Azerbaijan worked through traditional leaders, as they did in the remainder of north Iran. But Pishevari and his followers were allowed to operate openly in the province and with obvious Soviet favor. They were always careful, however, to insist that they were Iranian patriots.[25]

American oil interests persisted in treating the oil reserves of northern Iran as a potential American concession target. Through 1944 the Soviets tolerated this activity and gave no real indication that they harbored ambitions for gaining control of this resource of uncertain potential. Geological evidence suggested little grounds for optimism about the size and quality of the northern oil supplies. But, as later events would demonstrate, these estimates would not prevent a renewed Soviet interest in Iran's oil after 1944.

### The Azerbaijan Crisis

In 1945, with the war certain to end in an Allied victory, Soviet policy toward Iran changed directions. Two successive Iranian governments, headed by Prime Minister Sadr and Prime Minister Hakimi,[26] became the targets of hostile Soviet statements and hostile policy. There were three dimensions to this policy. First there was suddenly open activity in support of ethnic autonomy and ethnic separation. In Azerbaijan there was a sharp increase in support for Pishevari by Soviet occupation authorities. Increasingly newspapers in the area and official Soviet propaganda called for more respect for the distinctive Turkish culture of Azerbaijan, including the right to read, write, and be educated in Turkish. A political party, the Azerbaijan Democrat party, was formed from the Pishevari group, Tudeh party members, and Azerbaijani separatists. This newly formed party was correctly perceived in Tehran as being groomed to serve the purpose of the official party of an autonomous region.[27]

In September 1945 the Soviets, reversing themselves, suddenly turned a benign eye on Kurdish separatism. But the resulting policy was obviously ad hoc, clumsily executed, and indicative of the most superficial understanding of Kurdish nationalist politics. Using Soviet Azerbaijanis as contact persons, even though there were at least 100,000 Kurds in the Soviet Union and relations between Kurds and Azerbaijanis were often antagonistic, the Soviets bought into a young but vital Kurdish nationalist party, the Komeleh. In stark contrast to the situation in Azerbaijan, where separatist propaganda attracted little interest and the Azerbaijan Democrat party was viewed as an artificial creation, the Komeleh had the potential for speaking for

Kurdish nationalism especially among settled and urbanized Kurds. The Soviets in effect made an alliance with an outstanding Kurdish political leader, Qazi Mohammad, and the Komeleh. The so-called Mehabad Kurdish Republic attracted genuine popularity.[28]

George Kennan, speaking from the United States embassy in Moscow in 1946, commented that Soviet policy toward Azerbaijan and Kurdistan was in tune with a broad policy in the countries along the entire Soviet border of playing on ethnicity to set up autonomous, pro-Soviet regimes.[29] But what was the overall purpose this policy served? The Kurds, for example, were found in significant numbers in Iran, Iraq, Syria, Turkey, and the Soviet Union. Was the play on Kurdish nationalism designed to pressure host governments, to attract Kurds into joining with Soviet Kurds to form a Soviet regime, to constitute a puppet buffer state, to serve as a vehicle for further Soviet expansion in Iran and the southwest Asian region, or to serve some more mysterious purpose? Whatever the objective, Soviet policy over the next twelve months in Azerbaijan and Kurdistan was to lead to an international crisis that, along with Soviet policy in East Europe, was to generate what came to be known as the cold war perspective. In this view, the Soviet Union was seen as ineluctably aggressive and to be contained only by great will and determination and a full understanding of its devious and conspiratorial style. The Soviet purpose was a messianic one—to give to the world the blessings of communism, with Moscow the center of the communist universe. But as the following pages suggest, the policy in Azerbaijan that helped generate this view has been badly misrepresented in most U.S. accounts. This is true even though most of the Americans intimately involved with it at the time saw the policy with remarkable clarity.

Soviet complaints about the Iranian government in 1945 fell into two categories. The first was that two Iranian prime ministers, Sadr and Hakimi, were members of an Iranian ruling class that was antagonistic to the Soviet Union and whose antagonism constituted a threat to Soviet Azerbaijan and the oil refineries at Baku.[30] On the surface, this charge was so absurd as to be bewildering. Iran was under Allied occupation, Soviet troops were in full control of any invasion route, and the Iranian government was pathetically weak. Yet Stalin personally made the charge. The initial American response indicated that officials in Washington were flabbergasted that the

Soviets would seriously advance so ridiculous a proposition. But some diplomats on the field did understand what Stalin had left unsaid. By 1945, even before the Germans were finally defeated, Stalin was setting the stage for dealing with the inevitable conflict to follow. As Stalin described it, that conflict would be necessary to combat a persisting capitalist encirclement of the socialist homeland. Sadr and Hakimi were minor instruments in a British-led plan to use Iran as a base for advancing into the Soviet Caucasus. Lancelot Frank Lee Pyman, the Iranian desk officer of the British Foreign Office in 1947, described this view well: "The USSR is obsessed by the idea that America and/or British might move into northern Iran and use it as a base for attack against the USSR."[31] The second dimension of Soviet policy in 1945, therefore, was to insist on an Iranian government that would be independent of the British and at least not unfriendly with the Soviet Union. Ahmad Qavam, the Iranian prime minister throughout most of this crisis period, seemed to meet this requirement, at least at first.

The other area of complaint concerned northern Iranian oil. After a long period of apparent indifference to the question of a concession in that area as long as it remained out of British or German hands, the Soviets began manifesting an open interest in exploiting that resource and did so without subtlety. Given their repudiation of tsarist concessions in Iran and of extraterritoriality, the Soviets could not easily insist on being granted a concession. They proposed, rather, setting up a joint Soviet-Iranian company for the purpose of exploring and perhaps extracting oil.[32] Concern with Iran's oil constituted the third dimension of Soviet policy in Iran.

When they occupied Iran in 1941, the British and Soviets promised the Iranians they would evacuate Iran within six months of the cessation of hostilities. The Iranian government thought the date should be six months following the German surrender, but would have been more than satisfied were Iran free of foreign forces by March 2, 1946, six months after the Japanese surrender. The U.S. government made clear its determination to withdraw and called on the British and Soviets to do the same.[33] The British were agreeable, provided the Soviets left, but Soviet behavior, to say the least, was ominous. Far from showing signs of preparing to depart, Soviet activity in support of Azerbaijani and Kurdish separatism intensified. On November 19, 1945, Pishevari proclaimed the formation of an autonomous Democratic Republic of Azerbaijan that would be, except in matters of foreign policy, independent of Tehran. Soviet forces in the area kept the Iranian military confined to its barracks to prevent their taking action against the new autonomous republic.[34]

Robert A. Rossow, reporting for the U.S. consulate in Tabriz, provided the American government with a full description of the takeover. Rossow proved to be an aggressive and innovative reports officer. He made contact with Pishevari and set up a network of Iranian contacts who gave him reports of Soviet military movements in the area. Rossow's descriptions represent the earliest expression of the cold war view of the Soviet Union. He tended to see a strong rationale for Soviet actions and a Soviet ability to orchestrate both the political and the military environment with great skill.[35] Rossow years later wrote an article advancing his conclusion that the Azerbaijan crisis was part of a Soviet move on Greece, Turkey, and Iran. That it failed to achieve its objectives, Rossow concluded, like others who shared his view of reality, was due to the tough and determined stance adopted by President Truman and his representatives in the area.[36]

But neither Murray, Truman's ambassador in Iran, nor Ahmad Qavam saw the situation this way. Murray respected Rossow, and there is no indication in official American correspondence that the two opposing views of the Soviet Union and its intentions had crystalized. On the contrary, certain of Murray's reports approached the Rossow tenor. But far more frequently he saw genuine prospects for a Soviet withdrawal, if not by March 2, then shortly thereafter.[37] Soviet Ambassador Maximov had told the U.S. embassy of his suspicions of the purpose of British machinations in Iran, allegedly including efforts to undermine the position of U.S. advisers. Murray saw this as a continuing manifestation of the historic British-Russian competition for preeminence in Iran. He saw the British as more benign in intent, but he also saw little to choose between the two in terms of their intervention in Iran.[38]

American policy throughout the critical period from November 19, 1945, when the coup in Azerbaijan took place, to May 5, 1946, when the USSR withdrew from Iran, was focused on the United Nations Security Council. Both the embassy in Tehran and the department in Washington encouraged the Iranians to take their case to the Security Council and gave full and energetic support to the Iranian ambassador to the United Nations, Hossein Ala. Years after the fact, Harry Truman remembered having threatened the Soviets with sending a fleet into the Persian Gulf to emphasize America's seriousness of purpose. But government historians can find no documentary support for this recollection.[39] On the contrary, what is evident in the published documents is a full awareness by Ambassador Murray and his successor George Allen, and by the Department of State and the Department of War, of the United States' inability to give effective direct military assistance to Iran should the Soviets refuse to leave. Prime Minister Qavam on several occasions asked just exactly what assistance he could expect should the Soviets refuse to withdraw or should advance further into Iran. Each time the answer was that the United States would advance the Iranian case in the Security Council.[40] Both Americans and Iranians felt that in the event of Soviet intransigence the British would favor a de facto division of the country.[41]

Qavam was operating, therefore, from an exceedingly weak bargaining base. He could not expect significant direct support from any source and was denied any leverage that might accrue from a possible threat to resort to force. His only real leverage derived from whatever desire the Soviets might have for a favorable public opinion in Iran, the Middle East, Europe, and the United States. A brutal disregard for Iranian national sensitivities could, for example, reduce the Iranians' willingness to cooperate with local Marxists. Qavam and his foreign minister went to Moscow to negotiate, but they were painfully aware of the weakness of their position.

When Qavam returned to Tehran, he expressed the view to Murray that Iran's oil was the primary Soviet concern.[42] He concluded a working agreement with the Soviets that called for acceptance by the Iranian cabinet of a joint Soviet-Iranian oil company, 51 percent Soviet-controlled, that would explore, develop, and exploit oil fields in any part of northern Iran. But Dr. Musaddiq had proposed and the Majlis had passed legislation that denied any Iranian government the right to conclude an economic agreement involving concessions so long as foreign troops occupied Iran. Furthermore, ratification of the agreement would require the approval of a parliament elected after the evacuation of these troops. Qavam agreed that parliamentary approval would be sought within seven months.[43]

The Soviet government in this working agreement accepted the

Iranians' insistence that relations between Tehran and Tabriz were of domestic Iranian concern only. It was understood that negotiations would be entered into by Qavam and Pishevari and that the Soviet ambassador would serve as mediator. In return, the Soviet government agreed that all Soviet troops would leave Iran "in five or six weeks."[44]

On its face, this agreement was astonishingly favorable to weak Iran. Given the pessimism among geologists regarding the supply or accessibility of northern Iranian oil and the uncertainty of the ratification procedure, the Soviets would at best gain only a small return and possibly nothing at all. Rossow reported from Tabriz that Soviet military men posing as civilians were infiltrating the area, but Murray and the Department of State were willing to wait and see.

U.S. diplomatic correspondence is strangely silent on this Soviet generosity and whatever reasons lay behind it. Qavam felt that Iran had nothing to lose and much to gain in terms of its good relations with the Soviet Union by acceding to Ambassador Sadchikov's request that Iran withdraw the Azerbaijan case from the Security Council agenda. But Washington demurred. Without claiming publicly or privately that it was the leverage gained by keeping the case on the agenda that was responsible for Soviet behavior, the department was not willing to lose its one source of bargaining strength.[45] Qavam saw a great deal being risked for very little, but he did not want to offend the Americans and the British. However, when the Soviets expressed outrage, he instructed Hossein Ala to withdraw the case. Then, responding to American pressure, he agreed to allow it to remain quietly on the agenda until May 6.[46]

Negotiations began between Qavam and Pishevari with Sadchikov's mediation, but deadlocked over the issue of disbanding the Azerbaijan army. But, in spite of this, the Soviets completed their withdrawal on schedule. After May 5, Soviet personnel remained along the trans-Iranian railroad and in airports in Khorassan province. But the Soviet government insisted they had demonstrated without any question their sincerity of purpose and that both the government of Iran and the Security Council should recognize that fact by immediately withdrawing the Iranian case from the United Nations.[47]

But Azerbaijan and Kurdistan remained under the control of regimes that were in power because of blatant Soviet interference. The

USSR may have passed one test by withdrawing its troops from Iran, but a second and ultimately more important test remained. Would it allow the restoration of Iranian sovereignty over Azerbaijan and Kurdistan? Two very different answers to that question emerged in the Iranian government. The shah and his entourage were exhilarated by the Soviet withdrawal and the shah made clear both his diagnosis and his prescription. The Soviets withdrew because the Americans stood up to them, and they would not return if the United States showed the requisite will and determination. The prescription followed logically. The Iranian case must remain on the Security Council agenda and be given full support. Equally important, the United States must become intimately involved in Iranian affairs. By this the shah meant the United States must work internally in Iran with the British to give him full control of government policy. Qavam, he argued, would negotiate away control of Azerbaijan to Pishevari and the Soviet Union.[48] The shah's message was understood perfectly by Allen, who rejected his suggestion of internal involvement on the spot.[49] But the shah continued to push for his plan through the loyal royalist Hossein Ala. Ala was successful, and Secretary of State George Byrnes ordered Edward Stettinius at the United Nations to keep the Iranian case on the calendar.[50]

Ahmad Qavam saw the situation differently in every regard. He did not see, as the shah did, a highly aggressive Soviet Union seeking to impose communism on the world, but somehow easily containable by a strong U.S. position in the United Nations. He saw instead a continuation of the old Anglo-Russian struggle for preeminence in Iran. The British were openly interfering in the south, the Russians in the north. Their competition extended as always into the domestic political arena. The British were operating through their natural allies, the Freemasonry-connected landowners, tribal leaders, conservative clerics, and mercenary street leaders. Sayyid Zia was only the most obvious of their surrogates. Their real strength lay with the entourage of the shah and the shah himself. The Soviets, typically heavy-handed, operated through puppet leaders in Azerbaijan, many traditional landowners in the north, and with the left intelligentsia, particularly those associated with the Tudeh party.[51] Clearly, in Qavam's view, the British were in the stronger position and Qavam came close to entering into an electoral alliance with the Tudeh to balance off the British advantage. The leading nationalists in Iran, soon to be united in an umbrella organization called the National Front, were in general agreement with Qavam. Mohammad Musaddiq and his close allies in the Iran party went even further in effecting an alliance with the Tudeh for the coming elections.[52]

Americans concerned with Iran were not of one mind. Robert Rossow, for example, predicted that the Soviets would not only retain indirect control of Azerbaijan and Kurdistan but also subvert the government in Tehran. His view reflected in most particulars a rapidly crystallizing cold war perspective. But, unlike the shah, Rossow at this time did not claim that the Soviets withdrew because of manifest will and determination on the part of the United States. On the contrary, American officials across the board understood the USSR's geopolitical advantage in Iran. The belief that a tough U.S. stance explains Soviet behavior came to dominate American explanations in a few years and persists to this day. However, contemporaries most directly concerned—including even those most suspicious of the Soviet Union—were not so self-deceived.

The tendency was growing to define the situation in cold war terms. Yet George Allen in particular resisted this view. This is ironic, since Allen later came to be seen as an early cold war hero and the man most responsible for the belief that the USSR would reveal itself to be a paper tiger if only the United States were to stand up to it.

The U.S. bargaining position vis-à-vis Iranian politicians was excellent. The shah made painfully clear his wish in 1946 to enter into the kind of surrogate relationship with the United States that was established seven years later. Qavam, his chief competitor, was willing to risk Soviet wrath to retain U.S. favor. A battle quickly developed between the shah and Qavam to influence American policy in the Azerbaijan crisis.

The immediate issue of concern was whether the Iranian case should remain on the Security Council agenda. The shah won the first battle. Then, working through Hossein Ala who was willing to risk insubordination to serve the shah, he convinced the U.S. Department of State to support a British proposal to send a commission of inquiry to Iran.[53] The proposal would have been vetoed, but it would have maintained Anglo-American pressure on the Soviets. U.S. support was obtained by Ala through his claim that civil war had developed in Iran and that there was no indication as of May 20, 1946, that the Soviets had in fact withdrawn.

In Qavam's view, this was a fabrication designed to influence the political struggle inside Iran. He feared that an outraged Soviet Union would repudiate the agreement with him and insisted that the Iranian case be removed from the agenda. Allen's response to this was restrained. He told Washington, "It is important to keep Iranian attitude toward British in mind to interpret Iranian Government's attitude toward question of Soviet interference before the Security Council. I would suggest caution on our part to avoid getting too far out on a limb on question of Soviet interference without more positive evidence to support Ala's general accusations."[54] Allen saw dangers in Qavam's willingness to consider an alliance with the Tudeh. But he added, "On the other hand, Qavam's friendly attitude toward Tudeh has one political advantage in that it might tend to remove Tudeh feeling that Party must depend on Soviet support to prevent being suppressed. Any encouragement that could be given Tudeh to become genuine Iranian Party without looking abroad for support would of course be helpful."[55] This is a far cry from the rapidly developing image of a monolithic communism in which such parties as the Tudeh were seen as mindless agents of Soviet policy.

In early June 1946, a preliminary agreement was reached between the Iranian government and the Pishevari regime. By its terms the Azerbaijan parliament would be recognized as a provincial assembly; a governor would be chosen from a list submitted to Tehran by that assembly; the Azerbaijan army and gendarmerie would be integrated in an undefined way into the Iranian armed forces.[56] This was a standoff agreement that applied to Kurdistan as well. It did not substantiate fears of an expanding penetration by the Soviets, but neither did it promise Iranian reunification. The internal battle between the shah and Qavam continued and so did the external struggle for influence of American policy.

The British at this point proposed to Washington that there be an Anglo-American front formed in Tehran to urge on Qavam a more anti-Soviet stand. Allen saw this as reflecting the opinion of British Ambassador Sir John H. Le Rougetel and opposed the idea on the grounds that it would confirm Iran's expectation of the formation of a clever British–naive American front in support of policies identified with the shah. The department accepted Allen's recommendation and thus disappointed the shah and his supporters.[57]

From June to December 1946, the situation in Iran remained ambiguous. The critical unknown was the Soviet objective. Would the Soviets follow a forward policy, buoying up the regimes they had sponsored in Azerbaijan and Kurdistan and proceeding to dominate the government in Tehran through subversion? These were the expressed expectations of Americans such as Rossow and of the shah and his supporters.[58] Or would the Soviets acquiesce in Iran's reunification under a government that would be genuinely nonaligned? This was the fond hope of Ahmad Qavam. Ambassador Allen at no time allowed himself the optimism to predict this outcome, but his support to Qavam is evidence that he did not rule it out.[59]

Having been mildly rebuffed by the U.S. government, the British proceeded to behave in Iran much as they had before the days of Reza Shah. Interference with the internal politics of the southern tribes was so blatant that even Hossein Ala considered complaining to the United Nations.[60] Sayyid Zia continued to give the impression that he was the chosen instrument of British policy in Iran and the shah's collaboration with pro-British politicians was unconcealed. Ambassador Allen gained the impression that the British were now prepared to agree to a de facto partition of Iran, with Azerbaijan becoming one of many satellite regimes.[61]

The shah continued to make attracting official American support his primary objective. But he met with steady failure with Allen, who remarked to Washington that should the shah replace Qavam with a government composed of men seen as "British stooges," Iran would be badly weakened.[62] However, Hossein Ala had more success with American officials in Washington. Loy Henderson, director of the Office of Near Eastern and African Affairs and later the ambassador who would preside over the American role in overthrowing Musaddiq, wrote a memo favoring the shah's replacing Qavam with a stronger anti-Soviet prime minister.[63]

But Qavam was the man in control in Iran, and the policy he followed was one of cautious, exploratory pragmatism. In retrospect, his diplomacy in this critical six months appears to have been a tour de force. He gauged with apparent accuracy the freedom of action the international and domestic arenas granted him. Soviet behavior did not conform at all to cold war expectations. Pressure on Qavam was sporadic and largely verbal. Day by day it became more apparent to Qavam that he could restore Iranian control in Azerbaijan with Soviet acquiescence. In October 1946 he broke his tacit alliance with the Tudeh party and formed a new cabinet without Tudeh representation. The shah attempted to take credit for Qavam's move, but the new cabinet was composed entirely of Qavam loyalists.[64]

In November and early December Qavam made clear his intention to send the Iranian army into Azerbaijan, and he so informed the Security Council. The Soviets responded angrily, but Qavam was now convinced that if the Soviets were forced to choose between oil and Azerbaijan, they would choose the former. Qavam was ready to move into Azerbaijan while promising to stand by the oil agreement he had signed but could not ratify until a new parliament was elected. With considerable apprehension, Qavam sent the army toward the south Azerbaijan city of Mianeh with instructions to proceed cautiously, waiting for a possible Soviet reaction.[65] To everyone's relief and satisfaction, the army met no resistance and the citizens of Tabriz liberated their city before the army could arrive. Journalists and diplomats reported that the restoration of Iranian control was welcomed in Tabriz and elsewhere in Azerbaijan with jubilation reminiscent of the liberation of France.[66] In marked contrast, the Kurds resisted and, in the face of overwhelming force, sullenly accepted defeat.

Ambassador Allen reported that the Soviets had informed Pishevari that he could expect only moral support from them. But he reported as well that Iranians generally attributed the victory to the strong and forceful support the United States had given Iran in the Security Council. The shah, taking full credit for his government's actions, agreed but added high Iranian and low Azerbaijani morale as factors.[67]

Two Americans directly concerned with Iran, Allen and Walter Bedell Smith, the U.S. ambassador in Moscow, gave their answers to the question of why the Soviet Union behaved as it did in this crisis. Ambassador Smith already had accepted a cold war view of the Soviet Union. Ambassador Allen had not. Therefore the puzzle was greater for Smith than for Allen. Why had the ineluctably aggressive, monolithic, and conspiratorial Soviets permitted such a humiliation on their own border? Smith faced the question directly.

To us, most surprising element in situation was [that] weakness camouflaged Soviet military and political machine [in] Azerbaijan. . . . It . . . seems strange that USSR had not organized provincial force composed, if necessary, largely of Soviet Azerbaijanis adequate to resist timid tentative Iranian advance. Poor organization and over confidence may account for Soviet failure.

It must not be thought, however, that Kremlin will resign itself to this humiliating reverse. It will continue to maneuver not only for oil concessions but also for political (and strategic) ascendancy in Iran.[68]

The full-fledged cold war interpretation of this critical event, an interpretation that continues to dominate American accounts, dropped this element of surprise. The Soviets retreated, it was assumed, because of the strong will and determination manifested by the United States in the UN. Already, as we have seen, the view of Iranians associated with the shah accepted this interpretation.

Allen's explanation lacks the simplicity of that associated with a stereotyped cold war view. He saw a complex answer. "It is suggested that Soviet failure to send combat units to support Azerbaijan may have resulted from fact that Azerbaijan regime collapsed too fast, from internal considerations in USSR, from broader questions of foreign policy connected with Europe, from fear of SC [Security Council] and world opinion censure, or combination of all of them."[69]

The crisis was not yet at an end. Since Qavam believed the Soviets had made the choice of surrendering Azerbaijan for oil, he was understandably worried about what would happen if the agreement was not ratified. By the terms of his agreement, he was under an obligation to present it for ratification by a newly elected Majlis within a few weeks, and the election had not yet been held. His inclination was to procrastinate and, if possible, renegotiate the oil agreement he had signed. Ironically, his problem was magnified by the strangely acquiescent Soviet policy of the past year. Convinced as they were that the Soviet policy was a direct response to American firmness, most Iranian politicians saw no reason to approve the agreement. Had they not been so confident of the United States' ability and willingness to contain the Soviets, Qavam opined, they would quickly rush into the Soviet embrace.[70]

But Qavam had no illusions on this score. A strong stance in the United Nations, he felt, would have little bearing on a Soviet decision to invade. For the next ten months he was the source of alarming—Allen suspected alarmist—reports of Soviet troop concentrations.[71] Both the American embassy and Iranian politicians were the targets of these reports but neither evinced any real alarm. Had Qavam been privy to Washington's assessments, he would have felt more confirmed in his fears. A Department of State report to Allen stated flatly that, in the event of a Soviet military move, "It is not believed that at present any assistance could be brought to Iran which would appreciably enhance Iranian resistance."[72] The U.S. response to urgent pleas from both Qavam and the shah was a willingness to consider granting Iran modest military credits.

Ambassador Le Rougetel, Allen believed, favored Iran's ratifying the agreement. Division in the Foreign Office was apparent, but ultimately Foreign Minister Ernest Bevin came down strongly on Le Rougetel's side. Allen argued convincingly that this was a return to the 1907 partition mentality. He strongly disagreed and, with Washington's support, told Qavam that the United States felt Iran should decide for itself how to deal with the Soviets. Allen went so far as to make this point forcefully in a public address.[73]

The Iranian response was entirely predictable. The United States was willing to stand up to and oppose an Anglo-Russian conspiracy to partition Iran and to divide its great oil resources. Allen's audience was electrified. Memories of Shuster and Caldwell were revived, and American popularity momentarily was at the pre-Millspaugh level. But there was another side to this reaction. Iranian cynicism had not been disarmed by American policy. There must be some major U.S. interest in gaining for itself the oil concession. In their dealing with the Soviets, Iranians, including Qavam, explained their policy as dictated by American pressure.

This was the kind of explanation Soviet representatives were prepared to accept, and a major change took place in their attitudes. Britain, previously the focus of Soviet hostility, was forthcoming; the United States artlessly, even openly in public addresses, stirred Iranian public sentiment against the Soviet Union. Now the Americans alone were the target of a strongly negative Soviet and Tudeh party campaign. And any Soviet willingness to listen to a compromise plan by Qavam vanished.[74]

Now it was the Americans' turn to show some alarm. Had Allen encouraged the Iranians to expect more aid from Washington than could be realized? What exactly would the Soviets do in the face of this verbal provocation? Ambassador Smith, true to his cold war view, was pessimistic. He was convinced that the USSR had decided on a tough position toward Iran.[75] Allen disagreed. He saw insisting on the letter of the agreement a blundering mistake of the variety to be expected from a totalitarian regime.[76] The State Department added its wisdom here. The Soviets would follow one or more of the following: "1) start a Greek type guerrilla operation using ethnically-related Soviet citizens 2) cause disturbances in major cities to divert Iranian military forces from the northern frontier and/or 3) intensify anti-Iranian propaganda."[77] Since the latter was already occurring, this was one of State's safer predictions. At the same time, the State Department urged its ambassador to persuade the shah and Qavam to work together to push Iran toward progressive reforms and to make clear to the tribes that they should seek to achieve their objectives through parliamentary means. Recognizing the Americans' inability to help significantly but also understanding that U.S. policy had led the Iranians to adopt a strong position toward the Soviets, the best the department could do was to cajole the Iranians into strengthening their home base.[78]

Finally on October 23, 1947, the Majlis voted 102–2 against ratification. The Soviets blustered verbally saying that Iranians would be responsible for the consequences. But they took no further action. The Azerbaijan crisis had finally come to an end.

In the immediate aftermath of the wartime collaboration of the Soviet Union and the western Allies, there was some hope that sufficient trust had been generated that the world could enter an era of peaceful coexistence. But Soviet behavior in three areas, Eastern Europe, Greece, and Iran, shattered these hopes. By 1947 the era that is well characterized by the metaphor *cold war* had begun. In retrospect, however, the historical account of the Greek civil war that has mainstream American academic acceptance throws into question the earlier cold war–associated description of that episode.[79] Now the proposition that Stalin was by and large living up to his agreement with Churchill concerning Greece is widely accepted. But a cold war–related description of the Iranian crisis continued to have general acceptance.[80] What the preceding account suggests is that not only is the accepted interpretation wrong, but also it was not the accepted interpretation of most Americans intimately involved in the crisis at the time. Furthermore, those Americans, like Rossow and Smith, who did see events in a cold war perspective were consistently wrong in their predictions, as was the shah. Conversely, George Allen, whose complex picture of Soviet purpose in the area bore no resemblance to the stereotypical cold war view, was again and again proved correct in his expectations.

There never was any disputing the fact of brutal Soviet intervention in Iran. What was in dispute were estimates of basic Soviet intentions and specific Soviet strategic purposes. The Soviets themselves described their policy as defensive in purpose, a response to capitalist encirclement. Specifically in Iran this called for resisting Western, predominantly British, efforts to manipulate the Iranian political system to produce a pro-British, anti-Soviet regime.

Ambassador Allen and his predecessors witnessed, described, and were appalled by British and Soviet interference in Iran. On occasion American reports distinguished between the two policies in terms of ultimate purpose, but more frequently they condemned them equally. Allen and his predecessors did not view Soviet policy as ineluctably aggressive; that view does not dominate American reporting in Iran until well after the Azerbaijan crisis. But the question of Soviet purpose was never answered by Allen and those who saw the situation as he did. Certainly there was no credence given to the Soviets' assertion of a defensive purpose. Soviet policy was described as blundering, crude, ineffectual, brutal, and at least sluggishly aggressive, but of uncertain purpose.

Qavam and probably most Iranians assumed that the Russian purpose, under Stalin as under the tsars, was to gain control of Iranian resources. Considering the fact that Iran had been subject for a century to Anglo-Russian competition in the form of political interference and that the prize always seemed to take the form of some major economic concession, this conclusion was natural. And certainly the Soviets gave Qavam every reason to believe that their interest in Iran's northern oil was serious.

What proposition best explains Soviet behavior in this, one of the most critical episodes in the genesis of the cold war? As their record in predicting should tell us, those who saw a Soviet Union determined to impose the blessings of communism on the rest of the world, with the will to do so and the monolithic organization capable of orchestrating an elaborate strategy for the purpose, had greatest difficulty in explaining the flow of events. The retrospective claim that the Soviets retreated, like a paper tiger, in the face of a tough American stand was not made by contemporaries. Washington was honest in its estimates that the United States could not have restrained the Soviets if they had moved militarily.

The proposition that the Soviets were responding to a perception of threat is more defensible. Americans who were unaware of the history of Anglo-Russian competition for political preeminence in Iran saw the Soviet claim that they feared a pathetically weak Iranian government bewilderingly absurd. But if the hypothesis is accepted that the Soviets had in mind not the Iranian regime but their perceived masters, the British, Stalin's remarks are more understandable. The British, working through Sayyid Zia, the shah, and tribal elements, could well have appeared to confirm such views. But the studiedly correct behavior of the Americans and apparent British willingness to collaborate in dividing Iran may well have had the result of reducing the intensity of the perceived Soviet threat. Wanting to avoid a breakdown in hitherto good Soviet-American relations, wanting to protect as much as they could an already tarnished Soviet reputation as supporters of the victims of imperialism, and wanting to focus all available resources on internal Soviet reconstruction, the USSR was unwilling to pay a heavy price to protect its Azerbaijan protegés.

Likewise, Soviet behavior indicates that their interest in gaining an oil concession was real but of low intensity. They had shown almost no interest in the oil prior to 1944 and failed to go far beyond verbal protests when the oil agreement was rejected by the Iranian Majlis. Yet they pushed the Iranians hard and convinced both Qavam and the British ambassador that this was a primary concern. The American judgment that the USSR would have had access to good geological data indicating that there was likely little oil in the area was never confirmed by the Soviets. But Soviet technicians had to be aware of the evidence, and this could help explain the government's willingness to acquiesce in the rejection.

As long as Soviet documents remain unavailable, the answer to the question of Soviet purpose will be speculative. But the case is more harmonious with an image of sluggish rather than ineluctable aggressiveness on the part of the USSR.

## In Search of a Political Formula

With the end of the Azerbaijan crisis, Iran could begin to adjust to the post–Reza Shah period. As Iranians understood only too well, the sudden independence of the country from major external influence was precarious. The Soviet-American cold war was in its formative stages but, viewed in historical perspective, it was simply a new manifestation of the competitive patterns of the European era of Iranian history. Iran was a strategic prize, but its geopolitical position was such that the competitors were most reluctant to resolve their conflict through violent confrontation. Predictably, then, the battle for preeminent influence would continue to be waged within the Iranian domestic political arena.

The Iranian sociopolitical arena had undergone great change during the years of Reza Shah's dictatorship. Looking at, for example, levels of literacy and newspaper readership as indicators of receptivity for political involvement, one could argue that possibly as much as 10 to 15 percent of the population was disposed to take an interest in politics. This represents a vast increase over the number of potentially involved citizens when Iran was last relatively free in the early 1920s. And, of course, the percentage so predisposed was far greater in Tehran than in provincial cities and very small in rural areas. Much of this newly aware element could be described as middle-class, although there is no case to be made for strong class consciousness in Iran. But there was great variance along scales of religiosity, concern with freedom, views of a proper state role in the economy, and the locus of community identity.

What would be the characteristics of the political ruling elite that would prevail in this milieu? There quickly emerged several competing formulas for political control. But one that did not emerge was that of the traditional oligarchy with the shah primus inter pares in the old Qajar fashion. Apparently there was an intuitive understanding that pro-change elements were far too numerous now for the old elite to be able to reestablish control and to rule in the traditional way. But there was one formula that was close — that typified by both Sayyid Zia and the young shah. Both men counted as their closest allies members of the old oligarchy. And both saw the need to rule in an authoritarian manner. They both, however, recognized the necessity to adapt to social and economic change. The shah in particular, from his earliest days on the throne, made clear his desire to move Iran quickly along a modernizing path. The parallel continues in that both believed an alliance with one or more external powers was essential for control purposes. Iranians had to understand that even should the Iranian security forces appear inadequate, the external power would protect and preserve the regime. For Sayyid Zia, the external power was the United Kingdom. For the shah, joint Anglo-American support seemed to make more sense.

The Reza Shah formula, that of a strong dictator relying heavily for control on the military, had its strong proponents even though Reza Shah's son seemed to prefer a different path. Such a regime could rely even more on commercial middle-class elements than the old shah had in the late 1920s because that group now was much larger. Also it need not be as reliant on external support as Reza Shah had been in the early days of his rise to power and hence was more likely to be accepted as truly nationalistic. The man the oligarchy feared might well play this role was General Ali Razmara, who commanded the forces liberating Azerbaijan. The shah saw in Razmara a dangerous rival who could be expected gradually to attract the support of the military away from the court.[81] But the Iranian military was not yet strong enough to provide the necessary coercive base of support for a genuine military dictatorship. The aspiring dictator would be compelled, therefore, as Reza Khan had been, to ally himself with other elite groups and remain on good terms with external powers until a sufficiently strong military and internal security force could be constructed.

A third formula was represented by Ahmad Qavam, who took as his primary support base the progressive wing of the traditional elite. But he always understood that he must make alliances with groups that favored more rapid change and use them to balance off the court, the conservative oligarchs, including tribal leaders, and the external powers. As his performance described above in the Azerbaijan crisis indicates, Qavam's diplomatic skills were extraordinary. But survival in an era of rapid social change, with so weak a primary support base, would be problematic at best.

A fourth available formula was a Marxist leadership looking to the Soviet Union as its political mentor. Soviet behavior in the Azerbaijan crisis, brutal and insensitive to Iranian aspirations for national dignity as it had been, considerably weakened the prospects of this group. Iranians who were both Marxist and nationalist found much to complain of in Soviet behavior, and many left the Tudeh party and allied themselves with the secular nationalists. The real strength of the Marxists lay in their appeal to that section of the intelligentsia that saw few prospects for achieving the rapid transformation in values in the desired direction without strong, dedicated, and no doubt authoritarian leadership. But in this period the appeal outside the intelligentsia was slight; hence, the only real prospect for early power was through the assistance of the Soviet Union. And here the Soviet record in Azerbaijan was hardly one to inspire confidence. The Soviets had paid the full price in terms of alienating the nationalistic Iranians by their intervention, but then, inexplicably, were unwilling to give the necessary support to those who relied on them.

A fifth formula was the coming into power of a conglomerate of elements held together negatively by a shared hostility to the court, the old oligarchy, and external intervention and united positively by a fierce attachment to full sovereign independence for Iran. This group wished to see fundamental change, but differed widely regarding the direction of change. One strand, often upper- and upper-middle-class in social origin and self-identified as the intelligentsia, was deeply attached to Enlightenment values and favored a secular, liberal democratic institutional base. Another, less strong and more attached to the bazaar, was ideologically both liberal and Islamic. Then there were two strands that, while less well represented at the elite level, had the potential to furnish leadership with a powerful populist appeal. Most important of these were politically minded religious leaders who were following in the path of Modaress. The community of primary concern for them was the Islamic, and their objective was a government true to the tenets of Islam as they interpreted them. Liberal democratic institutions were instruments for achieving these objectives, not ends. Indeed, Enlightenment values were viewed as Western cultural manifestations and hence of no implicit interest. The populist appeal of a second and secular group was based on an intensely nationalistic appeal. Resemblance to European fascism, so recently defeated, was obvious.

American diplomacy in the war years and immediately after was already reflecting U.S. ambivalence with regard to involvement in Iran's internal political affairs. Arthur Millspaugh was one American without ambivalence. Iranians needed, he made clear, a long period of tutelage. Nor is there much question as to which of the above formulas he preferred. Sayyid Zia was his ally and like-thinker. But U.S. Ambassadors Murray and Allen consistently rejected explicit appeals from the shah and others to play the interventionist role this formula called for. Yet day by day the matters taken up by the ambassadors with Iranian officials moved more deeply into matters of domestic policy concern.

*Exploring the Alternatives*

Ahmad Qavam, after the rejection of the oil agreement with the Soviet Union, understood that he was in a perilous position. He attempted to mollify the Soviets by appearing to be even-handed in dealing with external powers. He began a campaign for the return of Bahrein to Iran.[82] The Iranians had a historical case to make, but there was no real possibility that this British protectorate with a majority Arab population and an Arab ruling class would come under Iranian sovereignty as long as Britain was a power of any significance. But Qavam needed a symbolic issue that would make his government appear independent both to the Soviets and to the nationalistic masses.

What Qavam hoped for was an American understanding of his dilemma. This called for a muted U.S. response (at most) to the Bahrein campaign and a representation to the shah on Qavam's behalf.[83] Allen made clear his favorable view of Qavam, but could not satisfy the implicitly contradictory demands of Qavam: to intervene on his behalf while at the same time permitting him to appear fully independent. Qavam's support base was insufficient and neither the oligarchy nor the nationalistic opposition saw him as an ally who could bring major strength to a coalition. Qavam fell, and with him fell the prospects of stability furnished by an alliance centered primarily on the progressive wing of the traditional ruling class.

For the next two and a half years, 1948–1950, Iranian politics focused on the efforts of the shah to achieve dictatorial control with Anglo-American support. The immediate issue was constitutional change that would give the shah the right to dissolve parliament. Everyone concerned recognized that this would be only a first step and George Allen responded quickly in the negative. His argument was that Iran was more likely to achieve stability through the democratic process.[84] Since the shah lacked effective control of the military, he had to have external support. Thus George Allen's opposition was a major obstacle.

However, Allen's tenure as ambassador was coming to a close and his successor, John C. Wiley, would be in one important respect his opposite. Wiley saw the Soviet Union in stereotypical cold war terms. Like Rossow and Smith in 1946, he was filled with forebodings of the USSR absorbing Iran into its political empire. Wiley's dark predictions happily never materialized, but his image of the Soviets nevertheless rigidified. His most persistent demand was that Washington urge Iran to renounce Article 6 of the 1921 Treaty of Friendship with the Soviet Union, which he saw as a calculated opening for intervention.[85] But in addition he was much more sympathetic with the shah's aspirations than Allen had been.[86] The view that Iran was not yet ready for democracy, one that would characterize official American thinking for the next generation, naturally coincided with an advocacy of an authoritarian, anti-Soviet regime.

But Wiley was ahead of the Department of State in adopting a view of the situation largely defined by the image of an ineluctably aggressive Soviet Union. After Allen's departure, Washington continued to advise against encouraging the shah in his aspirations for greater control in Iran.[87] Wiley's entreaties that Iran be encouraged to demand abrogation of the 1921 treaty with the Soviets were also rejected.[88] But there was a steady drift among those responsible for Iranian affairs in Washington toward the cold war perspective. This included reassessing the reasons for the USSR's failure to save its puppet regime in Azerbaijan. The question was now in fact rephrased. No longer was there any doubt as to Soviet objectives to establish control over Iran. The question now was, since the Soviets obviously desired to gain control, why did they allow Pishevari to fall? The answer was patently clear, and it was the same answer the shah had given over a year earlier: the show of American will and determination in the United Nations.[89] In the event of a Soviet invasion of Iran, it followed, the United States could achieve its ends by standing firm in the United Nations. By 1949, however, there were the first signs of a suggestion that, in addition, a small American force in the area might be useful in deterring Soviet aggression.

Washington's thinking shifted also with regard to the form of government and the particular group or individuals deserving support in Iran. In February 1949 the shah was wounded in an assassination attempt. He quickly parlayed the sympathy the attack generated into intensified efforts to revamp Iran's constitution to give him greater power. American resistance faded; by the fall of 1949 the State Department saw the shah as the key to stability in Iran: "The Department of State considers the development of the morale of the Shah, as Commander in Chief as well as Monarch of

Iran, of pressing importance. Iran's will to resist Soviet pressures short of war, and her spirit to engage in delaying action in case of invasion will depend almost conclusively on the Shah's point of view."[90] Yet there were regular expressions of dismay at the level of corruption and the lack of direction in Iran. American military and economic aid reflected both views. Iran's geographical central-ity for strategic purposes and the shah's centrality in Iranian politics were accepted, but many questioned Iran's ability to utilize aid ef-fectively. The result was a level of aid far lower than that given to the more respected Turkish government.

U.S. political analysis of Iran as reflected in documents in this period was suprisingly superficial, almost casual. It had three foci: a Tudeh party, "the only political party in Iran," that was danger-ously strong; a handful of political figures, in particular the shah, Prince Abdoreza, Sayyid Zia, and Ali Razmara; and "liberal ele-ments," never identified.[91] There is no indication of any awareness of a major political force developing with a strong populist appeal, the National Front. But disillusion with the shah was rapidly develop-ing and as it did so, a tendency also developed toward increasing involvement in the Iranian political arena. One American diplomat, Jerry Dooher, appeared to have succumbed to the temptation of as-sociating with a faction of Iranians who were anxious to be iden-tified as protégés of the American embassy, just as so many Iranians in the past had sought such identification with the British embassy. Dr. Taqi Nasr, documents suggest, was willing to work closely with Dooher and seems to have played an active role in approaching at different times both Prince Abdoreza and General Ali Razmara.[92] This is the one serious indication before 1952 of direct U.S. involve-ment in Iranian political affairs at the working level, and it seems to reflect the view that something must be done to create in Iran a government capable of providing stability in the face of Soviet ag-gression. A National Security Council Report of July 21, 1949, as-serted flatly that "Iran must be regarded as a continuing objective in the Soviet program of expansion."[93]

By the spring of 1950, the U.S. Department of State had given up on the shah. "All traces of effective leadership have virtually dis-appeared. The Shah, who for a while showed signs of being a force for progress and reform, has exhibited that he has neither the char-acter nor the ability to offer the people guidance."[94] Wiley was instructed to hint to the shah that he would be well advised to appoint either Minister of Interior Ardalan or General Razmara as prime minister.[95] Reading between the lines of official reports, one concludes that following these instructions, the embassy, and in particular the innovative Dooher, working through Dr. Taqi Nasr, maneuvered to have General Razmara appointed. Dooher met with Razmara and reported to the embassy the substance of his conversations with the general. Razmara presented Dooher with the assessment of the obstacles in his path and the program he was ready to endorse. The obstacles were the British embassy, the shah's family, Minister of Court Hakimi, and Prime Minister Ali Mansur, who was intriguing with the National Front. Razmara said his program would include (1) giving Dr. Taqi Nasr responsibility for economic and social planning, (2) conducting an anticorruption campaign to eliminate the likes of Mansur and Nikpur, (3) decentralizing politics, (4) dissolving the Majlis, (5) limiting the shah's power, and (6) getting an agreement with AIOC in line with other Middle Eastern agreements.[96]

Dooher doubtless understood that Razmara had in effect offered the embassy, through Dooher, an outline of the concessions he was prepared to make in return for the embassy's support. However, there is nothing in the published accounts to indicate that Ambassador Wiley had the same understanding. Nevertheless, Dooher, however calculating, had maneuvered the embassy into appearing to have made a basic choice. In the eyes of Iranian politicians, the embassy had thrown its support to General Razmara and thereby had blocked the shah's efforts, working through a malleable prime minister, to gain Anglo-American backing for his own authoritarian control. Since Mansur was attempting to get an agreement favorable to the AIOC approved, Razmara and others of the cognoscenti had reason to anticipate an underlying Anglo-American oil rivalry. Razmara had offered the United States the payoff he assumed was necessary. He would bring an American protégé into his cabinet in one area of U.S. concern, financial reform. He would bow to the American obsessions with corruption and decentralization. He would stop any appeasement of the dangerous National Front. And, most important, he would curb the pro-British court and oligarchy and adopt a tough stance toward the AIOC.

If this was indeed Razmara's thinking, he had misread the U.S.

embassy in several regards. First, Wiley had made clear his desire to see Mansur's AIOC plans succeed. Second, the embassy was singularly unconcerned with the National Front and continued to give lip service to democratic institutions. Third, there was nothing in the proposal that addressed the real concern of Wiley and his government: the Soviet threat.

Still, this episode was an instance of U.S. intervention, even though inadvertent, in Iranian internal affairs. The Iranians expected the Americans to behave as the British and Russians had before them. Since the pattern they knew was one of indirection and subtle maneuvering, they had always depended on reading (and misreading) between the lines. However, in this case there was a real U.S. decision to urge the shah to consider Razmara for the post of prime minister. Dooher's maneuvering gave emphasis to that recommendation and the shah treated it as an order. The impact was surely far greater than Wiley understood. In effect, the United States had made its choice among competing formulas for control of the Iranian government—that of military dictatorship.

Since this was a formative period in the United States' policy toward Iran, the personal role of the ambassador was of exceptional importance. Allen had operated with skill and clarity of mind in a crisis that in less able hands could have led to a major Soviet-American confrontation. His successor, Wiley, had a far less equivocal picture of Soviet intentions and during his tour American policy moved toward encouraging the formation of a strong, authoritarian and anti-Soviet Iranian government. But Henry Grady, Wiley's successor, was as different in world view from Wiley as Wiley had been from Allen. Grady, an Irish-American and a liberal, was suspicious of the British and strongly anti-imperialist. He was also anticommunist, but his view of the Soviets was not that of the stereotypical ineluctably aggressive force. Now, in contrast to the Wiley period, Washington was more belligerent than its ambassador in Tehran.

The British, understandably, believed the Americans were allowing Iran to play the two Western powers against each other. On October 26, 1950, following a high-level Anglo-American meeting, a joint policy toward Iran was agreed on. Its essence was that the "US will continue vigorous cold war action in Middle East" but considered "the area to be a British Commonwealth responsibility." The United States made clear its commitment to a "favorable AIOC settlement."[97] Grady remonstrated that by associating itself with the British, the United States sacrificed the possibility of strengthening the Iranian will to independence.[98] But he was sharply rebuffed.[99] Still, there remained in Washington a strong conviction that the British were allowing their interest in AIOC to blind them to changed circumstances and that the possibility of a major policy split between the two Western governments was real.

Having played a critical role in Razmara's coming to power, the U.S. embassy, even under a different ambassador, had difficulty withdrawing its commitment. The very forces that Razmara described as opposing his appointment were making a strong effort to remove him. A serious complication for American policymakers was the fact that Razmara, once appointed, made clear his independence from Washington by establishing the best relations an Iranian government had enjoyed with the Soviet Union since the early days of Qavam's tenure. It was a risky game for an Iranian leader to play at this moment. True enough, it was in tune with the time-honored Iranian diplomatic principle of negative balance and, in fact, internally stabilized Razmara's regime. But it underestimated the lethal quality of the American cold war view. Razmara was fortunate in having Grady, with his complex view of the Soviets, as ambassador. Even so, American support for Razmara diminished and his ability to survive became increasingly problematic.

Razmara's diplomatic skills were substantial, however. His strategies made clear his assessment of the demands of the situation if he were not only to survive but also to consolidate power. Having relied heavily on an only partially comprehending U.S. embassy to gain the premiership, he proceeded to mollify the Soviet Union and accepted the risks of distancing himself from the Americans. But he also had to appease the British—an effort which, if successful could neutralize opposition from the shah and from Sayyid Zia. Like Washington, Razmara apparently saw the British as primarily concerned with protecting their oil interests. He was successful in convincing them that he had the strength and courage to seek and gain the Majlis' approval for a new Anglo-Iranian modus vivendi regarding the AIOC.

In July 1949 the British had acceded to Iran's request to negotiate a supplemental oil agreement that was in all respects similar to the 1933 agreement. But it would have resulted in doubling the Iranian government's financial returns. The minister of finance signed the agreement but the government put off submitting it to the Majlis until the election of the Sixteenth Majlis in September 1949. After that election, the minister of finance asked that the agreement be modified before submission. The British refused, noting that opposition to the agreement was being led by a tiny delegation of five deputies, the representation of the National Front. It is easy to understand Britain's bewilderment. The large majority of Majlis deputies were of the variety that welcomes, even solicits, British involvement in Iranian affairs. Many were Freemasons, associates of Sayyid Zia having financial dealings with British commercial concerns. How could a handful of agitators so dominate such a Majlis? The British explanation seems to have been the personal weakness and deviousness of Iranian officials. Certainly there is no sign that they sensed an aroused public opinion capable of becoming the support base for a militantly nationalistic government.

However, if the British had difficulty taking a handful of nationalist "extremists" seriously, Razmara was fully aware of the degree to which public opinion limited his freedom of action regarding an oil settlement. Razmara's dilemma was difficult. His survival in office necessitated pleasing the British without alienating public opinion. He was caught in a deadly rhythm. Nationalistic and religious elements were gaining confidence in their strength almost daily, and as they did so their demands became steadily more radical. In late 1950 they were beginning to call for the nationalization of the AIOC. But British comprehension of this acceleration in assertiveness changed at a much slower pace.[100] The result was a steady reduction in Razmara's freedom of action.

On February 10, 1951, the British informed Razmara that they were ready to negotiate an entirely new agreement that would involve an equal sharing of income. In addition, they offered a major monetary advance to meet governmental expenses. Six months earlier, such an offer might well have led to an agreement and to Razmara's consolidating his position. But by February 1951 public opinion in Iran was aroused as it had not been since 1921. In this thirty-year interval, however, the percentage of the population that could be mobilized by popular leaders had multiplied several times. Razmara, now confronted with a demand for nationalization, did not dare make public an offer that the British considered extremely generous.[101]

On March 7, 1951, Ali Razmara was assassinated by a member

of Fadayan-i Islam, a religio-political organization with a small but dedicated membership that opposed any form of secular government. Almost immediately the Iranian Oil Commission headed by Dr. Mohammad Musaddiq called for nationalization, and on March 20 the Majlis endorsed a resolution proposing the formulation of a nationalization plan. Hossein Ala, whose faithfulness to the shah was well established, had been named prime minister. But carried by a tide of public opinion that regarded Razmara's assassin as a national hero and fully supported terminating British influence in Iran, the momentum for nationalization was unstoppable. On April 26 a Majlis composed largely of individuals representing traditional Iran approved nationalization unanimously.

Hossein Ala, unwilling either to support or oppose nationalization, resigned the premiership. Iran was on the edge of a new era. Public excitement was at an unprecedented level; crowds, huge by Iranian standards up to then, marched in Tehran and in all the major cities. An outside observer could easily have concluded that Iran had suddenly experienced the phenomenon of mass politics. But a closer look would have provided a different profile. Rural Iran, where the majority of Iranians still lived, was almost entirely unconcerned with the momentous developments in Tehran. Moreover, except for the few large cities, only a veneer of the population of urban areas in the provinces was caught up in the events. And even in the large cities, surely a majority of the population was nonparticipant and much of it unaware of what was occurring other than that it occasionally disrupted their daily routine.

Nevertheless, Iran was at a point of takeoff. Political leaders had appeared who were able to reach and to mobilize into political action those Iranians who had become aware of being part of the national community, the Islamic community, or both. Two of those leaders had achieved a level of personal popularity that no Iranian before them had even approached. One of them, Ayatullah Abol Qasem Kashani, was the preeminent political leader of the Islamic community. His aspirations for Iran were similar to those later associated with Ayatullah Khomeini. Indeed, Kashani and Khomeini were at this time friendly colleagues. But they had chosen to follow different strategies at this critical moment. Khomeini viewed secular nationalists much as had Fazlullah Nuri a half-century earlier. In his eyes they had rejected Islam and had become pathetic reflections of ungodly Europeans who were oppressing Islam and all the deprived peoples of the world. Khomeini saw no point in any form of political collaboration with such people. Kashani held this view as well, but like Modaress before him was willing to form a tactical alliance with the nationalists. He had good reason to believe that when the inevitable confrontation occurred he would be the clear victor in the struggle for mass support. Kashani approved of Razmara's assassination, but his own Warriors of Islam organization was of far greater political importance than was Fadayan-i Islam. There were other politico-religious leaders who had a far more benign view of secular nationalists and saw Enlightenment values as entirely compatible with—in fact, identical to—Islamic values. But they did not produce a great spokesman for their point of view.

The secular element calling for the nationalization of oil as a first and major step in a struggle for independence from perceived British domination were divided between Marxists and nationalists. The former were, by Iranian standards, well organized and disciplined. Their base of support was the intelligentsia and organized labor. The latter was fractionated along both personal and ideological lines. A number of prominent individuals who saw themselves, and were generally perceived, as the leaders of the struggle for real independence were accepted as general spokesmen and leaders of the national movement. But organized parties were forming as well. The Iran party, led by a group of prominent individuals, several of them from the upper class, adopted a program that was nationalistic, liberal, and social democratic. Its appeal was limited largely to the intelligentsia.

Another nascent party, the Toilers party, was in many respects more in tune with traditional Iranian politics. Its leader, Dr. Mozaffar Baqai, was initially the second most popular man among the secular nationalists. His party was a strange conglomeration. One section was the chosen home for many former Tudeh members who had left the party because of Soviet offenses to the nation. It included some of Iran's most sparkling intellectuals and attracted the imagination of many college students. The other section was personally loyal to Baqai and included individuals, often connected with organized labor, who could mobilize large but uncomprehending political mobs. This section had close ties to many religious leaders, including Kashani.[102]

Public demonstrations by the religious and two secular groups told much about their differences. Marxist demonstrations were tightly structured and disciplined. Those attending were generaly well dressed and young, obviously predominantly college students. Nationalist demonstrations had far more an appearance of spontaneity and those attending were more diverse. The core tended to be similar in age and class to the Marxists, but there were older people as well and more high school students, often followers of the nationalist populist Dariush Foruhar. Then there would be a sizable contingent of impoverished-looking individuals whose dress suggested that they had been paid to attend. Kashani's rallies were composed predominantly of such people. Frequently they arrived by the truckload from the poor sections of south Tehran.

But probably the most critical element in this new political equation was Dr. Mohammad Musaddiq, who by 1951 was already of advanced age. His mother was a Qajar and Musaddiq was socially at home in upper-class Iranian society. He had studied in France, had received a doctorate from the University of Geneva, and had returned to Iran a strong proponent of Enlightenment values. As a young man he had participated in the constitutional revolution and had operated on the margins of politics from that point on. American and British diplomats, the official correspondence suggests, took no real note of him until after World War II. But he was well known among the traditional elite and the intelligentsia as a sincere and highly emotional proponent of nationalism, liberalism, and abstract social justice. His personal honesty and integrity were rarely questioned, and he was viewed among political figures as a purist.

This is an unlikely background for a man destined to achieve a broad, charismatic appeal within the attentive Iranian public, now primarily composed of middle-class elements. That he should have received such exceptional popularity testifies to the conclusion that national aspirations rather than social and economic were most salient to this newly awakened mass public. But then national, social, and economic questions were closely intertwined. Imperialists, so nationalistic Iranians believed, wanted to perpetuate an Iran dominated by a traditional class that would welcome imperial protection for their vested position and would agree in return to protect the economic vested interests of Western capitalism. Thus the struggle for sovereign independence was essential for achieving social justice and economic development. This was very much the view of Musaddiq, and his speeches and policy recommendations struck a deeply responsive chord.

The national movement of Iran was composed of very diverse elements, united only by the objective of real, not merely formal, independence. But Musaddiq's personal appeal grew daily until it reached the charismatic level. Now the movement was united not only by a common objective but also by a willingness to place great and unquestioning trust in Mohammad Musaddiq. When Hossein Ala resigned as prime minister on April 26, 1951, the shah wanted to appoint Sayyid Zia, but he really had no alternative to accepting the fact of Mussadiq's charisma.[103] The fifth formula of those mentioned above—populist, anti-imperialist, and insisting on full sovereign independence—would operate in Iran for the next two and a half years.

## Anglo-American Responses to the Iranian National Movement

Britain's response to this revolutionary development was to deny its existence. The formula the British continued to advocate was the first one: to uphold the Iranian oligarchy with external protection. The leader they proposed was Sayyid Zia. If Musaddiq had come to symbolize Iran's struggle for independence and dignity, Sayyid Zia symbolized indirect, informal, but very real British control. That the British would persist in their efforts to place Sayyid Zia in the premiership in the middle of a populist explosion in which he was viewed as the most visible opponent of Iran's aspirations tells everything about the prevailing world view dominating the British government. For them Musaddiq was an absurd figure, given to fainting, weeping, and conducting his business from his bed. He was essentially a fanatic agitator, capable of manipulating his immature followers but incapable of conducting a rational course of action. The so-called nationalists, Musaddiq supporters, were fickle and childlike. They would accept a responsible leader like Sayyid Zia. No greater mistake could be made than to treat them as a manifestation of public opinion. For the next six months the British made no real effort to conceal their conviction that a resolution of the crisis necessitated Musaddiq's replacement by Sayyid Zia.[104]

The U.S. response in these first months was sharply different from that of the British, especially as long as Henry Grady remained as ambassador. Indeed, Grady was one of a very few foreigners who had some comprehension of the importance of the national movement. After leaving Iran, Grady did his best to persuade the American public of the necessity for the United States to accommodate itself to the appearance of nationalist aspirations in what would soon be known as the Third World.[105] But Grady's efforts were singularly unsuccessful. Americans, like the British, saw Musaddiq's behavior—so attractive in the Iranian culture—as comic theater. Nor did Musaddiq's supporters fare much better. Even in liberal intellectual circles they were viewed as irresponsible, fanatical, unaware of or unconcerned with the fact that they were improving the Soviets' subversive potential. The argument Iranian nationalists, aware of American preoccupation with a Soviet threat, assumed would be persuasive to the United States, that is, that a popular and nationalist Iranian government would be best able to withstand Soviet pressures, found little receptivity with the American public.

U.S. officials understood very well that the initial British response to Musaddiq's appointment was likely to exacerbate the situation.[106] These included an open display of naval force; an undisguised approach to elements the British traditionally worked through such as the Qashqai and Bakhtiari tribal leaders, conservative religious leaders, conservative members of the traditional class, and street leaders; and an open endorsement of the Sayyid Zia alternative. American officials were fully familiar with this British modus operandi, and they knew from countless conversations with the progressive wing of the traditional class that it was broadly resented in Iran.[107]

When little progress was being made in Anglo-Iranian conversations, the Truman administration sent Averell Harriman to Iran to explore the possibilities of playing a conciliatory role. Harriman proposed that a high-level British delegation be sent to negotiate in Iran. Sir Richard Stokes, Lord Privy Seal, was sent as the head of a British delegation, and on one level the proposals the British advanced appeared to be constructively responsive. The fact of the nationalization of Iranian oil was accepted, and generous arrangements for production and marketing were proposed.[108] But neither Stokes nor Harriman appeared to understand why the Iranians were so insistent on bringing the British staff under Iranian supervision. Both the British and Americans treated the problem as if it required quelling some natural, if irrational, manifestations of immature nationalism which should be satisfied by granting Iran the right to nationalize Iranian oil. That accomplished, the task of constructing a mutually beneficial arrangement for production, refinement, marketing, and transport of oil could be faced and worked out with technical proficiency.

But in fact the problem was political, not economic. It entailed control, not finding symbolic manifestations to satisfy Iranian dignity. Musaddiq and his followers saw an Iranian polity manipulated and controlled by British imperialism. Their instruments were, at the apex, Britons in the embassy, in British commercial enterprises, and in particular in AIOC.[109] These agents of British intelligence then operated through elaborate networks of Iranians headed by a few principal agents. Some of these agents, such as the Rashidian brothers, openly advertised their connection with Britain. Others, such as Sayyid Zia, were a little more discreet. But their influence was derived from perceived British sponsorship, and hence they not only had to advertise their connections but periodically to produce confirming evidence of them. British behavior following Musaddiq's appointment did in fact provide persuasive confirmation for this picture of Britain's imperialist control in Iran.

Iranian misunderstanding of British operations was not in seeing networks of individuals following the lead of a principal agent. The misunderstanding lay in grossly overestimating the degree of British control over individuals with whom these primary agents were directly or indirectly in touch. The Iranian nationalists' view of Freemasonry typified this misunderstanding. A great many of Iran's top social and political elite were members of Freemason orders. Some unquestionably were allied to men heading agent networks. But the common assumption that any member of the Freemasons was under British control and that this control was at the agent level had to be wrong. British operatives would have to have been superhuman to orchestrate such a large and diverse group, but of course this is precisely how such operatives were perceived.[110]

It follows that Musaddiq would see as the prime essential for achieving real control of Iranian destiny cutting off the apex of this British control. British oil technicians would be welcome to remain in Iran as the employees of the National Iranian Oil Company, but the use of the oil company as a cover for a major British intelligence force had to come to an end. Nationalization of oil would be an empty move if the oil company were to remain a "nest of spies." Political and economic independence and social justice could not be achieved. Had Harriman and Stokes comprehended this Iranian view of reality and had advanced proposals to convince Iranians that the oil company would be free of any intelligence connection, a settlement might well have occurred. Instead, Britain's partially overt moves to overthrow Musaddiq confirmed and rigidified the Iranian view.

In September 1951 the British finally did cease advocating a Sayyid Zia government. But they did so because of the continuing unwillingness of the United States to sanction their proposal. Indeed, for the time being they gave up on their preferred formula for an Iranian regime, that is, one supported by the British and the Americans, headed by a strong and comprehending leader, and operating through a traditional control system. The only clear alternative to Sayyid Zia for leadership was the shah; even though he had indicated often enough a willingness to play this role, the British like the Americans felt he lacked the necessary leadership abilities.[111]

Having given up hope of replacing Musaddiq in the immediate future—largely, as they saw it, because of the shah's weakness and Musaddiq's success in playing off the Americans and the British against each other—Britain moved to destabilize Musaddiq by instituting what amounted to an economic blockade. Musaddiq responded in September 1951 by ordering the British AIOC staff to leave Iran. At this point, Clement Atlee was prepared to consider the use of force by occupying Abadan Island. But Harry Truman replied bluntly that the United States would oppose such a proposal.[112] Atlee was unwilling to make such a move without American support and turned instead to the UN Security Council. But here too Musaddiq upstaged him. He headed the Iranian delegation to New York and put on a personal performance that was exceptionally effective. Furthermore, in consultations in Washington, Musaddiq broadened the distance between the United States' and Britain's policies.

As the British indicated on many occasions, a fundamental difference between London and Washington lay in their estimate of the internal communist threat in Iran. A second major difference lay in their assessment of the importance of Musaddiq and the National Front. The American estimate of the nationalists was downgraded after Henry Grady was replaced by Loy Henderson, but Dean Acheson persisted until the end of the Truman administration in seeing Iranian nationalism as a force from which American policy could not appear to be divorced. These differences led Washington to accept for a time the view that a popular nationalist regime would be able to stand against subversive Soviet efforts. It followed, therefore, that the United States should try to stabilize Mussadiq.[113]

Estimates of the impact of the economic crisis on Iran proved to be overly pessimistic. The situation was deteriorating. Without oil income, government officials could not be paid on time. Unemployment rose and so did inflation, although at a surprisingly slow rate. Fortunately for the government, the weather cooperated and the harvest was good. The British continued their efforts to bring Musaddiq down, but more directly, and this time through Ahmad Qavam and the progressive wing of the traditional class.

In the meantime, Musaddiq set the electoral machinery in motion. For technical and economic reasons, elections were staggered in Iran and several weeks would be required for their completion. The British predicted that in any case they would be rigged. But first results hardly supported that expectation. On the contrary, the returns gave an accurate picture of the rhythm of Iranian sociopolitical development. First returns were from Zanjan, a middle-sized city in southeastern Azerbaijan. The victors were the leading family of the district. The National Front vote was substantial, but the results suggested that in provincial cities of this size, the villagers and urban lower-class elements, who would vote as instructed by traditional leaders, could easily outpoll the people caught up in nationalist and/or religious fervor. In Tehran the top of the National Front list took between 50 and 70 percent of the vote. Marxist candidates mustered up to 20 percent and traditional candidates 5 percent. The results in Iran's second city, Tabriz, were similar, except that the National Front victories in Tehran were primarily secular, those in Tabriz mainly religious. This set the pattern. The National Front would carry the larger cities, traditional candidates would win in the rural areas. Since the majority of districts were rural, the National Front was headed for defeat. To obviate this, Musaddiq stopped the elections after a quorum in which urban deputies were overrepresented had been elected. Even so, the victory was precarious.[114]

Throughout these early months of the Musaddiq government,

British reports carried a continuing theme that Musaddiq was losing support. The outside observer looking at such indications as crowd size, proregime newspaper circulation, and the appearance of pro-government demonstrations in provincial areas would surely have come to an opposite conclusion. What the British were in fact watching was the ebbing of acquiescence in Musaddiq's control by the traditional elite and the wealthy. This old elite, overwhelmingly dominant in the Sixteenth Majlis and well represented in the truncated Seventeenth Majlis, had accommodated themselves to a nationalist mandate. They would not stand up to public opinion, especially in Tehran. But their unhappiness at what a nationalist revolution would mean for them led them to be willing to take some risks in opposing it. They were receptive to British overtures and, like most Iranians, felt that were there a combined Anglo-American plan for Musaddiq's replacement, it would have an excellent prospect for success.

In July 1952 the shah, as he was constitutionally entitled to do, dismissed Musaddiq as premier and appointed in his stead Ahmad Qavam. A majority of the deputies in the Majlis voted their approval. The maneuvering that preceded this event continues to be a matter of mystery. But Hassan Arsenjani, a loyal and devoted lieutenant of Qavam, has described it in close detail. Claiming to have been the contact between Qavam, the shah, and the British and U.S. embassies, Arsenjani painted a credible picture. The shah by this account participated reluctantly.[115] Sir Francis Sheppard, the British ambassador, was the instigator but Loy Henderson a cautious but indispensable collaborator. Qavam, understanding as always Iranian political complexity, knew the great risk he was taking and the onerous consequences that threatened any Iranian willing to replace a man who had become a popular symbol. He agreed because of his overestimation of Anglo-American ability to amass the necessary support.

This event led to one of the really great outpourings of popular sentiment in Iran. It was not to be surpassed until Khomeini's revolution. Included was the entire range of support groups for the National Front and the Marxists as well. After a few days Qavam resigned and Musaddiq was reappointed. Forgotten were Qavam's services to Iran six years earlier. His property was confiscated and his reputation destroyed. The Majlis, true to form, now overwhelmingly endorsed Musaddiq.

But a negative target was necessary for this display of unity. Shortly thereafter the alliance began to disintegrate. The Marxists went their own way. Their propaganda had been attempting for a year to portray the United States as the number one imperialist power, with the British an enervated partner. Few non-Marxists agreed with this view. A decline in the British resource base was apparent. But a popular cliche, "British brains and American money" well summarized a widespread Iranian attitude. Therefore, as they explored their options, marginal allies of Musaddiq who were on the edge of defecting were at least open to indirect contact with the British. With Qavam's political demise and his Anglo-American allies unable to save him, these moves were made tentatively.

British government reports began taking increasing note of General Fazlullah Zahedi.[116] Zahedi had been arrested by British officers in Iran in the war years as a German agent and taken to Palestine. Presumably there the British gained at the least a full reading of Zahedi's leadership potential. He was described in 1952 as the clearest alternative to Musaddiq. His closest ally, the British agreed, was the conservative right. But he was moving as well to capitalize on the spinoff from the National Front. Those defecting included three of the most popular associates of Musaddiq: Hossein Maki, Mozaffar Baqai, and Abul Qasem Kashani. Maki's defection was tentative and least significant since his support base was narrow. He had gained wide recognition and popularity by his prominence in the struggle to nationalize Iran's oil, but he had no independent organization. Baqai did have his own organization and had worked energetically with the cooperation of Musaddiq to gain control of the trade union movement. In this he failed badly. He had worked through individuals who had little credibility with the workers and made no real inroads in Marxist dominated unions. As he began to toy openly with defection from Musaddiq, the intellectual base of his party split off under the leadership of Khalil Maleki and took with them Baqai's claim to ideological legitimacy.

Most important by far was the defection of Ayatullah Kashani. This friend and associate of Khomeini was Musaddiq's only real competitor for mass charismatic appeal. Kashani's natural constituency, like that of Khomeini a generation later, was the urban lower and lower-middle class. In 1952 most members of these groups were little concerned with politics. They were respectful of their religious leaders, but it was difficult to mobilize them into sustained political activity. Large numbers could be stimulated or hired to participate on a day-to-day basis, and this was the procedure that Kashani's organizers used. But Musaddiq's support base was the urban middle class which was by now alive politically and not only fully capable of sustained participation but also willing to take serious risks. Still, despite Musaddiq's relative advantage, the defection of Kashani was certain to seriously weaken the government. In fact, Kashani's defection was to prove decisive in the success of the Anglo–American-orchestrated coup against Musaddiq.

The U.S. Department of State, under the leadership of Dean Acheson, persisted in the view that, however irrational he appeared to be, Musaddiq and his movement were the source of great strength in dealing with the Soviet threat. Acheson percieved—and British documents now released indicate he perceived correctly—that the British were preoccupied with their oil interests and only marginally concerned with a Soviet threat to Iran.[117] He therefore placed considerable pressure on Britain to negotiate the oil question with Musaddiq. There is reason to believe that Loy Henderson shared the British view of Musaddiq but not of their concern with oil. His role in bringing Qavam to power and statements by the British chargé in Tehran that Henderson shared his views are evidence of this. But in the fall and winter of 1952–1953, after Musaddiq had broken diplomatic relations with the British, Henderson proceeded with skill and persistence to attempt to bring about an oil settlement. Britain's reluctance is self-evident in the documents. But Musaddiq was surprisingly forthcoming and was willing to meet most British objections. The U.S. Department of State, for its part, demonstrated a seriousness of purpose by being willing to offer Musaddiq immediate financial support when the agreement was signed: $100 million.[118]

However, Musaddiq was able to be thus flexible only by maintaining the strictest secrecy regarding the negotiations. The Tudeh party was proclaiming in its wide-circulation press its contention that Musaddiq was an American surrogate and was prepared to capitulate to U.S. oil interests. Maki, Baqai, and Kashani voiced similar suspicions. And British support for General Zahedi, which was only just below the surface, led Musaddiq's close associates and no doubt Musaddiq himself to be deeply suspicious of some deviousness of purpose on the part of the British. Confronted with these pressures,

Musaddiq retreated from positions he had taken and negotiations collapsed.

With the distraction of possible negotiations removed, the agenda became the overthrow of Musaddiq. When Dean Acheson was replaced as secretary of state by John Foster Dulles in January 1953, there was instantly a new official definition of the situation. There was little discernible difference in the American assessment of Soviet aggressive intent. In this area, the American and British views continued to be very different; British official correspondence indicates that this American preoccupation was always a factor the British had in mind when attempting to influence American policy. But now the American view of Musaddiq and the importance of his movement shifted and became more harmonious with the British view. Both agreed that Musaddiq would bring terrible consequences if not quickly removed.[119] But for the British the consequences were damage to British prestige, influence, and vital commercial interests. To the Americans they were weakening Iran and increasing its vulnerability to Soviet penetration.

In April 1953 Musaddiq's chief of police, Mohammad Afshartus, was murdered in the home of Hossein Khatibi, a lieutenant of Baqai and a man thoroughly at home in Tehran's political underworld. Khatibi's connections with Kashani and General Zahedi were well established, and he would be later a confidant of the shah. No one in Tehran doubted the conclusion of investigators that this act reflected a working relationship not only of all the above but also of the British. The modus operandi was only too clear. De facto collaboration of Kashani and his associates with the British was now accepted as a fact, and this opinion continues to be accepted by secular nationalists even today.

According to Kermit Roosevelt, the grandson of Theodore Roosevelt and the man who claimed in his book *Countercoup* primary personal responsibility for Musaddiq's overthrow, close Anglo-American collaboration in support of a coup began in February 1953.[120] What it amounted to essentially was the CIA's buying into an alliance of British intelligence and a diverse group of Iranians centered on General Zahedi. Orchestration would be provided by the United States, since the British had been expelled from Iran. But the key to success was the smooth functioning of elaborate British networks of agents and contacts centered on a few principal agents. The nets embraced military officers, a broad array of conservative politicians (many indeed members of Freemason orders), conservative religious leaders, mob and labor leaders, tribal leaders (especially of the Bakhtiari and Qashqai tribes), and the court. Maki, Baqai, and Kashani were in close contact with one or more of these networks. Events such as the Afshartous murder and a February 1953 assault on Musaddiq's house by a howling mob of mercenaries led by a notorious strong-arm leader, Shaban Jafari, "the Brainless," revealed the pattern of events.

Obviously, such a large operation as this could not be concealed. Musaddiq was fully aware of it. Indeed, the problem for him, as for most Iranians, was a tendency to see greater intelligence and skill in the operation than actually existed and, more important, far greater control. Kashani's hatred of the British was surely genuine. His mortal combat with Musaddiq no doubt led him into de facto collaboration with agents of Britain, but there was surely no British control over him. Yet the general perception that he was a controlled agent was only to be expected. Also of consequence was the deep distrust of this type of activity on the part of the British generated in Musaddiq and his lieutenants. The collapse of oil negotiations, which could have led to a consolidation of a National Front government, was only one of the many direct results.

Musaddiq's efforts to counter the coup plan included eliminating the cover positions of British intelligence, both commercial and official. This necessitated taking the drastic action of breaking diplomatic relations with Britain even though the diplomacy of negative balance on which Musaddiq was raised required a strong Russian and British presence in Iran. But the Americans were available to balance off the Russians. Musaddiq's strategy included a prolonged effort to prevent Anglo-American collaboration, and the British gave Musaddiq high grades for that effort until Dulles replaced Acheson. It also included an effort to keep the court from full participation in the plot. To accomplish this, Musaddiq was able to force the pro-British Hossein Ala out as minister of court and to replace him with Abol Qasem Amini, a Qajar aristocrat with some sympathy for the National Front. But most critical was the effort to wrest control of the military from the shah. Conservatives in the Majlis, along with National Front defectors, were able to block formal approval of a proposal to accomplish this. However, informally Musaddiq was beginning to gain control over the military by virtue of some critical appointments.[121]

In the summer of 1953, Musaddiq was ready to forego liberal democratic niceties and reconstitute an effective and supportive Majlis. He had his supporters resign from the Majlis and then held a popular referendum to approve its dissolution. He won 99 percent of the vote, a result that confirmed Musaddiq's readiness to resort to totalitarian techniques to preserve his regime. There is little doubt that a new Majlis, had it been elected, would have been overwhelmingly National Frontist. Furthermore, Musaddiq was able to achieve this degree of control even though his hold on the military was tentative. He was popular with junior officers, but many senior officers were protégés of the Pahlavis and loyal to them. It was Musaddiq's populist appeal that provided the basis for his ability to exercise coercive control along with his control of the Ministry of the Interior and its associated internal security forces. Musaddiq was the clear victor over Kashani in the important arena of the religious community. The large majority of clerics who were active in politics, including those in parliament, sided with Musaddiq. So did the majority of the influential leaders of the bazaar. In general, the National Front could count on the majority of the religious community that was sufficiently interested and involved to be capable of sustained political activity. Of the secular middle class, support was divided between the National Front and Tudeh, but at this critical moment Tudeh leaders cooperated with Musaddiq's efforts to prevent a coup even though there was no agreement to do so.

However, National Front weakness was also apparent. Most significant was its inability to count on the military for support. But beyond this it depended totally on the support of those Iranians who had become politically conscious and favored rapid social change. This was a strong support base in Tehran and other large cities, but of little significance in the remainder of the country. Even in Tehran the majority of the population was not yet really politically aware. Wherever political consciousness remained low, traditional political patterns and traditional leaders prevailed. It was precisely in this area of traditional politics that British understanding was greatest and the British political networks most effective.

Traditional political domination of the countryside and of provincial towns was not of critical importance to the National Front at this juncture. The drama would be acted out largely in Tehran; Musaddiq had no other base to fall back on. The real problem was in south Tehran where traditional leaders could mobilize by purchase and by demagoguery large, uncomprehending mobs. Labor leaders, so-called, such as those associated with Baqai, were usually ideologically unconcerned and capable of producing large numbers of demonstrators on order. Strong-arm leaders usually associated with athletic societies served the same function. It amounted to a political underworld with more than casual resemblance to those of large American cities in the early twentieth century. Of most significance were conservative clerics to whom many in this area turned for personal guidance. The ability of the British acting through their principal agents to reach all of these elements was well established. Indeed, the cynicism among the British toward Iranian public opinion is explainable given their long experience with purchased demonstrations.

In this context, the defections of Baqai and Kashani were to prove fatally significant. Both men had had a support base that was in part traditional and in part radical revolutionary. As long as they were allied with Musaddiq, they were able to deny to the traditional urban leaders effective control of south Tehran. But when they broke with Musaddiq and lost their progressive support base, they renewed their alliances with the old traditional leaders. Since many of these leaders were involved directly or indirectly with principal British agents, this was the basis of the de facto alliance of Kashani and Baqai with the British. But they were not the direct instruments of the Anglo-American effort. Strong-arm leaders, especially Hassan Arab and Shaban Jafari, and conservative religious leaders, especially Sayyid Mohammad Behbehani, served this function.

The coup plan was a relatively simple one.[122] The shah would issue an order dismissing Musaddiq and appointing Zahedi as prime minister. Since this was a constitutional procedure, the military would honor it. Should the National Front bring out their middle-class supporters, the traditional leaders of south Tehran would counter with huge, essentially mercenary mobs hired for the occasion. The new regime would quickly take control of the radio station and proclaim martial law. Military officers involved in the plan would take over critical command posts. Generous U.S. financial support would be immediately forthcoming, and General Zahedi, with the aid and assistance of American and British technicians, would establish the institutional base for dictatorship. The support base would be the traditional elite. The formula was in every particular that preferred by the British for the past decade, and really for the past half-century.

The primary obstacle—given the expectation that so simple a plan could oust a regime with a large and dedicated support base—was the shah's diffidence toward the scheme. The shah, Hamlet-like in his ambivalence regarding power, was in one of his down periods. Of course it had to be self-evident to him that success for the coup would mean dictatorial powers for Zahedi, not for him. His role was simply to replace one dominant prime minister with another. Still, Musaddiq was in the process of wresting control from the military. The shah's comments to Ambassador Henderson made clear his bitterness at this development. On the other hand, he, unlike the coup proponents, had considerable respect for the force that would oppose the coup and was far from sanguine regarding the prospects for its success.

A major campaign was launched to win him over. Henderson was eloquent and forceful in advancing the case. The shah's twin sister, Ashraf, whom the allies saw as a more forceful personality than her brother, was enlisted in the campaign. Then finally Norman Schwartzkopf, whom the shah respected from his days as police adviser, traveled to Iran and argued the case. Ultimately, the shah agreed, and on August 16, 1953, the order dismissing Musaddiq was delivered. Musaddiq, of course, knew what to expect. When the order was delivered he rejected it, announced that it was a forgery, and arrested Colonel Nematollah Nassiri who delivered it. With that, the coup collapsed. The shah, who was not surprised by the results, fled the country, going first to Baghdad and then to Rome. Zahedi in hiding made a pathetic effort to convince the public that the order was legal; however, when it appeared that few cared, Zahedi began thinking in terms of some area in Iran where he could set up a rival government. Loy Henderson, who chose to be in Switzerland during the coup, flew back to Tehran and openly and feverishly attempted to reverse the course of events.[123]

But two developments occurred that in tandem seem to have been decisive in producing Musaddiq's overthrow. The first was the response of the Tudeh party. Moving quickly to take optimal advantage of the failed Anglo-American effort, the Tudeh leadership apparently sanctioned large public demonstrations against the Pahlavis. But the demonstrators also attacked religious symbols, including mosques. In doing so they not only offended the religiously inclined, including enlisted personnel in army units and the security forces, but also raised the spectre for many of Musaddiq's middle-class supporters of a Tudeh takeover. Recognizing this mistake, two U.S. agents with access to mercenary mobs paid to have their people join in the attacks on the religious symbols. It is impossible to assess the importance of their contribution. But it is clear that the Tudeh miscalculation was critical in turning defeat into victory for Zahedi. On the night of August 18, Musaddiq ordered police to attack Tudeh demonstrators.

The following morning, crowds began moving from south Tehran toward the center of the city shouting their support for the shah. The instigators of this mob were apparently the Rashidian brothers whose net embraced the strong-arm leaders and religious leaders who already had been paid to bring out the mercenary mob.[124] In addition, they instructed Ahamd Aramesh, one of the most resourceful of British agents, to contact Kashani and request his assistance. Kashani, who apparently had not been advised of the coup plan, reportedly cooperated. If this is true, he deserves critical responsibility for the successful outcome of the Anglo-American effort.[125]

The timing of the movement could not have been more fortuitous. Police and enlisted army personnel, thoroughly angered by the actions of the Tudeh crowds, joined the mob, as did a great many people from the bazaar. The Tudeh, having been attacked the previous night, did not respond to this unexpected, even bizarre development. And most important, Musaddiq's core supporters remained indoors. Musaddiq too failed to recognize the seriousness of the development and did not order his loyal officers to turn back the swelling mob. An astonished Zahedi and his military co-conspirators moved decisively. They seized the radio station, imposed martial law, and quickly secured the city. Pro-Musaddiq responses in the bazaar and in some provincial cities, such as Isfahan, came much too late.

In retrospect, neither the Americans nor the Iranian victims of their success were willing to face the unavoidable conclusion of the above description, that is, that the success of the coup was a consequence of, first, a major Tudeh miscalculation, and, second, the timing of a counterdemonstration that was critically fortuitous.[126] The American involved saw the results a demonstration of the effectiveness of the CIA's covert operations arm—an illusion that persisted until the abortive Bay of Pigs invasion of June 1961. The Iranian victims found an explanation of Anglo-American cleverness more comforting than an explanation that would force them to examine their own vulnerability. The CIA–MI-6 plans reflected a fundamental misassessment of Iranian sociopolitical developments. The coup effort led to a demonstration of the difficulty of Iranian secular nationalism, even with a charismatic leader, to deal with its traditional opponents. And yet the Musaddiq movement in Iran surely provided the optimal moment for a secular liberal nationalist elite to gain control of the direction of Iran's development. Among the many ironies of the events of August 1953 in Iran, two are particularly noteworthy. First, the Americans, who prided themselves on being the primary proponents of liberal democratic nationalist values, played a decisive role in denying to Iran a regime that conceivably could have incorporated those ideals as the prevailing political values in Iran. Second, the very elements of the population that would later be the core support base for the bitterly anti-American Ayatullah Khomeini, the urban lower and lower-middle class, provided the crowds that granted the British and the Americans their victory.

# 4

## CONSOLIDATING THE ROYAL DICTATORSHIP

When the shah was in Baghdad after the coup had apparently failed, he asked both the Americans and British for advice. In mulling over an answer, the British government made some revealing observations:

It may be argued that the Shah, by running away with so little dignity, must have forfeited any audience his message might have commanded in Persia; that he will not necessarily take any advice that is given to him; and that since, in any case, he cannot be relied on at any future time to exercise effective leadership, it is of no use keeping him in being as a possible leader or focus of loyalty.

On the other hand, we should not entirely discount the Shah as a possible leader of opposition to Musaddiq. His continued claims, if kept before his people, will provide a rallying point for anti-Communist and patriotic sentiment; and it is conceivable that he might one day play a useful part as a figurehead leader in a truncated non-Communist Persia.[1]

Britain's fascination with a partition of Iran, with the southern oil-producing area under the control of their man, is still apparent. Also apparent is the British assessment of the shah as a leader. The latter is important to note, because the impression was later to become so pervasive that the anti-Musaddiq coup established the royal dictatorship of Mohammad Reza Pahlavi. In fact, the dictatorship established was that of General Zahedi, and the formula was essentially the one the British had long advocated. The differences were that Zahedi was the chosen instrument rather than Sayyid Zia, and the external support was Anglo-American rather than simply British. But the support base was the same: the Iranian traditional elite. Further, the mode of control of the country was the same: the security forces plus conservative clergy and street leaders. Obviously, for the British the National Front phenomenon was of no fundamental importance. The Americans such as Henry Grady and Dean Ache-

110

son who saw it otherwise were no longer making decisions. Those who were agreed with the British about Iran but not about the Soviet Union. The idea of partitioning Iran—with the Soviets getting the north, for example—had no attraction for any official American group.

The best supporting evidence for the Anglo-American view of Iran in 1953 was that the Zahedi regime survived for two years. How could a movement capable of attracting crowds of 100,000 demonstrators, that excited the university students and the intelligentsia, that could win overwhelming victories in relatively free elections in urban Iran, that attracted open support from so many junior officers in the security forces, be swept aside so easily? Until the mass politics convulsion of 1978–1979, the prevailing British view that the strength of Iranian populist nationalism was illusory had to be taken seriously. But the outbreak of revolution one generation later, one of the most spectacular manifestations of mass politics in human history, strongly suggests that the national movement was an early precursor of that phenomenon and that the growth in mass political participation was already substantial and accelerating at the time of the Musaddiq government.

There is an additional reason for the survival of Zahedi's dictatorship. All politically conscious Iranians in 1953 regarded the successful coup as the result of Anglo-American manipulation. As they saw it, once again external powers, operating through elements of the population willing to trade the national interest for self-interest, had proved capable of controlling Iranian politics. And this time they had removed the first truly popular regime in Iran's long history. The result was destructive to the morale of Iranians caught up in rapid change. The belief that no basic change could occur in Iran without the acquiescence of the interfering great powers—a belief that had begun to fade—was reinforced and rigidified.

Then, finally, U.S. financial support for Zahedi was immediately forthcoming and very generous. In the first three months after Musaddiq's overthrow, it amounted to $73 million, a figure equal to almost half of all Iranian government expenditures for the year 1952.[2] For the commercial middle class that had suffered severe losses from the British blockade and the internal chaos, for government employees who were owed months of back pay, and for the urban unemployed, the prospects of an improved standard of living had to be appealing. Even for those who had followed Musaddiq, the process of accommodation had begun.

In 1954 American grants-in-aid amounted to 54.9 percent of Iranian government expenditures, and the $110 million was three times greater than Iran's oil revenues had been in 1950, the last year of full production.[3] Premier Zahedi's finance minister, Ali Amini, took on the task of working out an oil agreement that would insure a large and regular income but would also be something the public could acquiesce in. The principle of nationalization had to be accepted and the monopoly of the Anglo-Iranian Oil Company ended. The negotiations were difficult and the political risks for Amini and Zahedi substantial. But an agreement was signed in September 1954 that established a production and marketing consortium. AIOC's share was reduced to 40 percent, although the share of all British companies, including AIOC, was 52 percent. American companies held 40 percent of the shares. And as far as a great many Iranians and not a few Britons were concerned, this was the United States' purpose all along. In fact, the U.S. government had to do a good deal of arm-twisting to persuade American companies to take the risks of participation. Most were not overly sanguine concerning the prospects for survival of the new Iranian regime.[4]

The following year, oil income was double what it had been in 1952 but still $13 million less than American aid to the government. Together these sums amounted to 59 percent of government income.[5] Quite literally, the United States was purchasing the acquiescence of the Iranian public in the regime that succeeded Musaddiq.

However, the regime differed in important respects from previous traditional elite–external power alliances. The massive size of American financial support was only one indication of drastically changed circumstances. More significant still was the regime's necessary reliance on a coercive force that bore little resemblance to past terror instruments. In the transition period during which a modern coercive system was being developed, the strong-arm leaders and the conservative clerics, since they could mobilize large mobs, were essential for control. As a reward, Shaban the Brainless, for example, was given a great sports palace and the aristocratic elite came to do him honor. The conservative clerics were favored with a campaign against Bahais. The military governor of Tehran and chief coercive officer of the regime, General Timur Bakhtiar, swung the first axe in the symbolic act of removing the dome of the Bahai temple. However, when the covered bazaar, in time-honored fashion, closed its doors to protest government excesses, General Zahedi engaged in another symbolic act, the removal of the roof of the bazaar, to demonstrate to the *bazaaris* that even if the traditional elite was back in power, the traditional system of protest was gone forever.

But Zahedi was not the man to inaugurate the new system. Britons who knew him well commented on his corruptibility. Judging from his personal expenditures, his two years as prime minister must have been extraordinarily lucrative. It was not the kind of behavior to attract support and respect. His interest in government affairs was limited and much of his time was spent in widely noted extracurricular activities. When Loy Henderson was advancing the case to the shah for supporting a coup to place Zahedi in the premiership, the shah commented on Zahedi's limited intellectual abilities.[6] In all likelihood, the shah anticipated reasonably well the level of Zahedi's performance and in November 1955 dismissed him. From that point until 1978, the shah was dictator of Iran.

The case is easily made that in 1955 the shah could have opted to follow a path to restore some lost legitimacy to the regime. It was well known that he had been a reluctant participant in the coup. And it was General Zahedi who had to bear the onus of having signed a new oil agreement that placed Iran's oil effectively in Anglo-American hands. Then the shah dismissed the corrupt, repressive, and sycophantic regime placed in power by a foreign-backed coup. The Americans had effectively placed all their eggs in the basket of his leadership and really had no option but to give Iran a generous subsidy even were the shah to distance himself from them. A strategy the shah could have followed was to have appointed Musaddiqists to the cabinet. Such an act would have had real promise of producing stability and legitimacy as a consequence. But it would have involved sharing power, and it was quickly apparent that the shah had no interest in doing that. He clearly preferred maintaining for five years the working relationship he had established with the traditional ruling class.

However, the shah did signal his attraction to the modernization of his country and his willingness to turn to members of the technocratically proficient intelligentsia to achieve this purpose. He did so by accepting the advice and the leadership of the thoroughly competent Abol Hassan Ebtehaj in the Plan Organization.[7] That institution would serve as a recruitment and training base for a new technocratic elite, which would soon become a mainstay of the regime. In retrospect, this was a move of exceptional importance. It was an indication of the shah's understanding that he could, with offers of material and symbolic rewards, coopt individuals who were vital to the National Front support base.

The shah signaled also a willingness to grant a great deal of entrepreneurial freedom in Iran. This applied both to foreign enterprise and to the most progressive elements of the Iranian commercial community. Rumors that the shah and his family would tolerate — even cooperate in — corrupt business practices also became widespread. Evaluating such rumors is impossible, but there is no doubt that aggressive entrepreneurs came to understand the influence channels that could lead to remunerative contracts and that these channels frequently emanated from the court.

Most important, the shah had to strive for and ultimately to achieve a perception of invulnerability to assure the survival of his regime. In the Zahedi years, a sense of invulnerability was attached to the image of Anglo-American omnipotence and dedication to preserving the regime. Thus the reconstruction of the police and the military as reliable forces was the shah's number one objective; immediately after the coup, the project was begun. General Bakhtiar was appointed military governor of Tehran and the institution he constructed would be the basis for Iran's primary internal security force — to be known by its acronym SAVAK. American advisers were brought in to oversee the development of this organization, as well as the police, the secret police, and the gendarmerie. And a U.S. military mission was sent to advise the armed forces. Something less than half of the huge American aid package to Iran over the next decade was spent for these purposes.[8] Under the shah's dictatorship, these programs developed rapidly. Politically unreliable officers were retired and the shah set up a system of personal access for security and military officers that was to guard effectively against any temptation for officers to think of a military coup. The security forces were kept hydra-headed for this reason. By 1960 the shah felt he had constructed a sufficient coercive base to permit dispensing with his alliance with the old traditional elite. He was ready to inaugurate a new era in Iran.

*The External Factor*

U.S. policy after August 19, 1953, was effectively to give the new regime total and unquestioning support. Fear of a Soviet take-over was uppermost in policymakers' minds, and there was a full appreciation of Iran's exceptional weakness. Why indeed didn't the Soviets make a move to take advantage of this situation? In 1954 Iranian security officials captured a document that listed the names of over four hundred Iranian officers who were members of a Tudeh military network. This in turn led to the uncovering of a maze of Tudeh infiltrations in all ranks of the security forces. The officers involved were, with few exceptions, not in critical command posts. Even so, the Tudeh military potential had been substantial. Yet there is nothing to indicate even the preliminaries of a military coup plan.[9]

However, the primary opportunity for the Soviets did not lie with the Tudeh and the attraction of Marxism for a minority of the in-telligentsia. The opportunity offered the Soviets by the Anglo-American–assisted coup was the disaffection of Iranian nationalists with the United States. There was a serious difficulty involved in tak-ing advantage of this disaffection, however. For most Iranians, the Soviet Union was still imperial Russia, which had shown signs of coveting Iranian territory during the reign of Peter the Great and throughout the nineteenth and early twentieth centuries. The Anglo-Soviet occupation of Iran and the Azerbaijan crisis reversed what-ever decline there may have been in the perceived threat from Russia during the Reza Shah era. Furthermore, there was a lingering hope that the United States would again break with the British and cham-pion the cause of Iranian sovereign independence.

In 1954 the Tudeh party published a pamphlet, "28 Mordad" (the date by the Iranian calendar of Musaddiq's overthrow), which was severely self-critical. It argued the case for a popular front and lamented the failure to have achieved one in time to have prevented the coup. It recognized fully that there now was a major opportu-nity to form a popular front and appealed to Musaddiq's followers to recognize the community of purpose. But for this to have oc-curred, there would have had to have been some indication that such a popular front could expect support from the Soviet Union and, most difficult of all, that such support would be disinterested. No such indications were forthcoming. To the contrary, Soviet policy toward a regime supported by the United States for the ostensible purpose of preventing Soviet subversion was more than correct. It was friendly. The Iranian nationalist opposition, now operating underground, did not seriously consider the option of a cooperative relationship with the Soviet Union and rejected overtures from the Tudeh party. The Tudeh leadership was placed in the difficult position of having to argue a case for friendship with the Soviets in spite of their good relationship with the shah.

Soviet policy toward post-Musaddiq Iran soured briefly in 1959, but until then had been one of economic cooperation, favorable trade relations, and vigorous cultural exchange. There was no serious effort to exploit political opportunities with ethnic groups or major opposition forces. Yet by all indications, American policy in Iran in this period was primarily concerned with helping Iran gain the kind of stability and economic well-being necessary to contain Soviet subversive efforts. There is no indication whatsoever that the Soviet failure to exploit real opportunities in Iran led to the United States' reconsideration of assumptions regarding Soviet intentions in Iran or more broadly in the region.

There are three obvious explanations for the unwillingness to consider, as a few people such as George Kennan were doing,[10] the Soviet Union as increasingly a status quo power. First, the USSR's failure to take advantage of nationalist disaffection in Iran was not even noticed by U.S. policymakers who had convinced themselves that the overthrow of Musaddiq was desirable. They, like the British, simply did not see a strong nationalist movement or indeed much in the way of assertive Iranian public opinion. Second, a central aspect of cold war imagery is that if the United States shows sufficient will and determination, the Soviet Union will prove to be respectful and even cooperative—a paper tiger. Third, and surely most important, the United States was a universal not a regional power. Policy in Iran was one aspect of general U.S. policy in the Middle East, and, especially after 1955, American policymakers saw many manifestations of aggressive Soviet behavior elsewhere, especially in the Arab world. Hence there was no challenge to the assumption that the USSR was following an aggressive policy in Iran.

U.S. policy in the Middle East in the 1950s began to fall into some clear patterns. The problem was to find some formula for achieving three difficult-to-reconcile objectives: to contain perceived Soviet expansionism, to maintain the flow of oil to Western economies, and to provide for the security and well-being of Israel. As was apparent in the Iranian case, some American policymakers saw in the growth of strong and assertive indigenous nationalist movements the best hope for containing Soviet expansionism. Gamal Abdul Nasser in the Arab world appeared to some Americans to be particularly likely to achieve this purpose. Nasser was both a nationalist and an authoritarian. Therefore, unlike Musaddiq whose brief role in Iran was chaotic and tolerant of internal communist activity, Nasser brought stability and order to Egypt and tightly controlled Egyptian communists. Kermit Roosevelt, who gloried in his role in the overthrow of Musaddiq, was a friend of Nasser and an advocate of U.S. cooperation with his regime.[11] But what inevitably emerged was that Nasser, as the self-proclaimed defender of the Arab nation, would be perceived in Israel as the most threatening of Arab leaders. During 1955, events demonstrated the difficulty for the United States in continuing to support both Nasser and the government of Israel.

In addition, Nasser and the forces of Arab nationalism were perceived as seriously threatening to oil-rich Iraq by the Anglophile oligarchy who ruled that Arab state. In this oil-producing part of the Arab world, Arab nationalism was the same kind of destabilizing force for oil interests as was Iranian nationalism in Iran. It follows that local leaders that had evolved comfortable relations with oil interests were viewed by Arab nationalists just as their Iranian counterparts were viewed by Iranian nationalists. Even the Saudi royal family, which had allied themselves with Egypt because of a dynastic quarrel with the Hashemites in Jordan and Iraq, was becoming nervous about the implications of the Arab nationalist movement.

It was John Foster Dulles's hope that a Middle East Defense Pact could be formed that would satisfy U.S. and "free world" objectives in the area. In his vision, this pact would attract both Nasser and the Iraqi leaders and would be viewed as acceptable by the Israelis. But the vision was innocent of any understanding of Middle Eastern attitudes. Nasser, embroiled in the final stages of a struggle to eliminate the British imperial presence from Egypt, was hardly likely to ally his country with an Iraqi regime that he and Arab nationalists generally viewed as an informal British colony. Israeli leaders, equally suspicious of the British, could only see the pact as a device for arming their enemies.

But Britain saw great advantages in a regional defense pact and its enthusiasm was certainly not diminished by Nasser's refusal to join and by the denunciations of Arab and Iranian nationalists. As it took shape, the pact would be a means for institutionalizing British and American support for regimes characterized as "moderate" and "responsible." Nuri Said, the gifted leader of the Iraqi oligarchy, and the shah of Iran saw it the same way. Pakistani leaders saw it as a means for strengthening their military in its contest with India. And Turkey, which alone of the emerging alliance agreed with Dulles about the Soviet threat, saw it as a means for deterring the Soviet Union militarily and politically.

American policy was evolving toward a formula that would reconcile the three basic and somewhat contradictory objectives.[12] That formula was an alliance with traditional regional regimes and opposition to strongly pro-change and nationalist regimes. Because Israel was unhappy with the prospects of American support for an alliance that would include Arab states, Israeli opposition was sufficient to prevent formal U.S. membership in the alliance, finalized in 1955, that came to be known as the Baghdad Pact. Israeli leaders understood, however, that the alliance as it developed was anti-Nasser and anti–Arab nationalist and, from that perspective, useful for them. They therefore acquiesced in an informal but vigorous U.S. participation in the pact. Conservative, oil-producing Arab regimes other than Iraq did not join the pact but obviously approved of its purposes.

In 1957, following the diplomatic disaster of the Suez crisis, in the course of which the United States found itself for a time a de facto ally of the Soviet Union against Britain, France and Israel, American policy further crystallized. Dulles steered Saudi Arabia away from Nasser into a close bilateral relationship with the United States. Then he made an attempt to isolate Nasser. In April he supported the successful royal coup of King Hossein in Jordan. The coup was directed against the government of Prime Minister Suleiman Nabulsi, a leader similar to Musaddiq in terms of his support base, his intense nationalism, and his espousal of liberal democratic values. An attempted coup against President Shukri al Quwatli of Syria in August was comparable to that in Iran in its direction and the logistic support given by the CIA. It was comparable as well in its clumsy execution and in the ease of attribution.[13] However, this coup failed, but in doing so brought an end to Syria's brief experience as a liberal democray and strengthened the communists internally. Ironically, Syria was saved from going communist by Nasser, who reluctantly agreed to a Syrian-Egyptian union in the United Arab Republic.

Following these developments, the Arab world was sharply polarized. Nasser was the leader, active and symbolic, of Arab nationalism. Given U.S. enmity, he had no other recourse than to turn to the Soviet Union for support against what was seen as a Zionist-imperialist alliance. Soviet support in the form of arms sales was forthcoming. But even when local communists were strong, there was little hard evidence of significant Soviet involvement in internal affairs. The parallel with Iran, therefore, was close. U.S. policy in Iran in 1957 was in full harmony with American policy in the Arab world and in the region. It appeared to be securely grounded in a set of intersecting bilateral relationships, with Israel, with the Turkey of Adnan Menderes, with the Iraq of Nuri Said, and with the Iran of the shah.

But in July 14, 1958, an almost casually executed military coup overturned the government of Iraq. The young king, the regent, and Nuri Said were killed. In the days that followed, rumors abounded of a royalist force or some external force that would restore the royal regime. How is it possible that the government of Iraq, seemingly the most stable of Arab regimes and one with the full and unequivocal support of the United States, Britain, Turkey, and Iran, could be overturned with such ease? The shah was in Turkey when this event occurred, and he delayed his return to Iran for several days. His concern was understandable. The regime of Iran, like that of Iraq, relied on the popular belief that in a crisis it would be protected by Britain and the United States. Were that belief to fail, the regime would be in serious danger of challenge. The Iraqi regime was overturned with stunning ease, and no external force had materialized or shown signs of attempting to restore it. It was a dangerous moment. When the shah did return to Iran, his armed forces took every precaution to ensure his safety.

The new regime in Baghdad, led by General Abdul Karim Qassem, mirrored the diversity of the opposition to the old order. Among its leaders were individuals enamored of Gamal Abdul Nasser, Arab nationalists of Baathist persuasion, parochial nationalists, and Marxists. It was of more than symbolic significance that no invitation was issued to Nasser to make a triumphant visit to Baghdad—another great Arab city yearning for the formation of an Arab nation-state. On the contrary, factional conflict quickly flared, and in a few months the pro-Nasser leaders had been defeated. But in the eyes of the Eisenhower administration, this was the moment of confrontation with the Soviet Union and its primary Arab client, Nasser. Iraq was seen as having entered that camp. The British sent armed forces to sustain King Hossein in Jordan; Eisenhower sent American marines into Lebanon. Secretary Dulles then initiated a series of bilateral discussions with remaining members of the old Baghdad Pact, now referred to by its acronym CENTO, to provide the needed reassurance of American support. The shah took advantage of this move to make lavish demands, including an American promise to come to Iran's aid in case of attack and to equip two new army divisions.

However, American attitudes were beginning to change. The dramatic moves made following the Iraqi coup were based on an assumption of a Soviet-orchestrated move, acting through the United Arab Republic and directed against Nuri Said, King Hossein, and Lebanese President Camille Chamoun. But the course of events that followed disconfirmed American expectations. The leaders of the Lebanese forces opposed to Chamoun proved in negotiations to be rather conservative nationalists who were quite willing to enter a government of national unity. Pro-Nasser elements in Iraq were waging a losing battle against President Qassem and his Marxist allies. President Nasser was expressing concern at communist inroads in Iraq, while the Soviet Union was doing very little to exploit what was a most favorable situation for doing so. The sense of urgency that would have been necessary for U.S. acceptance of the shah's demands, therefore, was lacking; the demands were either rejected outright or put off for later discussion.

A bilateral agreement that fell far short of the shah's demands was negotiated and scheduled for signing January 29, 1959, at a CENTO meeting in Karachi. Sometime prior to that meeting, talks were initiated—by whom is a matter of dispute—between the shah and the Soviet government. On January 29, while the CENTO meeting was in progress, a high-level Soviet delegation appeared in Tehran announcing that it was there to negotiate a nonaggression treaty with the Iranian government. The central terms would be an Iranian promise not to sign the bilateral agreement with the United States and a Soviet renunciation of Article Six of the 1921 treaty.[14]

The United States and its allies took this development seriously. Eisenhower and the heads of state of the other CENTO powers sent direct appeals to the shah not to sign. What followed is instructive for anyone seeking to understand the behavior of the Soviet super-power toward a relatively weak state on its southern border. Just as it appeared that the treaty with the Soviets was about to be signed, the shah announced he was ill and Prime Minister Manuchehr Eqbal left town. A Soviet delegation, including a deputy foreign minister, was left without anyone to negotiate with. Shortly after the depar-ture of the chagrined delegation, a U.S. delegation arrived to hear Iranian demands for more economic and military assistance. For six months the Soviet radio blistered Iran, and then relations returned to their previous cooperative, if not friendly level.[15]

The shah was to demonstrate later in oil negotiations that he could play a tough bargaining game. But the implications of this episode, a relatively minor one in cold war annals, are too important not to spell out. The case is strong evidence that the shah felt little real threat from Soviet aggression. He chose to offend an enormously powerful neighbor six months after his own great-power allies had lost con-siderable credibility in the region. The Soviet response was the best he could expect; apparently it was just what he did expect.

The possibility cannot be dismissed that the shah was serious about the negotiations with the Soviets. The United States and the United Kingdom had been unable to reverse the situation in Iraq and had not insisted on President Chamoun's remaining in power in Lebanon. Since the shah's own position in Iran depended on the sup-port of these powers, he would be wise to consider his options seri-ously. One such option would be to present himself to his people as a nonaligned leader and to seek thereby to restore an increased measure of public support. But if this was his intent, he did nothing to prepare his public for such a radical change in policy and the con-sequence was more public bewilderment than support.

## The Shah's Change of Direction

The shah in 1959 clearly was preparing for a radical change in both domestic policy and in his domestic political alliances. He could think in these terms because of the growing strength of his internal control. Income from oil was steadily mounting and Iran's economy was prospering. Professional, technocratic, and middle-class elements were doing well in particular and appeared to have become reconciled to the regime. But even more important, SAVAK—and the internal security force generally—were, in the shah's judgment, capable of meeting any domestic political challenge. The shah's dependence on his traditional political allies at home had declined to the point where he felt he could dispense with them.

But just as he was not willing to follow through by exploring the option of nonalignment, the shah was unwilling to consider an alliance with nationalist leaders. In many respects, such an alliance would have been natural. Programmatically, the shah and the nationalists were in agreement in many areas. The form of economic and social development the shah favored was fully in tune with the mix of state planning and free entrepreneurship advocated by the old base of Musaddiq support. Land reform, educational policies, labor legislation, and social welfare measures—all programs the shah would sponsor—were close to the National Front philosophy. And if the shah were to terminate his alliance with the traditional elements, he would need a new support base.

There is no evidence the shah seriously considered or explored this option. But he did wish to establish at least the trappings of a parliamentary democracy. Rather than create a single authoritarian party as the institutional base for his regime and a career path for regime functionaires, he promulgated two parties. One would serve as His Majesty's government and the other His Majesty's loyal opposition. Thus he appointed his prime minister, Manuchehr Eqbal, leader of the majority, "conservative," government party, the Melliyun or National party. As leader of the opposition, "liberal," party, he appointed his loyal friend and one of Iran's great landowners, Amir Assadolah Alam. Neither party, it was quickly apparent, would have any real independence, and political wiseacres saw the entire operation as a charade. Speculation about the real reason for inaugurating such a grotesquerie centered on the United States. Naive, innocent, and yet sincere as they were, the Americans wanted their client to be democratic but would be entirely happy with the mere facade of democracy.[16]

But as the shah would shortly demonstrate, he was serious about inaugurating a system with a strong institutional resemblance to a

European constitutional monarchy. He said his father had failed to provide the monarchy with a solid institutional foundation and he would do better by his own son. Thus in 1960 he announced that there would be new and free elections for seats in the Majlis based on party competition. The world press decided to take him seriously, and a large press corps was sent to observe. They were not disappointed. What followed was the initiation of a three-year crisis that in many respects foreshadowed the revolution that would follow a generation later—in particular the shah's behavior in that revolution. Dr. Mozaffar Baqai, who had preserved a core party organization while suffering disgrace for his role in Musaddiq's overthrow, took advantage of the relaxation of coercive control to launch a real electoral campaign. His fierce attacks, focused on the prime minister, were ultimately almost unrestrained. Charges were made of corruption, nepotism, denial of the rule of law, brutality, and insensitivity in the realm of social justice. Veiled references to foreign control of the country began appearing, and Baqai went so far as to refer to Eqbal as a "traitor."

What began as a charade had become real; the shah was beginning to lose control. National Front elements began to join demonstrations, and even within the "opposition" Mardom party, attacks on the government became serious. But no alteration of the shah's plan was made. When the election results were reported, charges of rigging seemed to be validated. Melliyun won its expected handsome majority, and Mardom a respectable minority. But there had been no effort to give an appearance of closely fought elections within districts; evidently, some districts had been previously designated as Melliyun and others as Mardom. In almost every case, the designated party won its district easily. Since a fair amount of free expression had been granted, outraged protest greeted what was described as an electoral travesty. The shah responded by nullifying the election, dismissing Dr. Eqbal, and appointing as prime minister Jafaar Sharif-Imami, a politician with advertised good relations within the National Front and religious communities.[17]

In 1960 the shah was demonstrating an ambivalence that would be fatal eighteen years later. Driven by an ambition to be as absolute a ruler as his father had been, yet almost equally determined to be recognized by his people as their benign master, he searched for the institutional formula that would give his tutorial position consensual legitimacy. His compromises with external powers, he would explain, were realpolitik exigencies to be abandoned as soon as new power realities allowed. He could be arrogantly dictatorial in his relations with his lieutenants, but the appearance of widespread public support for rivals, such as Musaddiq, or of opposition to his rule, left him bewildered and depressed. At such moments, he became not merely indecisive but also self-destructive.

The shah's failure to make overtures to men with genuine popular support, it follows, reflected an unwillingness to recognize independent and assertive public opinion in Iran. In this regard he closely resembled Western imperialists. His people needed his benevolent guidance to lead them gradually into a new era, he reasoned. Thus the party institutions should come first. In time, possibly, they would be allowed some measure of independence. However, for the immediate future, both should accept his guidance. A strong coercive force would be essential to restrain irresponsible agitators such as Musaddiq who played on the emotions of a politically immature people, but as the people came to understand how much his royal benevolence was helping them, coercion could be relaxed. By 1960 the shah felt he had reached the point at which his new system could be inaugurated and control relaxed. Yet when this relaxation led to internal disruption and chaos, he somehow could not bring himself to reimpose a brutal coercive control, even though he had the capability to do so.

The shah's decision to appoint Sharif-Imami as prime minister remains a puzzle. Since he would turn again in 1978 to the same man to deal with a public that was now out of control, he clearly saw in Sharif-Imami a possible answer to his dilemma. A proposition that cannot be ruled out is that the shah sensed the imperialist hidden hand in both situations. In his final tormented account of his fall from power, *Answer to History,* he makes the point explicitly that the CIA had turned against him and was responsible for at least some of the popular agitation.[18] The fact that he appointed Ahmad Aramesh as the head of the important Plan Organization is instructive. There is little question that the shah believed Aramesh was an agent of MI-6.[19] His overt role in the coup against Musaddiq was comparable to that of the Rashidian brothers in its openness. Sharif-Imami and Aramesh were brothers-in-law and Sharif-Imami was closely associated with the Freemason group. The appointment therefore may well have been a move to appease the British and to enlist their support in restoring control.

In fact, Sharif-Imami had no real constituency, and the shah granted him no real authority. His strategy was one of attempting, through personal dealings with leaders with whom he was acquainted, to persuade nationalist and religious elements to cooperate with the regime. Since the opposition was sensing a vulnerability in the regime that might well be fatal, they rejected all his overtures. The opposition's momentum continued to develop, and it was abetted by an impending financial crisis.

Undaunted, Sharif-Imami held new elections that, though obviously rigged, resulted in a Majlis far less subservient to the shah than its predecessors had been. Then when opposition continued to mount, the shah dismissed most of his top security force leaders, including Timur Bakhtiar, and attempted to make scapegoats of them. He would follow this tactic again in 1978, even though in 1961 it simply gave further evidence of the regime's vulnerability. A teachers' strike that culminated in riots in which two teachers died proved to be the climactic moment for Sharif-Imami. He was dismissed and Ali Amini appointed in his stead.

Ali Amini was a political leader who in many respects paralleled his kinsman Ahmad Qavam. In fact, Amini brought Qavam's protégé, Hassan Arsenjani, into the government with him. Like Qavam, Amini represented the progressive wing of the upper class; indeed, the shah thought of him and feared him as a Qajar and a possible proponent of a Qajar restoration.[20] Amini was considered by Americans who had known him as Zahedi's minister of finance as intelligent, skillful in negotiations, pragmatic, tough, and courageous. But Amini lacked Qavam's acute sense of politics. He had little more understanding of the force of an aroused public opinion than did the shah. Establishing a working relationship between him and the nationalist leadership would have been difficult for two reasons. First, popular sentiment was so strongly in favor of the nationalists that the argument for their making significant compromises was not strong. Second, Amini's role in restoring effective foreign control of Iran's oil had led to a public view that he served foreign interests. In any case, Amini, despite the weakness of his own base of support, did not make a serious effort to effect an alliance with nationalist leaders.

The image of Amini as an instrument of foreign interests was not confined to the pro-Musaddiqist element. Indeed, the view was held almost universally that Amini was the United States' choice for prime minister and, moreover, that the Americans wanted him to be a strong prime minister. Admiration for Amini on the part of leading Americans had been long noted in official Tehran, and the shah was personally well aware of them. He understood as well that it was a common opinion in the embassy that the kind of understanding and strength Amini could offer was necessary to deal with Iran's serious economic difficulties.[21]

But the signals the shah had received were broader than these. When John F. Kennedy was inaugurated president in 1961, the quality of U.S. support for the shah's dictatorial rule began to shift. Kennedy was the one American president of the cold war era who inclined toward the view that Third World nationalism should be enlisted in the United States' struggle with the Soviet Union. Furthermore, in several parts of the world—Peru, the Dominican Republic, Laos—Kennedy used his influence to advance democratic forces. He was therefore receptive to the argument of the shah's liberal opponents and was critical of the shah's role in Iran. Whereas in 1960 the shah had felt that he was now sufficiently strong to reduce his dependence on external support, by 1961 he was in serious trouble and needed clear evidence of American favor. His people had to believe the U.S. government would support him if he were strongly challenged. If this meant accepting as prime minister a man he disliked and feared but who could ensure continued American support, he was ready to make the appointment. This may well have been the shah's thinking in appointing Ali Amini.

As matters turned out, the appointment of Amini was fortuitous for the shah. Amini symbolized U.S. support for the regime and thus improved the shah's control of the situation. He failed totally to strengthen his own hand against the shah by negotiating alliances with opposition elements. Moreover, he put into effect an austerity program which, with generous American financial assistance, helped the Iranian economy on its path to recovery. Since Amini, not the shah, was the focus of dissatisfaction produced by these austerity measures, the shah came through the episode politically stronger.

In the spring of 1962, the shah visited Washington with the clear intent of discovering what the U.S. government's attitude would be if he were to dismiss Ali Amini. Official Washington, which only a decade after Musaddiq's overthrow had no functional memory of that deed and its consequences, was bemused. To be sure, many admired Amini and believed he had furnished exactly the leadership Iran had needed for the past year. But the shah was a sovereign ruler; dismissing and appointing prime ministers was his constitutional prerogative. Shortly after his return to Tehran, the shah dismissed Amini and appointed the most loyal of Iranian politicians, Amir Assadolah Alam.

Alam commenced negotiations with nationalist leaders in an apparently more serious and certainly more informed manner than Amini had done.[22] But the nationalists were still confident that they could not be denied a return to power. Their demands were no less than free elections—including, of course, the freedom of press, assembly, and speech necessary to make them meaningful. Negotiations were broken off, and in January 1963 virtually the entire top leadership of the national movement was arrested. The security forces exercised effective control and the nationalist leadership was decimated without significant public protest. In retrospect, it is clear that this act marked the end of the dominance of secular liberal nationalists in the Iranian opposition.

When the shah dismissed Amini, he retained Hassan Arsenjani as minister of agriculture. Arsenjani's role in the quarter-century of Iranian history dating from the Allied invasion was extraordinary. He first achieved major visibility as editor of the Marxist and pro-Soviet newspaper *Darya* and established a reputation for brilliance and unpredictability. He next appeared in the entourage of Ahmad Qavam and ultimately became Qavam's loyal and devoted confidant. This position took Arsenjani out of the mainstream of either the Marxist or secular nationalist camps where an intellectual with his talents and lowly social origins normally would be found. It gave him access to Iran's established social and political elite, and that ultimately included regular sessions with the shah. Arsenjani was a natural strategist, and apparently it was these talents that made him so valuable to his mentors. He claimed, for example, to have persuaded the shah to pursue a pro-Israeli policy on the grounds that the geopolitical positions of Iran and Israel made them natural allies against the Arabs.[23]

Until his last year, Arsenjani's influence was exercised through three successive mentors, Qavam, Amini, and the shah. It is impossible to know, therefore, what that influence was. He is important to this account for two reasons. First, his relationship with the shah tells a good deal about the shah as a leader, as a decision maker, and as a man.

In the spring of 1958, a group of conspirators led by General Vali Qarani had planned a coup against the shah. The group involved neither the National Front nor the Tudeh party, but it did include a broad array of conservative political leaders. Qarani, who briefly was to be commander of the Army of the Islamic Republic before being assassinated, seems to have had a Nasser-type role in mind. But most of the conspirators were civilians. Because Arsanjani was among them, of course, the assumption was that this meant Amini, at the time ambassador in Washington, and possibly the Americans were as well. However, the shah learned about the plans, and Arsenjani was among those arrested. Three years later, Amini was prime minister, and Arsenjani was not only in the cabinet but also back in regular contact with the shah. The episode illustrates the point that the shah trusted almost no one and assumed disloyalty even among his closest officers. Because Arsenjani's ideas were useful to him, the shah was obviously quite willing to overlook documented betrayal to keep him in his employ.

The second reason for Arsenjani's importance to this account is the strong possibility that he was one of the shah's primary strategists in 1963. Arsenjani believed that the shah had erred badly in 1960 in assuming that old pro-Musaddiq supporters were reconciled to his regime. His proposed strategy was to create a new and intensely loyal support base. He saw potential support coming from the peasantry and from labor. The former could be mobilized through the application of a drastic land reform program, one that would go far beyond the timid and tentative proposals of the National Front.[24] The latter could be attracted by further development of some already advanced labor legislation and by such schemes as workers owning shares in the companies that employed them. What Arsenjani was proposing in fact was that the shah turn for support to the very element of the population that was most rapidly coming into political awareness and had hitherto looked for direction to religious leaders or to Marxist labor leaders, not to the nationalists.

## The Political Debut of Khomeini

In early 1963, the shah proclaimed his White Revolution, which fully incorporated Arsenjani's strategic approach. In addition to the focus on land reform, workers' rights, education, health, and social welfare, it called for a major emphasis on women's rights and opportunities. Following several weeks of intensive publicity for the program, he put it to a referendum. The vote was 5,598,711 for and 4,115 against. Indications of the level of U.S. journalistic concern with Iran was the editorial comment of the *New York Times* on this vote: "The great mass of the Iranian people are doubtless behind the shah in his bold new reform efforts. The national plebiscite he called early this year gave emphatic evidence of this."[25]

What the plebiscite gave evidence of, of course, was the totalitarian nature of the shah's control. What the editorial illustrated was the extraordinary willingness of American journalism, including most liberal journals, to view in symbolically favorable terms a regime seen as a necessary ally for containing the Soviet Union. *Times* reporters only a few months earlier had described antigovernment demonstrations in Iran, largely middle-class in composition, involving up to 100,000 participants. And the above editorial was written only four days after violent riots in Tehran, Qom, Shiraz, Mashad, and other Iranian cities that came close to getting out of control. The government admitted that eighty-six people were killed, the U.S. embassy indicated two hundred, and the opposition claimed more than a thousand dead.[26] The riots, which were a portent of the revolution to come, marked the entry of Ayatullah Ruhollah Khomeini into the consciousness not only of the United States and the shah's government, but also of the secular nationalists who previously had dominated the opposition.

The shah's White Revolution incorporated reforms that most Musaddiqists were skeptical of but could hardly oppose. As such, it was disarming for them. But it was directed, explicitly in Arsenjani's formulations, at the sector of the population with whom religious leaders had their greatest influence. The angry response of Khomeini and his followers was viewed by the U.S. embassy as a violent reaction to modernization and to a challenge to vested interests, since church properties would be subject to land reform. The shah saw the hand of Egypt's Gamal Abdul Nasser and his allies among Iranian nationalists. The Soviet radio broadcasts dismissed as absurd the notion that the riots were religious-led and saw them as reflecting working-class revulsion against the shah's regime.[27]

But much the most interesting response was that of the Musaddiqists. Immediately after Musaddiq's overthrow, one group of his supporters, calling itself the National Resistance Movement (NRM), split from the main body of the National Front. Led by Mehdi Bazargan and Ayatullah Mahmud Taleqani, it drew heavily for both leadership and its rank and file from progressive clerics. The NRM ideologically was liberal, reformist, and equally devoted to the national and Islamic communities. The National Front, in contrast, tended to be self-consciously secular, with anticlericalism never far beneath the surface.

The response to the rioting, as might be expected, differed from one group to another. The secular element was shocked and totally unprepared to take advantage of this appearance of mass dissatisfaction. The religious element incorporated in the NRM, now calling itself the Freedom Movement, saw immediately the significance of the development and moved to join it. The rioting lasted two days, with Freedom Movement participation notable on the second day. Furthermore, from that day on Mehdi Bazargan in particular fully understood the charismatic potential of Ayatullah Khomeini and was determined to harness it for the achievement of Bazargan's image of an ideal future for Iran.[28]

The demonstrations and rioting of 1963 were a clear indication of the change in direction produced by Musaddiq's overthrow. Middle-class, professional, and student elements had given every indication in the 1960–1963 crisis period that the Musaddiqist leadership spoke for them. But the ease with which that leadership was suppressed in January 1963 now stood in contrast to the shah's great difficulty in suppressing Khomeini's supporters. In the ten years since the coup, the percentage of the population predisposed to political participation had obviously grown rapidly and was continuing to grow. The newly politically conscious were to be found predominantly in the urban lower-middle- and lower-class communities. They tended to be religious and looked to religious leaders for guidance in personal affairs. And quite obviously they were attracted to clerics such as Khomeini who understood them and could speak to their anger, anxieties, and aspirations. These leaders served as the socializing agents of this awakening mass. The Musaddiq phenomenon had ended before they became politically conscious, and Musaddiq's secular followers had lacked either access to or interest in them.

However, the Freedom Movement did attract the support of many outstanding clerics and religious laymen. It provided a ready-made organizational apparatus for underground activities and was led by men with impeccable religious credentials. Khomeini had opposed Kashani's tactical decision to cooperate with secular nationalists, but he clearly respected and trusted Mehdi Bazargan and his liberal religio-nationalist associates. The immediate stimulus to Khomeini's anger and of the rioting that followed was the shah's granting something close to extraterritoriality to U.S. military personnel in Iran. To Khomeini this symbolized the surrender of Iranian and Islamic dignity that characterized what the shah's supporters called Westernization. To characterize Khomeini's response as focused on opposition to anything as specific as land reform or women's rights is surely in error. To depict it as reactionary or against change is even more off the mark. It was rather an early manifestation of a preference for the radical change in direction that was to follow sixteen years later. Arsenjani's hope that the shah could attract the support of the element of the population that would back the revolution indicates his prescience. But the hope was to be in vain. Arsenjani finally lost the favor of the shah when he made a personal effort to appeal to the beneficiaries of land reform and was removed from the cabinet. The shah was to find his core support base among the newly rich and made no real effort after 1963 to follow Arsenjani's advice.

Forced into exile by the shah in 1964, Khomeini eventually settled in Najaf, Iraq—an important center of the Shiite world. There he was in regular contact with Freedom Movement figures. His role was that of abstract theorist and communicator. Strategy, tactics, and organization were largely in Bazargan's hands. As events were to demonstrate, however, Khomeini charted his own ideological course. His developing charisma gave him a potential power far greater than that of the sum of Bazargan and his Freedom Movement associates.

*A Decade of Stability*

Between 1964 and 1974 Iran enjoyed political stability, exceptionally rapid economic growth, low inflation, and a rising standard of living for most of its citizens. It was the high point of the shah's rule, an era in which he exuded confidence. His control of policy in Iran, domestic and foreign, was close to absolute. Of twentieth-century leaders, probably only Fidel Castro rivaled him in personal dominance over decision making. The shah was able to perform at this level, first, because of the stability of his authoritarian control of his country; second, because of his willingness to immerse himself in the details of most important policy areas and his ability to gain a basic understanding of complicated and technically demanding policy questions; and, third, because of his refusal to allow imaginative and independent-minded subordinates any real decisional freedom. The second level of decision making soon became the province of technocratically competent individuals who well understood and accepted their limited role.[29] Gone from the administration were men of the likes of Abol Hassan Ebethaj—brilliant, confident and strong-minded.

Iranian policy, domestic and foreign, reflected this decisional profile.[30] Ideas abounded, but programmatic development was mechanical. In foreign policy there were strong strategic notions but no real tactical constructions that would allow the achievement of strategic objectives. High-level government employees were handsomely rewarded in terms of salary and perquisities as well as the clear availability of extralegal profits. No "Young Turk" movement developed by which imaginative policy programs could have been proposed and sufficient bureaucratic pressure generated to have them seriously considered. Income from oil increased steadily, but at a rate that did not exceed the easy absorption capacity of the economic system. Plans for development were prepared by well-trained Iranians and foreign advisers. Major problems, such as the lack of sufficient training programs for Iranians, could easily be identified,[31] and the norms of social justice intervened little in policy determination, but still this was a decade of major economic and social achievements.[32]

Yet in 1979 the shah's system of internal control collapsed with a totality that is usually seen only as a consequence of military collapse in war. Obviously, therefore, there was a fundamental vulnerability to the shah's system of control. The stability of the 1964–1974 decade was real and the shah's control solid. But to explain the decade of stability, I must describe both the bases of solid control and the regime's underlying vulnerability.

Of first importance was control through coercion. The shah's success in putting down the June 1963 riots was a demonstration of the efficiency and the reliability of his security forces.[33] To be sure, he had been compelled to make use of the military in dealing with rioters, but his success was a message to those unhappy with his regime that they lacked the ability to overturn it by force. In the following months and years, the internal security apparatus improved in quality and increased in size. The primary responsibility for internal security rested with SAVAK. With both internal and external jurisdiction, it was functionally parallel to the KGB. But as in other totalitarian regimes, the authorities well understood the need to have other organizations, independent of SAVAK, which could serve to monitor and check SAVAK. There was, as a consequence, an elaborate and overlapping internal control system whose major components all had direct access to the shah.[34]

The real success of an internal security complex is to be measured in how it is perceived by the public. In the case of Iran, the internal security apparatus came to be perceived as omnipotent, omniscient, and omnipresent. So complete was its apparent control that an individual who had the temerity to engage in oppositionist activities came under suspicion as a probable agent of SAVAK. Who else would dare challenge so powerful and all-embracing an organization? This myth was sufficiently compelling that fathers who had fought in the streets for Musaddiq did not describe that part of Iran's history to their sons and daughters. Typically, Iranian students discovered Iran's recent history only when they went abroad to study. And even abroad they believed that some among their friends and colleagues were certainly covert agents of SAVAK.[35]

The effect of this propaganda was sufficient to make open opposition to the regime unimaginable for the vast majority of Iranians. For those who disliked the regime, accommodation or at least acquiescence were the only alternatives to voluntary exile. Core opposition elements continued to exist within the country, but their activities were generally limited to the salon where they deplored the regime in conversations with trusted friends and relatives. Open dissent was not comparable even to that within the Soviet Union.

Prior to 1964, the Iranian armed forces, particularly the army, were essential parts of the internal security forces. Their task was far greater than securing tribal areas and dealing with insurrections in mountainous and unpopulated regions. They had to be prepared as well to deal with urban rioting, such as that of June 1963, which had threatened to get out of control. By 1964 the assumption was strongly held that henceforth the armed forces could be concerned virtually completely with external security and achieving other foreign policy objectives. As the Iranian revolution began to develop momentum, their lack of training for and preparedness to deal with internal political disturbances was only too apparent.

There was another side to coercive control that the shah apparently considered very little in the 1964–1974 decade but very seriously after that. This was the belief on the part of the Iranian people that the U.S. Central Intelligence Agency was capable of destroying even the most broad-based political movement. Events would demonstrate the illusory quality of this image; but the belief that the Americans, when the chips were down, would maintain the shah in power complemented the image of omnipotence that SAVAK had achieved. It is fair to say that this estimate of the United States' ability to intervene and its willingness to do so came close in importance to a parallel view of Eastern Europeans regarding the Soviet Union. Through 1974 and 1975, the shah's coercive system appeared to be so overpowering that no thought of rebellion occurred except at the guerrilla warfare level. After that, however, the notion of American help became critical for the stability of the regime.

Of equal importance to coercion in explaining the regime's stability was the ability of the shah and his government to satisfy the material and influence needs of his people. The shah's success in granting material satisfaction through prosperity was far greater than his ability to gratify demands for influence. Some elements of the population really did suffer, compared to those doing very well. Landless peasants who benefited little from land reform and emigrated in large numbers to urban slums are the most important example.[36] But employment for unskilled labor was so plentiful that many Afghanis and other non-Iranians slipped into Iran seeking employment. For all but the very lowest stratum, in fact, people could look forward to next year's being better than last. Real income for most

Iranians climbed in this decade. For some, the improvement in standard of living exceeded their wildest expectations.

A vital aspect of the shah's control in this utilitarian category is difficult to prove, yet is pointed to by most acute participant-observers: corruption. The institutionalized corruption of the traditional system in Iran resembled very little that of the last royal dictatorship. In traditional Iran, payments were made to officials at a widely agreed-upon rate, and division of these revenues among a group of officials followed a well-understood protocol. But in the 1960s and 1970s the possible returns from graft were astronomical. Cognoscenti understood the process, including how to reach those with critical access to lucrative contracts. Certain families and individuals were understood to play key roles in the exchange. Most frequently, people pointed to members of the shah's and the empress's families. Great fortunes obviously could be made; the percentages claimed by those controlling access to such rewards could quickly mount into many millions. Periodically there were crackdowns on this practice, but participants assumed the de facto sanction of the regime. No aspect of the political process in many Third World countries is more deserving of careful study than this, but because of the difficulties of research, it must remain, with regard to the shah's Iran, inconclusive.

Given the shah's decisional style and apparent temperamental inability to share power, the development of institutions that could satisfy the desires of politically participant Iranians to exercise more influence over their political destinies was never sufficient. Institutions that might have served this purpose were the political parties, the parliament, and more interest-specific groups such as chambers of commerce, lawyers' associations, and theological associations. After surmounting the 1963 crisis, the shah replaced the Melliyun party with the Iran Novin party as His Majesty's government party. Since Iran Novin was originally an association of politically ambitious technocrats, there was at least a possibility that it would develop as the vehicle for a single-party authoritarian system.[37] If so, it could serve as a career path for the ambitious and as a source of technocratically inspired policy programs. But instead the shah persisted in maintaining the charade of multiparty competition and did not allow Iran Novin even the freedom to serve a primary recruitment function for technocratic leadership. Arbitrary appointments and dismissals of high-level officials characterized the shah's administrative style. Without question, that style helped maintain his personal control over institutions, but it could hardly generate loyalty among subordinates.

The shah recognized the need to provide an institutional base for his regime. As noted earlier, he seemed committed to the model of a constitutional monarchy in which the monarch played a strong but not absolute role. The monarchy would be complemented and supported by institutions that would provide for systematized public participation. But the shah made clear in countless public statements his view that the Iranian public had not reached the level of maturity necessary to play its role.[38] Therefore it needed more years of his tutelage. However, the institutional structure for this eventual participation was established and allowed to go through the motions of playing a decisional role, even though no decisional freedom was granted. The obvious dilemma was how to create credibility for institutions not granted any real authority but compelled to operate as though they did. The shah was directing a charade in which participants were expected to act as if they believed fully in what they were doing. There was some danger that the participants might take their roles seriously. A case in point developed when the executive director of the Mardom party, Nasser Ameri, took his role as a leader of the opposition seriously. He proposed a platform that would have amounted to a real programmatic alternative to that of the government. Ameri was dismissed and shortly later died as the result of an automobile accident. His death, it was widely believed, was not entirely accidental.[39]

Following the Ameri incident, the shah established an authoritarian single party, the Rastakhiz or Resurgence party, that was more in keeping with a totalitarian system. He made clear his expectation that anyone who hoped for a position of any influence in Iran, public or private, would join this party. But even so, he was unwilling to give up his constitutional model. Two factions were arbitrarily created, one supposedly conservative and the other progressive, and essentially mock factional conflict took place over policy. In addition, he allowed some minor parties to survive. As revolutionary momentum developed, these small parties began manifesting some independence. But Rastakhiz quickly became moribund.

Parliament, both the Majlis and Senate, were the products of systematic rigging. Electoral campaigns were conducted, but determining the victor was an involved influence process in which voters played no role. Seats in parliament were much sought after, however. They offered visibility and access to channels of influence for gaining lucrative contracts. Unlike the single party, Rastakhiz, parliament began to develop signs of vitality as the regime's vulnerability developed. By the time of the revolution, it had passed beyond the shah's control. However, its moment of rebellion was insufficient to restore legitimacy to its members. None survived politically.

The shah's decade of stability was thus a product of two factors: his ability to offer material rewards to major elements of the elite and an improved standard of living to most Iranians, plus a coercive capability perceived by his people to be so overpowering that the regime was essentially invulnerable. But despite this illusion of permanence, the regime did not achieve real legitimacy. Even in a period of unprecedented prosperity, the shah was unwilling to relax his coercive control. The belief that he had as many as 50,000–100,000 political prisoners—certainly vastly exaggerated—and that torture was being applied in the most sadistic manner was allowed to persist. There was enough real evidence of political oppression to maintain the belief, however, and the belief itself was a major control factor.

To be willing to risk relaxing his coercive control, the shah needed to see indications of a positive consensus, not a fear-induced consensus, in support of the regime's basic institutions. Such indications of consensus are generally best seen in popular attraction to symbolic representations of the regime. Regimes with real legitimacy are able to manipulate patriotic symbols that in times of crisis can induce public willingness to make great sacrifices in the name of the national and/or religious community. But it is precisely here that the shah's difficulties were most apparent. He made a strong effort to persuade his people that he represented "positive nationalism" in contrast to Musaddiq's "negative nationalism," but with no apparent success. Even in the days of his—and through him Iran's—greatest international influence, he was unable to appeal to a sense of national grandeur. His most important foreign military adventure—the successful if not glorious suppression of a rebellion in the Omani province of Dhofar—received surprisingly little attention even in his own tightly controlled press. Apparently he and his communications technocrats sensed little public interest in the event. The man who achieved total power as a consequence of a foreign-directed coup against the symbol of Iranian nationalist aspirations was never able to convince his people of his own deep nationalism. At least with regard to nationalism, the shah made some effort to overcome his difficulties. However, in contrast, he clearly underestimated the importance of projecting himself symbolically as representing the religious community. After 1964 he systematically reduced the influence of religious leaders in public life. The irony was that the shah was mystically attached to Shia Islam and believed he was the beneficiary of personal protection from the twelfth *imam*.[40] Yet he could not project this attachment symbolically or put it to political use.

The shah made his greatest efforts to achieve legitimacy through symbolic appeals in two other areas, failing badly in one and partially succeeding in the other. His failure was in an area that he deemed of great personal importance: the dynasty. He made a major effort, as his father had done, to describe the dynasty in symbolically appealing terms. His father had coopted the family name of Pahlavi, a great name from pre-Islamic Iran. Mohammad Reza Pahlavi added to the already impressive title of *Shan-in-Shah,* the king of kings, that of *Aryamehr,* the Light of the Aryans. In military circles, he was also referred to as *Khodaigan,* a name that implies illustriousness of leadership that goes beyond that of mere mortals.

The shah orchestrated two extravaganzas to project himself as one in a glorious tradition of great Iranian monarchs. In 1967 on his birthday he held a long-delayed coronation. Four years later, he hosted at Persepolis a celebration of 2,500 years of monarchical rule. Unfortunately for him, the world's press described that $100 million event as the ultimate in high camp; domestic criticisms were so severe that the shah had to take public note of them. To project himself as a true successor of his favorite king, Cyrus, seemed to many Iranians the height of presumption. The reaction underlined the failure of his longstanding campaign to generate a deep affection for the dynasty.

The regime was more successful in depicting itself as the agent of modernization. Slogans such as the "White Revolution" and "the Shah-People Revolution" may have been overdrawn, but "modernization" did come to symbolize achievement in technology, industrialization, and such major social endeavors as women's rights. The appeal, of course, was highly differential. For the upper-middle class, professional people, and the secular intelligentsia, the appeal was strong. Since this was the natural support base of the National Front, this attractiveness was of significant importance for the shah. Yet there was some negative response even in this section of society. The term "stricken by the West" was an unflattering reference to those seeking to immerse themselves in the West to the point of losing their own identity.[41]

For much of the religious lower-middle class and urban lower-class elements, "modernization" as symbol generally had a negative impact. It conjured up the view of those who occupied the favorable end of a widening income gap, who tended to look on "non-Western" Iranians with contempt, and who treated them arrogantly. Khomeini's charge that the "modernization" the regime spoke of really meant an abject acceptance of another, spiritually demeaned culture was widely appreciated.

Across Iranian society, the shah's regime had the enthusiastic support of some, accommodation from far more, and acquiescence from most. The enthusiasts were primarily those who could attribute their upward mobility or material improvements to the regime. These included the officer corps of the security forces, the newly rich, a *kulak* class of peasants who had benefited most from land reform, and industrial workers. Most important of these numerically and in terms of potential mobilization was the large, ostentatiously affluent nouveau riche. Indeed, to describe the regime as the dictatorship of the parvenu would not be far off the mark. But the shah did little to institutionalize support from these or any of the groups classified as enthusiasts. Industrial workers, for example, were well paid but denied the right to have independent unions and dealt with brutally when they resorted to occasional unauthorized strikes. When deep trouble developed for the regime, there was no institutional means for mobilizing effective support from those who owed most to it except from the security forces.

Included among those who accommodated themselves to the regime were those whose skills were important to the government and who were well rewarded materially but who did not owe their status to the regime. These people questioned the regime's legitimacy. The old land-based aristocracy, by and large, were in this category as well. They were unhappy with their diminished influence, but unable to see a more attractive alternative. But most important were the professional and upper-middle classes who provided the technocratic basis for the regime and the economy. Members of religious minorities who fell into this category — Christians, Jews, Bahais, and (to a lesser degree) Zoroastrians — were considerably more inclined to support the regime than their Moslem counterparts. The shah's very lack of nationalist legitimacy was a factor in his favor, since the religious minorities felt threatened by the populist appeal of nationalism.

Merely acquiescing in the regime were those whose material rewards were relatively declining. As long as they could expect next year to bring an improvement in their standard of living, they accepted the regime. But they were very conscious of and resentful of the growing disparity between their standard of living and that of those, many of whom were seen as corrupt, who profited most from the regime. The urban lower and lower-middle classes were reminded of their relative position in the four daily traffic rush hours when the streets were clogged with automobiles they could not dream of owning. Landless peasants who remained in rural areas were also in this category, but were no more mobilizable in support of the revolution than their *kulak* brethren were in support of the regime.

## The Shah: World Leader

At the beginning of his decade of stability, the shah was perceived internationally as being dependent for his survival on Anglo-American support. By the close of the decade, he was exercising an influence in world affairs at a level far greater than Iran's national power would seem to warrant. In part this is to be explained by the shah's aggressive adeptness in manipulating his oil leverage. But, even more important, the shah was the beneficiary of the intersection of major power strategies in the region.

As his internal position improved and his program of training and equipping a large military force progressed, the shah came to be seen by American authorities as a major security asset in the area.[42] Whereas previously Iran's military and economy relative to that of Turkey and Pakistan had been denigrated in U.S. estimates and those of most other countries, by 1974 Iran was perceived as a major regional military power. At the very least Iran could serve a "tripwire" role in the event of Soviet aggression. It could hold off Soviet forces long enough to grant Americans time to prepare a strategic faceoff. Thus Iran, and this meant the shah's regime, should be given full and unequivocal American diplomatic support.[43] This granted Iran great derivative bargaining strength. The shah could credibly promise or threaten a negotiating partner with the tacit understanding that the United States would back him diplomatically. Thus by 1974 the shah's Iran was perceived by American authorities as a primary regional surrogate, a lesser ally willing to advance U.S. interests in the Middle East.

This decade also witnessed the intensification of the Sino-Soviet conflict and the rapprochement of the People's Republic of China with the United States. As a major power in a region in which Iran was at the western limit, the PRC saw Iran as a natural ally in its own containment strategy directed against the USSR. PRC policy in southwest Asia tended to be dictated by its conflict with the USSR. Chinese rhetoric was as effusive as American rhetoric in support of the shah.[44] They depicted him as a vanguard figure in the Third World struggle for independence and dignity. There was indeed no real indication that the Chinese understood—or, if they understood, cared—that their words would appear grotesquely cynical to nationalists and leftists in the area. They appeared no less willing than Americans had been to leave progressive and nationalistic Iranians no alternative to exploring an alliance with the Soviet Union. The consequence in power terms for the shah was entirely favorable. The shah's Iran was viewed as a surrogate by both the Americans and Chinese, and the bargaining advantage this granted Iran was enormous.

There could have been major risks for the shah in accepting these relationships. Had the USSR taken advantage of its opportunities to ally itself with antiregime elements in Iran, the subversive potential could have been substantial. In that event the shah would have needed a good deal of external support, and his bargaining position would have deteriorated. But in fact, as the shah freely asserts in *Answer to History,* relations with the Soviet Union in this decade were good to excellent.[45] Why the Soviets maintained good political and excellent economic relations with the shah even though his alliance with the United States granted the Americans a major presence in Iran, is not easily explained. Using Iran as a tripwire could be seen as a dubious proposition by any detached observer. But the presence of major electronic listening devices directed against the USSR manned by Americans should surely have generated hostile responses from the Soviets. However, Soviet responses indicated otherwise. Far from feeling threatened by the shah's military machine, the Soviets were only too willing to add to Iran's proficiency by selling it artillery and ground transport equipment. Furthermore, the USSR gave every appearance of applauding and encouraging the vigorous economic relations of Iran and East Europe. In 1959, when for a few months Soviet-Iranian relations were poor, Khrushchev had compared Iran to a ripe plum that was sure some day soon to fall.[46] That remark seemed an apt explanation for Americans of the cold war persuasion for this strange Soviet reluctance to oppose this regime which the USSR's two primary enemies saw as their surrogate. A decade of friendly Soviet-Iranian relations did nothing to reduce the force of the U.S. conviction that the Soviets were simply waiting for the plum to fall.

The shah began the decade of stability by occupying an unenviable regional position. His quick conclusion in June 1963 that Nasser was orchestrating those first Khomeini riots tells much about his sense of weakness and isolation. Turkey and Pakistan, his allies, had little respect for Iran's military capability. The militarily most important Arab states, Egypt, Iraq, and Syria, were his bitter foes. India saw Iran as another American client, along with Pakistan. And the shah's friendship with Israel seemed to all his enemies an open confirmation of their view that he was, like Israel, a willing part of the American imperial control scheme.

By mid-1975, the regional picture was completely different. Turkish skepticism regarding Iranian military capability, although still present, was much reduced. Pakistan viewed Iran as an essential ally against India. Nasser was dead and his successor, Anwar Sadat, was becoming the shah's closest personal ally. Iraq had signed an agreement with Iran and enmity was giving way to friendliness between the two regimes. Iran's friendly relations with Israel, although by now even closer, were less noticeable, as Egypt by the Sinai II agreement was telegraphing its willingness to consider a separate peace. A civil war was developing in Lebanon that would see the shah, Israel, the United States, Jordan, and Saudi Arabia carrying out parallel covert policies. The organization of oil-producing states, of which Iran was vying with Saudi Arabia for leadership, was a major factor in world politics. And the shah's military was demonstrating a capacity to supply an Iranian armed force in Oman's Dhofar province and to be capable of defeating a Soviet-supported rebellion there. Only Syria, Libya, The People's Democratic Republic of Yemen, and factions of the Palestine Liberation Organization stood adamantly against him.

The shah's foreign policy reflected well his decisional style. It was assertive, ambitious, and imaginative in its general thrust. The shah was creating one of the world's most splendid military forces and gave every indication of wanting a foreign policy to match. His moves were sometimes adventurous. But there was a formless quality to the policy that reflected a failure to develop the tactics to support his general strategic objectives. For one thing, especially after the 1975 settlement with Iraq, he had no clearly defined enemy. The Soviets were obviously pleased with their good relations with Iran, and on more than one occasion the shah made clear his acceptance of Iran's inability ever to challenge the Soviets in direct military action.[47] Arabs, even those whose governments were on good terms with Iran, asked themselves nervously against whom the shah was preparing to move. Seeing no obvious regional enemy threatening Iran, they had to consider the possibility that the shah was arming for offensive, not defensive, purposes, and that they were the most likely target.

By any objective standards, Iran's national power in the early 1970s was a modest one. Its industry was rapidly expanding, but lacked any immediate potential to serve as a basis for an independent military force. Its population of 35 million or so lacked the education and training necessary to become a significant industrial power any time soon. And there was little to indicate that the shah could generate the kind of public enthusiasm that would be essential for an aggressive foreign policy. Yet when the shah asserted, as he often did, that Iran was moving rapidly to a second-class power position equivalent to, for example, that of West Germany,[48] he was taken seriously. The case could be made that, in terms of influence exercised in regional and in world affairs, by 1975 the shah's Iran was indeed a second-level world power.

The shah's ability to exercise influence rested not on a strong industrial and military base but rather on an exceptionally strong bargaining base. A $20 billion income from oil sales, the major source of Iran's income, appears puny when viewed in terms of the income available to West Germany. But, given the state of development of the Iranian economy, these revenues enabled the shah to purchase a major war machine and to attract the active interest of the Western corporate world. In addition, in 1975 the oil-consuming world was sharply sensitive to their dependence on OPEC, an organization within which Iran's voice was strong. Still, the leverage derived directly or indirectly from Iran's oil resources and from Iran's impressive military machine was small compared with that derived from Iran's strategic importance, as the United States and the PRC saw it. Iran's neighbors understood well that the shah could gain the support of both for his foreign policy objectives. They also understood, even if the American and Chinese governments did not, that the shah had little reason to fear Soviet opposition to the achievement of these objectives.

To maintain his exceptionally close relations with the United States, the shah had to confirm the American view that his primary concern was to oppose Soviet expansionism. He apparently was able to do that remarkably well in private conversations with American policy leaders. Henry Kissinger for one speaks glowingly of the shah's acumen in assessing the international situation. He had to do the same with the Chinese. Kissinger expresses an understanding, however, of the shah's need to avoid provoking a superpower neighbor. Thus the fact that the shah's public remarks were rarely offensive to the Soviets did not disconfirm American and Chinese assessments of his basically friendly foreign policy purpose.[49]

However, the policies the shah actually carried out suggests a very different picture from that seen by his American and Chinese allies. It suggests a four-tiered set of strategic objectives, the first and least equivocal of which was to become the hegemonic power in the Persian Gulf. When the British in 1971 announced their plan to withdraw militarily from the Gulf area, the shah proclaimed his intention to replace them—a policy Americans such as Kissinger interpreted as a move to deny the area to the Soviet Union, and hence eminently acceptable.[50]

The shah executed his strategy in this arena deftly. His purchase of naval equipment including a hovercraft fleet gave him an easy superiority over the combined forces of the other littoral states of the Gulf. In 1970 he moved to allay Arab suspicions by surrendering historic Iranian claims to the island state of Bahrein. But he then made two unilateral moves that demonstrated his military superiority. In 1971 he announced that the thalweg or navigation channel of the Shatt al Arab would henceforth be the southernmost boundary of Iran and Iraq, despite Iraq's legal claim to the entire river. This assured Iran freedom of navigation to the port of Khorramshahr, but it also demonstrated Iran's superiority over Iraq, its only real military rival in the area. Then in 1972 the shah seized three small islands in the Strait of Hormuz that were part of the United Arab Emirates. For the most part, however, the shah's policy toward the Persian Gulf states was in the Concert of Europe mode: serving to perpetuate a favorable status quo. Having established his military preeminence, he would intervene to preserve regimes dedicated to that status quo. Thus in 1973 when Sultan Qabus of Oman asked for his assistance in putting down a rebellion in his western province of Dhofar, the shah willingly complied. Since the rebellion was supported by the People's Democratic Republic of Yemen and through it was receiving support from both the Soviet Union and China, it was perceived by the Nixon and Ford administrations as proof of communist expansionism. The shah used his leverage with the PRC to effect a withdrawal of Chinese support from the rebels.[51] Then he sent a contingent of around 3,500 troops to Dhofar and supplied them by air from Iran. Militarily the Iranian record was something less than glorious, but the Iranian contingent was a decisive factor in the defeat of the rebellion. The shah's behavior was in tune with the American view of him as regional protector against Soviet-inspired insurrection and subversion. His own description of his target made to C. L. Sulzberger of the *New York Times* suggests a different interpretation. "Imagine if these savages took over the other side of the Hormuz Strait at the entrance to the Persian Gulf. Our life depends on this. And these people fighting against the Sultan are savages. They could be even worse than Communists."[52] Throughout the episode, Soviet-Iranian relations remained friendly. The shah had the best of both worlds: full Sino-American support for his expanding influence in the Arabian peninsula without incurring the enmity of the Soviet Union.

Iraq remained a problem. It had provided a haven for the shah's most dangerous opponents: Ayatullah Khomeini and General Timur Bakhtiar, the one representing a potential mass opposition movement and the other the opposition of pro-British conservatives. The shah, always sensitive to the possibility of an externally sponsored coup, apparently was most fearful of Bakhtiar. In 1970 Bakhtiar was killed on a hunting trip in Iraq. There is little doubt that his death was not accidental but rather a SAVAK execution.[53] In addition, the shah made two unsuccessful attempts to overturn the Iraqi regime and to place in its stead a government prepared to accept Iranian regional leadership. Failing in this, the shah made a direct appeal for American assistance in dealing with Iraq. The result was an American-Iranian-Israeli cooperative venture working through Mullah Mostafa Barzani, a tribal leader in Iraqi Kurdistan. This important episode reveals much about cold war American policy in the Middle East and will be discussed below.

The Persian Gulf arena was the major foreign policy preoccupation of the shah, but he was also clearly thinking in terms of a far more ambitious role for his government. This second tier of his foreign policy concern was to challenge India for preeminence in the Arabian Sea–Indian Ocean arena. He had great plans for a naval base at the eastern end of the Gulf of Oman giving him direct access to the Arabian Sea. In addition, he had plans to use his oil wealth to make Iran the primary power in an Indian Ocean Common Market. His closest area friend was Pakistan. But in the mid-1970s he had gained considerable influence in Afghanistan and had negotiated commercial agreements with India and other regional governments. His travel itinerary made clear his interests in all the Indian Ocean littoral states, including Australia and eastern and southern Africa.

The third tier of foreign policy concern was the East Mediterranean–Red Sea area. The shah's relations with Israel, Sadat, King Hossein, and the Saudi royal family ranged from good to excellent. He was most ambivalent toward Israel and Saudi Arabia. He had long recognized Israel as a natural geopolitical ally and his collaboration with the Israelis in security and intelligence matters was intimate. Just how intimate became clear during the trials of his generals after the revolution. Each one detailed training missions in Israel and close contacts with Israelis in Iran. But this collaboration was also an embarrassment because of the enmity of Islam toward Israel. Indeed, the shah's remarks about Israel indicated often a good deal of annoyance. As the shah's relations with Arab regimes improved, the argument for collaboration with Israel weakened, and by the late 1970s there were signs the shah was beginning to distance himself from them. Still, the shah and Israelis had parallel policies in Lebanon, and the shah was entirely positive regarding the Camp David process.

Ambivalence toward Saudi Arabia was inescapable. The two governments embraced a similar world view, and an alliance with the United States was central to the foreign policy of each. Both favored the same kind of conservative, status-quo regimes in the area and would have liked to have helped establish such a regime in Iraq. But Saudi Arabia could hardly be happy with Iranian hegemony in the Persian Gulf and Iran was rarely pleased with Saudi policy as the leading oil producer and strongest voice in OPEC.

The fourth and highest tier of the shah's foreign policy concerns was the world economic arena. Iranian investments in major corporations in the Western world underlined his ambitions. The shah coupled a promise never to use oil as a "weapon" with a brilliant use of his oil income and his oil-pricing policies to gain significant influence in world affairs. Major world leaders included Tehran in their travel plans and the shah's views on world affairs were listened to with an apparent genuine respect.

## American Policy in the Decade of Stability

Henry Kissinger's role as a formulator of American foreign policy coincided with eight of the years of the golden decade of the shah's rule in Iran. And Kissinger's memoirs include an emphatic assertion of the importance of Iran in American foreign policy. But of the almost 2,700 pages Kissinger devotes to these years in his memoirs, references to Iran occupy only a few. Furthermore, most of these few pages are given over to an angry essay, essentially the same essay in both volumes, lamenting Jimmy Carter's failure to keep the shah in power and the bad press the shah received after his fall. Like other critics of Carter's handling of the Iranian revolution, Kissinger gives his readers no hint as to what could have been done to preserve the shah's regime. Much is made of the shah's faithfulness as an ally and his acumen as an analyst. There is no evidence whatsoever of any awareness of the history of American-Iranian relations or of any understanding of the basis of the shah's vulnerability. Iranians are depicted as a people who have known only authoritarian rule and the shah's mistake was simply to modernize too rapidly.

Summary State Department reports prepared in this decade, now available, demonstrate that Kissinger's account was not shared by the bureaucracy. On the contrary, there is in these accounts a well-developed though necessarily brief description of social change in Iran, an analysis of the shah's inability to attract greater support, and a full understanding of the independence of the shah's foreign policy.[54]

It was the shah's good fortune that this decade of stability coincided with American administrations, those of Johnson, Nixon, and Ford, that viewed the shah in the image that appears in Kissinger's memoirs, not in the Department of State's Bureau of Intelligence and Research accounts. For these administrations and the ambassadors they sent to Iran, the shah was viewed almost uncritically. As the Department of State admits, the ambassadors of this era refused to risk incurring the shah's displeasure by allowing members of their staff even to meet with members of the opposition.[55] The obvious point that such meetings, although creating annoyance and hence some small discomfort for the ambassador, would also have generated leverage that could have been used to pressure the shah into taking measures to broaden his base of support, apparently did not occur to them. Kissinger saw no need to take measures that could result in a more stable Iranian regime. The result was that the shah had every reason to believe that U.S. support was unqualified and unquestioning.

The relationship of the CIA and SAVAK in this era took the form of an essentially liaison relationship. The CIA could count on SAVAK assistance in operations against the Soviet Union. This included especially the vital listening-post activity. But the CIA was dependent on certainly self-serving reports from SAVAK for their internal intelligence yield. This pattern is common with the United States' authoritarian allies and is an important part of the explanation for the poor quality of American intelligence concerning such regimes.

Henry Kissinger takes note of the reluctance within the Defense Department to sell Iran some of the advanced weaponry the shah was so enamored of. But he dismisses this as objections of individuals who were jealous of American inventories.[56] He takes no note of the central argument that the weaponry purchased served no clear strategic-tactical purpose and could not easily be absorbed in the Iranian weapons system. In addition, he denies the claim that there was heavy pressure from U.S. manufacturers to sell these weapons for reasons of economic interest. But the importance of arms sales to Iran in this period for the American arms industry was openly admitted by both industrial and governmental sources and widely reported in the press.[57] If the economic factor was minor in the decision to overturn Musaddiq, as contended above, by the mid-1970s it had become a significant determinant of U.S. policy toward Iran. And it provided an added pressure for the kind of unquestioning support of the shah's regime favored by the three administrations.

The lack of attention Iran received in Kissinger's memoirs, far from suggesting unconcern, reflects accurately the totality of confidence the Nixon administration felt regarding the mutuality of American and Iranian interests. Their common purpose was, they felt, the containment of Soviet expansionism. The idea that easily occurred to Arabs and Indians that the shah had another agenda reflecting an imperial purpose motivated by the shah's own desire for grandeur did not occur to the Americans. U.S. strategies in the Persian Gulf, Indian Ocean, and Eastern Mediterranean arenas always entailed close cooperation with the United States' "loyal" Iranian ally. Specific U.S. policies in the three arenas illustrate this point.

Probably most revealing of the extraordinary extent of American-Iranian collaboration is to be found in the case of the Iraqi Kurds mentioned above. A good deal is known about that case because of the leaks to the press in 1976 of the Pike Committee study of American clandestine diplomacy.[58] According to this study, the collaboration was initiated by the shah when Richard Nixon visited Iran in 1972. The shah apparently decided to enlist American support to weaken and perhaps even to replace the Iraqi regime by fomenting a rebellion of Iraqi Kurds. As the shah well understood, the Nixon administration viewed Iraq as a client of the Soviet Union. Therefore the United States should be attracted to a plan that could alter that status. The shah proposed that an alliance be made with the most powerful of traditional Kurdish leaders, Mullah Mostafa Barzani. Since the Iraqi government had granted the Kurds an autonomy agreement far more liberal than that enjoyed by Kurds in Iran, the shah's proposal was not without risk. He must have understood that Barzani would agree to collaborate only if he were to envision virtual independence as the outcome. Since independence for Iraqi Kurdistan would lead to similar demands in Iranian Kurdistan, the shah could not afford to risk permitting it. And, indeed, as the Pike study makes clear, the shah and Nixon agreed privately that their Kurdish allies should not ultimately prevail. The Pike Committee reported: "They preferred instead that the insurgents simply continue a level of hostilities sufficient to sap the resources of our ally's neighboring country (i.e., Iraq). This policy was not imparted to our clients, who were encouraged to continue fighting. Even in the context of covert action, ours was a cynical enterprise."[59]

Henry Kissinger agreed to the shah's proposal with enthusiasm, and suggested that Soviet arms captured by the Israelis be secreted into Iraqi Kurdistan. His suggestion was accepted, and Israel became third partner to the conspiracy. The implications of this suggestion are startling. It not only implied contempt for Iraqi intelligence, which presumably was expected to believe that their Soviet allies were dumping old weapons in Kurdish areas and hence inexplicably weakening seriously an ally with whom they had a treaty of friendship; even more important, it implied that neither Iran nor the United States believed that the Soviets would be annoyed to the point of responding violently to this gross subterfuge taking place only a few miles from their border and involving an ethnic group well represented in the Soviet Union. That such expectations of no Soviet response in the face of a major provocation could be reconciled with the Nixon-Kissinger review of ineluctable Soviet aggressiveness is puzzling. However, as I have mentioned, the diabolical enemy stereotype does incorporate the view that if one stands up to the evil foe with will and determination, it will behave like a paper tiger.

In any event, the Kurdish rebellion was triggered in 1974. But, to the dismay of the three governments, the Iraqi forces quickly gained the upper hand militarily. The shah was faced with a decision of either openly intervening and thus engaging in hostilities with a Soviet ally, or allowing the Kurds to be defeated. He chose the latter course, apparently with American acquiescence. In early 1975 he accepted an Algerian-mediated agreement by which he would abandon his support of the Kurds. For their part, the Iraqis agreed to restrict the activities of Khomeini's supporters, to halt their support for ethnic Arab and Baluchi separatists in Iran, and formally accept the thalweg of the Shatt al Arab as the southernmost border of the two countries.[60]

The consequences of this episode were ironic. Soviet-Iraqi relations deteriorated in the months that followed. The Soviet Union's failure to give any real support to its Iraqi ally in the face of an Israeli-Iranian-American plot to weaken it, has to have been a factor in that deterioration. Iranian-Iraqi relations, in sharp contrast, improved. The Iraqis were true to their agreement to curb Khomeini's activities and ultimately when his movement was gaining great momentum in Iran, forced Khomeini to leave Iraq. Thus, as their old enemy the shah was faced with a deadly internal challenge, the Iraqi government chose to follow a course of action of implicit support for the man who had three times attempted to overthrow them. Their actions added to the enmity of the soon-to-be-victorious Iranian revolutionaries toward the Iraqi regime. Even more startling, there is no evidence that the American government recognized the irony of this outcome. Certainly it did not lead to any reconsideration of the assumptions on which U.S. policy was based.

The Dhofar case, outlined above, was in contrast more amenable to a classical cold war interpretation. There was operating from the PDRY, and no doubt with Soviet assistance, an organization known as the Popular Front for the Liberation of Oman and the Arab Gulf (PFLOAG). The shah was doubtless correct in assuming, as his remarks quoted above to the *New York Times* suggest, that the Dhofar rebels were an indigenous rebel force rather than agents of PFLOAG. But the rebels were receiving assistance from Marxist groups and the American interpretation that this was part of the shah's anti-Soviet policy is at least defensible.[61]

The 1971 India-Pakistan crisis that developed as a consequence of the breakaway rebellion of East Pakistan was an exceptionally dangerous episode in cold war annals and one with a serious potential for accidental war. It occurred in the months following the Nixon-Kissinger realization of the bargaining advantage the Sino-Soviet split granted the United States, described metaphorically as the Chinese card. But as the crisis developed, there appeared a real possibility that a new and lethal alliance pattern was crystallizing. There were on one side the United States, the PRC, Pakistan, and Iran, and on the other side the Soviet Union, India, Bangladesh, and Iraq. The potential for confrontation was demonstrated by the willingness of the Nixon administration to send the aircraft carrier *Enterprise* as the flagship of a naval task force into the Bay of Bengal even though it understood that the Pakistanis had lost their eastern province irremediably. The objective, Kissinger makes clear in his memoirs, was to prevent India, viewed as a Soviet client, from invading and dismembering West Pakistan.[62] Iran's role in the crisis was viewed as critically important. And indeed the shah saw both risk and great opportunity in it. He would give his Pakistani friends his full support, but if disintegration occurred he would grant his "protection" to some of the parts.

The crisis passed when it became obvious that India had no intention of dismembering Pakistan. Of course, Kissinger could believe that his sending the task force into the Bay of Bengal telegraphed American will and determination, despite the reluctance of the bureaucracy to support him, and thus that he was responsible for the restraint of India, and India's mentor the Soviet Union. But the PRC surprised him by its caution as the crisis came to a climax, and he apparently soon lost interest in the South Asian arena.[63]

The shah came through this episode brilliantly. He had confirmed once again to his allies, especially the United States and the PRC, his dedication to the mutual cause. But as the Nixon administration lost interest and the situation became more fluid, the shah moved quickly to establish good relations with both India and the new state of Bangladesh, tantalizing both with suggestions of favorable commercial and financial arrangements. At the same time, he consolidated his close friendship with a grateful Pakistan. And, through it all, Soviet-Iranian relations were excellent.

In the eastern Mediterranean arena, U.S. and Iranian strategies dovetailed just as nicely. King Hossein's decision to force the PLO infrastructure out of Jordan in September 1970 was welcomed by both. The shah recognized more quickly than did the Nixon administration the radical shift in Egypt's foreign policy stance when Nasser died and was replaced by Anwar Sadat. For the shah the appearance of an Egyptian regime that was prepared to move away from the Soviet Union and to surrender any pretense to the leadership of an Arab national movement was a welcome relief. The shah had no doubt exaggerated the intensity of Nasser's hostility toward him. But there was no question that Sadat was sincerely interested in establishing close and friendly relations. This new Egyptian policy decreased markedly the shah's need to rely on Israel. In the October 1973 war, the shah's sympathy for the Egyptians was obvious.[64]

Kissinger's step-by-step diplomacy following the 1973 war, designed to keep the Soviet Union on the sidelines and to take full advantage of Sadat's willingness to break with Nasser's pan-Arabism, received the shah's encouragement. Then, as Lebanon moved toward civil war, the shah's preference among Lebanese factions, particularly the Phalangists and their Shia traditional allies, paralleled that of the United States.

As a major customer of the oil-producing states, the United States presumably would not appreciate the shah's oil-pricing policies. But Henry Kissinger makes the point several times over that no one could fault the shah for seeking the natural market price for oil.[65] Kissinger denied emphatically the rumor that the Nixon administration in fact welcomed the price rise because of the enhanced ability of oil producers to purchase arms from and make other economic arrangements with American corporations. He apparently did feel that using the oil lever negatively by cutting or threatening to cut production levels was unfriendly. Since the shah made only positive use of the lever and refused to cut production, he was judged still a good and faithful friend.

The case is remarkably clear. Throughout the decade of royal stability, American administrations chose to view Iran as an entirely dependable regional ally. Bureaucratic unease regarding the regime's stability was never apparent at the top policy level. In terms of bargaining advantage, the relationship was sharply assymetrical in Iran's favor. And the shah's neighbors fully comprehended his ability to influence the American superpower for his own ends. The shah's domestic opponents comprehended equally well that their ruler could count on full American cooperation in doing whatever he asked to strengthen his hand internally.

There was an equally clear mesh of American and Iranian foreign policy objectives. Iranian cooperation in the Bangladesh crisis, the Dhofar insurrection, the effort to weaken the Iraqi government, and the Kissinger formula for a step-by-step peace process in the Arab-Israeli conflict—all fit nicely an American policy focused on containing the Soviet Union. The proposition that the shah was primarily motivated in all these cases by a quest for personal and dynastic grandeur was simply not considered. The shah's excellent relations, including the purchase of military transport and artillery, with the Soviet Union did not lead to any questioning of his largely privately expressed claims to be playing a central role in containing the Soviet Union in the area. For his part, the shah was frequently dissatisfied with the strength of American resolve. Beneficiary as he had been of an activist U.S. foreign policy, the shah could only deplore signs of declining American interest. This was particularly apparent in his judgment of the tentative and uncertain American role in the Bangladesh crisis.[66] The shah, like Sadat, wanted and needed for the fulfillment of his own objectives a Pax Americana in which the United States would work through major regional surrogates to preserve a global status quo. But the best he could get was a U.S. policy reacting to a perceived threat from the Soviet Union—a perception, the evidence suggests, the shah during the decade only partially shared.

# 5

## THE COLLAPSE OF THE SHAH

In the days of Iran's greatest stability, in the early to mid-1970s, the shah reveled in his success. He was not only the absolute ruler of the Iranian people, but also one of the world's leaders. In interview after interview, he heaped scorn on the weakness and instability of democratic societies. Yes, Iran was a coercive state. His people had to have strong leadership and he had no apologies for providing it. Love and affection were not what he asked from his people; awe and respect were what he wanted. His 1973 interview with the brilliant journalistic portrait artist, Oriana Fallacci, which occurred at the moment of his greatest self-confidence, is strikingly revealing of the cynical arrogance of his world view.[1] It was apparently inconceivable to him, as it was to most of the world's governments, that his regime was in any serious sense vulnerable.

The case presented here is that the vulnerability of the shah's regime was caused by its lack of nationalist legitimacy and the shah's indifference to the welfare and the desire for political participation among the majority of his population. The regime's stability rested on a coercive force that effectively denied the dissatisfied the option of active opposition. It also depended on a growth in real income for most Iranians. Compared to that of most Third World regimes, the basis of stability in Iran was solid. Surely Iran should be able to survive even a serious internal crisis.

In fact, the crisis that did occur was only moderately serious. Iran's economic growth was uneven, corruption was hardly concealed, the income gap was widening, and financial resources were lavished on state-of-the-art weapons and technology of dubious utility. But until 1974 inflation had not been a serious problem in Iran, employment was high, and even those who realized that the income gap was widening at their expense expected a materially better tomorrow. However, in 1974 the Iranian economy became overheated and strong inflationary pressures developed. The reason for this, ironically, was the sudden spectacular advance in oil prices and hence a multiplication of government revenues. The shah chose to seek to translate this income bonanza into an accelerated economic development program. Inflation, which had for a decade been less than 4 percent, now began to rise and at times approached the 45 percent mark. Yet even that rate was far below that of other regimes that have remained stable.[2] The individual costs and benefits of this inflationary expansionism reflected accurately the regime's support base. Speculators and recipients of governmental largesse, the elements of society classified here as "enthusiasts," were most likely to profit from the situation. Fixed-income groups, largely among those social elements who were willing to acquiesce and accommodate themselves to the regime, were most likely to suffer. For them real income fell, and with it expectations of material betterment. As a natural development, those suffering were predisposed to listen to opponents of the regime.

The formula for dealing with this crisis is easily stated in the abstract. The regime's coercive instruments should have intensified their activities to suppress potentially active opponents and to make clear to the public the dangers of listening to agitating elements. Also, corrective measures should have been taken to slow the rise in prices even if that involved punishing some of the regime's strongest supporters. But the shah made only sporadic efforts to curb prices and profiteering until 1978, while dissatisfaction continued to develop. The regime's resource base was sufficiently sound that this failure to take corrective measures need not have been overly serious. However, intensified coercion was required. The failure of the regime to take the necessary measures in this area is the real mystery of the shah's policy.

## Human Rights Policy and the Revolution

There is little doubt in retrospect that much of the explanation for the shah's failure to act in this area lies in his interpretation of U.S. policy toward Iran during the Carter administration. In *Power and Principle* Zbigniew Brzezinski tells us that, as a self-proclaimed policy activist, he favored an American foreign policy that took the ideological offensive.[3] Simply opposing and containing Soviet expansionism was not enough. The United States should stress concern for human dignity and freedom and U.S. policy should stand with a sensitivity to American honor. Creatively developing policy based on these principles would in turn enhance American power and not only help to meet U.S. security needs but also benefit mankind generally. But abstract principles advanced by American foreign policy formulators had to be implemented within the framework of U.S. relations with other states. How were Iranians to interpret the Carter administration's pronouncement that human rights would be a central concern of American foreign policy? Informed Iranians, whether supporters or opponents of the shah, believed the United States was primarily responsible for overturning the liberal Musaddiq government and replacing it with a dictatorship that openly defended its policy of suppressing human rights in Iran. They believed as well that U.S. government support was necessary for the regime's stability. Now the new American administration was calling for an observation of human rights by other governments. Could that mean that U.S. support for the shah would be withdrawn unless he granted his people far more freedom and concerned himself far more with elemental social justice?

Apparently, both the shah and his liberal opponents interpreted U.S. policy similarly. Both saw a major difference between the two American parties in their attitudes towards Iran. To be sure, Lyndon Johnson had behaved much like his Republican successors. But Truman, Kennedy, and now Carter were more equivocal in their attitudes toward the shah. In his *Answer to History* the shah explicates his suspicions regarding American opposition to him and in particular indicates his belief that the Carter administration had to be mollified on the matter of human rights.[4]

The general underlying thesis of the Carter human rights policy toward friendly authoritarian regimes was simple. Liberalization by such a regime should not only result in an improved human condition but also result in a broadening of the regime's support base. This in turn should make the regime less vulnerable to Soviet-sponsored subversion and hence would serve the American strategic purpose doubly well.

But the application of this policy was not so straightforward. If a friendly authoritarian regime lacked nationalist legitimacy, as the shah's regime did, a relaxation of coercive control could result in less rather than greater willingness among the population to accept the regime's authority. Opposition groups, seeing a regime they could not identify with on nationalist grounds reducing its coercive force, might well take advantage of their expanded freedom of action to increase their efforts to overturn the regime. If—as was also true of Iran in 1977—the regime were in trouble economically, embarking on a program described as liberalization could lead the opposition to sense a vulnerability in the regime's authority position that they could not resist exploring. For Iran, the possibility that the United States' official advocacy of human rights abroad would have a destabilizing effect was made even more likely by the fact that the U.S. government was viewed as the mentor of the Iranian regime.

As suggested in the previous chapter, the shah could have adopted policies, especially in this decade of stability, that could have restored a degree of nationalist legitimacy to his regime. But to do so he would have had to have shared power with individuals who were avowed Iranian nationalists. But in periods of stability the shah proved consistently unwilling to share political power. Thus when his economic difficulties led to a moderately severe crisis in authority, he was unable to call on his people to make the sacrifices necessary to deal with the crisis. As the crisis deepened, the shah's rhetoric changed sharply. There were no more contemptuous remarks about democratic government. Now he stressed his devotion to human rights. To underline this, he took several measures to improve the situation of incarcerated political opponents. They were to be granted due process of law. Torture was eliminated, at least in prisons of high visibility, and living conditions improved. A sizable number of political prisoners were released.[5]

Among core opposition elements, those who thought of themselves as followers of Musaddiq were much encouraged by the prospects of a change in U.S. policy. To them it gave promise of a return to the policy role the United States had followed through 1952. They saw a real possibility that American pressure would compel the shah to return to the rule of law and open the Iranian political process to free participation. The shah's change in attitude toward political prisoners was the first concrete evidence that their most optimistic expectations might be realized.

The initial response of these elements was to explore the new boundaries of freedom of activity that the regime would now permit. They began cautiously. Several well-known leaders from the Musaddiq period wrote and distributed open letters to the shah and his government. Most noteworthy of these were the brilliant and pointed essays of Ali Asghar Haj Sayyad Javadi. A small organization, the Radical Movement of Iran, headed by Rahmatollah Moqadam Maraghei, published and distributed clandestinely highly critical accounts of the regime's scorn for rule of law, its corruption, and its insensitivity to social justice. But direct attacks on the shah or references to his mode of achieving absolute power were notably absent.[6] The opposition press operating outside Iran suffered no such restraint. Brutality, corruption, and treason were its constant themes, and there was no question that these would be the themes advanced internally if freedom of the press were allowed.[7]

By the summer of 1977, evidence of the government's willingness to tolerate a fair degree of internal opposition was such that organized activity by groups calling for reform began to take place. This included the emergence of a group of jurists, including members of the Ministry of Justice, who issued a critical review of the administration of justice in Iran. A group of artists, composers, and litterateurs demanded and were allowed to form an organization independent of government control. But in retrospect it is clear that the most important activity was beginning to occur in the mosques. Mehdi Bazargan and his Freedom Movement had provided a loose organizational base for the activities of the religious opposition to the regime. As I mentioned above, in June 1963 the charismatic appeal of Ayatullah Ruhullah Khomeini was recognized by Bazargan and his group, and an effort was made to establish a working relationship with him, his sons, and his personal followers—including several of his most outstanding students.[8] The deep differences that were to crystallize later between liberals such as Bazargan, radical progressives such as Ayatullah Mahmud Taleqani, and radical advocates of a religio-political government were not yet apparent. But the potential appeal of an effort to demonstrate that Islam could provide the moral base for dealing with the political, social, and personal problems of the twentieth century in Iran was made clear by the electric appeal of the lectures and writings of Dr. Ali Shariati.[9] Shariati, a French-trained sociologist, lectured in Iran from 1966 to 1973 when he was arrested. The popularity of his message was one of the few clear signs of the deep dismay felt particularly among Iranian youth at the loss of Iranian cultural identity that was occurring in the milieu, dominated by parvenus and consumerism, the shah called "modern."

The institutional center of Shariati's influence was the Hosseiniya

Irshad, a religious educational facility in Tehran. But in 1977 sermons were delivered in mosques throughout Iran that contained increasingly open criticisms of the regime. Attendance at these sermons was often large. This reflected the fact that those who were suffering most from the effects of the inflationary pressures were precisely that section of the population most responsive to religious leadership. As revolutionary momentum began to pick up, the role of the mosque bureaucracy emerged as an organizational base for revolutionary activity. A year later, public demonstrations were surprisingly well disciplined, with participants organized into marching companies. They appeared more like the organized efforts of an authoritarian regime than like public demonstrations against an authoritarian regime mounted by people who understood they were risking their physical safety.

In the summer of 1977, two events occurred that were significant in influencing the evolution of the revolution. Early in June, Shariati was released from prison and sent into exile. On June 19 he suddenly died, ostensibly of heart failure, in London. Few Iranians doubted he was another victim of SAVAK. Then Ayatullah Taleqani was sentenced to ten years in prison. There is no evidence to suggest that SAVAK was engaging in a sophisticated strategy to eliminate or reduce the influence of religious spokesmen that were rivals of Khomeini. But the failure of SAVAK to arrest and incarcerate many of the most influential religious leaders who were associates of Khomeini, has to have been the consequence of a fateful policy decision whose rationale is still unclear.

The core of the leftist opposition took advantage of the relaxation of coercive pressure in this period, but there is no evidence that they shared the liberals' sanguine view that American policy was shifting away from uncritical support for the shah. The battle for mass support was in this early stage clearly being won by religious leaders. The left had no forum comparable to the mosques, and SAVAK was much better prepared to deal with the leftist opposition, its longtime primary target.

Actual U.S. policy toward Iran bore little resemblance to that imagined by the shah and his liberal opponents. Human rights were defended at the abstract level only. There was not really a human rights strategy. Human rights for Iran was no more than a vague, high-level objective. Furthermore, there is no evidence that the Carter administration understood that the great risks being taken by liberal opponents of the regime were a consequence of this policy, or that the shah's "liberalization" measures were calculated to please Americans more than to effect any serious changes.

A number of Carter administration policies in 1977 should have served to reduce the shah's suspicions that the United States was considering withdrawing or reducing its support of his regime. The choice of William Sullivan as ambassador to Iran was viewed symbolically. Because of his two previous posts, as ambassador to Laos in the waning days of the Vietnam War and as ambassador to the Philippines under President Marcos, he was seen as another in a long line of American ambassadors who saw their role as giving unequivocal support to the shah. Sullivan was to become the first ambassador since Seldon Chapin to view the shah skeptically,[10] but the symbolism of his appointment was depressing to the opposition. Then the Carter administration, quite contrary to its posture during the election and Carter's first days in office, pushed hard for and succeeded in gaining congressional approval for the sale of aircraft equipped with the sophisticated electronic warning system known as AWACS. Possibly most important was the total silence with which the administration met the prison sentence of Ayatullah Taleqani. The liberal opposition feared that this was a negative signal to them and a positive signal to the shah. Taleqani was second in popularity to Khomeini among religious leaders, and unlike Khomeini, had demonstrated throughout his life the same kind of concern for human rights that Carter and Brzezinski were advancing. In fact, the Carter administration appeared totally oblivious of Taleqani and his importance and took no note of his arrest.[11]

Skepticism regarding the United States' sincerity was growing among the opposition. But they remained uncertain, not because of American actions but because of the shah's inaction. Would the shah continue to liberalize even though the Americans had obviously telegraphed their unconcern in this matter? That seemed unlikely; yet the shah persisted in his course of action. The shah did respond occasionally and sporadically with brutality. However, his chosen instrument for this was commonly strong-arm bands acting ostensibly as vigilantes outside any formal government organization and committing acts of violence against seemingly arbitrarily chosen targets. This mode of behavior infuriated the opposition, and yet was not systematic enough to deter opposition activities. The rhythm seemed mindless, a display of brutality reflecting weakness and lack of resolve. The shah's terrible and much feared instruments of coercion were inexplicably restrained.

Revolutionary momentum continued to develop, and with it a parallel decline in hope for support from the United States. Yet the liberal leadership of the revolution had not completely given up hope for American assistance. When Jimmy Carter scheduled a trip abroad in the early winter of 1977–1978 that would include a New Year's stop in Tehran, leading liberal and leftist opposition figures made an overture to Washington. They prepared a major statement in the form of a letter to Secretary-General Kurt Waldheim calling for a restoration of rule of law in Iran. It was a hard-hitting critique, but more reformist than revolutionary in tone and entirely congruent with Carter's human rights stance. A month before its publication on December 22, 1977, the group sent the statement and a partial list of the signatories to the Carter administration. Their hope, ultimately, was that U.S. pressure would be applied to persuade the shah to accept a position as constitutional monarch and to permit free debate and a free election—an election that, considering the prominence of the individuals involved and the unpopularity of the regime, they had a reasonable expectation of winning.

This overture was, arguably, the last opportunity the United States government had for exercising any serious influence over the course of the Iranian revolution. Throughout 1977, disillusion had been growing regarding the seriousness of purpose of the Carter human rights policy—at least as applied to Iran. Increasingly it appeared as empty rhetoric except insofar as it served an instrumental purpose in dealing with the Soviet Union and its allies. Yet so important to the longevity of the shah's regime was American support of the shah that U.S. policy was a matter of central concern for liberals right up to the moment of the revolutionary victory. But by 1978 efforts were directed more toward producing American neutrality rather than enlisting positive American support for fundamental reform—a prospect that seemed still possible when the overture was made. Throughout 1977 the Carter administration had evinced no awareness of the encouragement that its human rights policy had given Iranian oppositionists or that Iranians were taking risks in the hope that American influence with the regime would furnish them some protection. By sending the letter in advance to the American government, the liberal leadership hoped to make all of this clear. Should Carter decide to persist in giving full support to the shah, the least they could hope for was that they would be told not to expect any U.S. support if they went ahead with their plan to publish the letter.

The absence of any mention of the letter in published accounts of this era by Americans involved in policy, and the failure of any official to attempt to communicate in any way with the Iranians involved suggests that none of the officials who had been directly made aware of the letter placed any significance on it, if indeed they even took mental note of it.[12] Still, Carter's New Year's toast to the shah several days after the publication of the letter was an effective answer. A few days before, in Warsaw, Carter had made stirring reference to human rights, thus embarrassing the Polish government and its Soviet mentor. But in Tehran he remarked that Iran was an "island of stability" and the shah was "beloved of his people." Carter gave no hint in public that there might be a human rights problem there. He thus signaled both to the shah and to the opposition that the United States had no intention of applying any real pressure. The shah's response came in the form of official vigilante action, now against several of the signatories and their families. For the opposition, this meant the end of any real hope that Carter's human rights program was meant for them. Whatever the explanation for the shah's ineffective and inconsistent policy of persecution, it was not a response to pressure from the U.S. government.

## The Preeminence of Khomeini in the Revolution

In retrospect, it is apparent that whereas 1977 had been a year in which the old pro-Musaddiqist leadership group had given a reformist definition to the burgeoning opposition, 1978 saw the relative decline of this group and the relative growth in importance of radical clerical elements. This change reflected the rapidly increasing willingness to participate in revolutionary activity among the urban lower and lower-middle classes. The primary pattern of the revolution was developing. Leadership of the revolution was concentrated in the hands of liberals, both secular and religious. But the early base of mass support came from the element of society that looked to clerics for direction. The pattern that had first become apparent in 1963 was now the defining characteristic of the revolution. Secular nationalism, especially liberal secular nationalism after Musaddiq's overthrow, had been unable to serve as the major socializing agent of the rapidly accelerating percentage of the population predisposed to become politically active. By 1978 it was apparent to any serious observer, including members of the Iranian government, that the large urban mass that was coming to life politically saw in Ayatullah Khomeini a man who understood their anguish and aspirations. He had a charismatic attraction for them. Thus a fatal asymmetry was developing in the revolutionary movement. The liberals and leftists who dominated the leadership core inside Iran lacked a significant base of mass support, whereas Ayatullah Khomeini, the sole major spokesman of religious activism, attracted the intense support and adulation of a large and easily mobilized public. In January 1978 the first really significant demonstration occurred protesting Taleqani's imprisonment and demanding that Khomeini be allowed to return from exile. Religious leaders called for the demonstrations in part because of an obviously officially sanctioned article that appeared in the large-circulation newspaper, *Ettelaat*.[13] The article, a crude and offensive attempt to defame Khomeini, demonstrated both an understanding on the part of the regime of Khomeini's vast appeal and its almost total lack of understanding of how to counter that appeal. Far from raising doubts about Khomeini, the article enraged his followers and ensured the success of the demonstration. By January 1978 the enormous personal popularity of Ayatullah Khomeini was the central fact of the revolutionary movement. The signs were already clear that the Iranian revolution was becoming populist. But it was not at all clear in 1978 that it would ultimately produce an authoritarian populist regime.

Zbigniew Brzezinski quotes with scorn a cable from Ambassador Sullivan suggesting that Khomeini could become Iran's Gandhi.[14] But among the Iranians who knew him best, this outcome, while optimal, was seen as a serious possibility. Khomeini had shown little interest in the universe of conventional politics. He was largely ignorant of the rivalries and factions within the political opposition and deplored the divisions that existed among the sincere Moslems involved in the revolution. In his image of the future, Iranian political leaders would seek and follow the guidance of those Islamic leaders who had a true and profound understanding of the just society as revealed in the Qoran. He was convinced that his own role was in accordance with divine preference. It was his task to show the oppressed peoples of the world that they need not bow to the great oppressors, in particular the United States and the Soviet Union. With faith, courage, and divine favor they could prevail. But it was also his task to bring first to Iranians, then to Islam, and ultimately to all mankind, the Islamic ideology. In his view Iran had drifted far from this path in the Pahlavi era. It had accepted the materialistic values of the Europeans and had lost sight of spiritual values. Liberal secular nationalism was a major deviation from the spiritual path. Real freedom and human self-realization were possible only within the context of a full acceptance of Islam and total willingness to follow the guidance of those few and rare individuals who had a holistic conception of God's revealed plan.[15]

Khomeini neither before nor after the revolution evinced any serious interest in a programmatic translation of this Islamic ideology. He called for a society in which spiritual rather than material values prevail, where true social justice exists, and where brotherhood and compassion characterize the relationships of the faithful. In such a society tyranny is impossible. But since the struggle between good and evil, the forces of God and those of Satan, is ubiquitous and since good must prevail, the forces of evil must be met with a firm and unwavering resolve. Compromise with evil is unacceptable; mercy is reserved for the faithful and those sincerely seeking to understand the path of God. However, the question of what program of action is best suited for producing these ends was never his concern. In the days before the revolution's success his contribution to the strategy and tactics of the opposition was largely to strengthen its stance. There he stood for uncompromising firmness. Lacking any detailed understanding of either the international or the domestic Iranian political environments and apparently uninterested in acquiring any, Khomeini would leave the formulation of general strategy and tactical specifics to those who had such an understanding.

The fact of Khomeini's extraordinary charismatic appeal was recognized by some governmental officials and some opposition leaders, but certainly not by all. Many secular-minded Iranians had long viewed clerics with a mixture of contempt and fear. They could not deny the influence the clerics could exert on the uneducated mass and they feared the force of their demagoguery. But they saw them as ignorant, superstitious, and hopelessly unable to comprehend and deal with the modern world. They saw them, in addition, as hypocritical and open to corruption. The suspicion that the clerics would willingly accept British monetary support and follow British directions may have begun to atrophy, but in 1978 was still strongly held. The question was less whether the British, and their less-informed and more innocent American cousins, were behind Khomeini than why. And the answer commonly given to that question was that the Anglo-Americans saw Khomeini as a more effective instrument in opposing the Soviets than the shah had been and also as likely to be less assertive on matters of oil production and pricing. The shah himself was inclined to accept this view. The thesis of the U.S. Labor party, regarded broadly as on the lunatic fringe in the United States, that the British hoped to keep Iran from industrializing was highly credible to Iranians, especially to royalists.[16]

Government supporters who viewed Khomeini in this way believed he could be countered by restoring subsidies to religious leaders and organizations that the shah in his days of supreme confidence had canceled. In addition, they focused much activity on convincing the Anglo-Americans that the *mullah*s could not be for them reliable allies. There is little doubt that the shah's efforts to satisfy Carter on human rights was grounded in his suspicions of the United States' attraction to Khomeini. This response of the shah and his supporters thus was deeply embedded in the traditional mode of dealing with the religious leaders. Among secular opposition leaders, too, there was a strong tendency to discount the qualitative difference between Khomeini's support and that of his popular predecessors such as Kashani. Men like Shapur Bakhtiar discounted the importance of the mass support for Khomeini, seeing it as impossible to sustain. In the twenty-five years since Musaddiq's overthrow, Iran had moved into the mass politics era, but few of its leaders were as yet ready to recognize that fact.

Government supporters who did see the power of Khomeini's appeal and his burgeoning support base, began to call for a drastic crackdown on the regime's opponents, including the religious network. This view increasingly characterized the military and security officer corps.[17] They saw little point in appeasing an opposition elite which every day sensed greater regime vulnerability. Readjustments in the regime's relationship with the religious hierarchy could take place later, but the need of the moment was to cripple their ability to mobilize a large public in opposition to the regime. American policy, and in particular Carter's New Year testimonial, indicated that the United States would not oppose a crackdown. But the shah persisted in his policy of allowing sporadic acts of coercion but refusing to agree to a systematic crackdown on the religious opposition.

Opposition leaders who recognized the charismatic potential in Khomeini and who understood Khomeini's aloofness from concrete policy came quickly to see the possibilities of manipulating him to serve their own policy ends and personal ambition. In 1978 the three individuals who were in the best position to take personal advantage of Khomeini's power were Ibrahim Yazdi, Sadeq Qotbzadeh, and Abul Hassan Bani Sadr. Yazdi was with Khomeini that year both in Iraq and later in Paris, and Qotbzadeh and Bani Sadr were in constant attendance in Paris. Given Khomeini's unconcern with tactics, the three were able to advance tactical plans they understood would be favorably received by Khomeini. This granted three rather obscure individuals an enormous advantage over far better-known opposition leaders in Iran. All three were later to recognize Khomeini's leadership as destructive of the values they believed in and to see a Khomeini far less vague, far less concerned with other worldly abstractions, and far more personally cunning and devious than they had believed.[18] But as 1978 was coming to a close, they saw their relationships with Khomeini as catapulting them into positions of great influence in revolutionary Iran.

The opposition leaders in Iran who best understood both the exiled Khomeini's potential power and his unconcern with day-to-day affairs were Mehdi Bazargan and his associates in the Freedom Movement. Bazargan would be the first prime minister in the Islamic Republic. The Iran he wished to see emerge was liberal, nationalistic, and Islamic. The last meant for him primarily the obligation to bring social justice and a concern for public morality to government. In terms of strategy, Bazargan was a major proponent of the unity of democratic forces, including especially the secular liberals of the National Front. He was highly skeptical of the far left, the Mujahaddin and Fadayan, and opposed any dealings with the Tudeh and others of the pro-Soviet left. He made every effort to tie opposition activities in Iran to the human rights banner and in so doing to explore fully any potential there still might be in showing some attempts to adhere to Carter's human rights program as a means of gaining American political encouragement. The Iranian Committee for Human Rights and Liberty was formed and affiliated itself with the International League for Human Rights. Effectively it was the central committee of the revolutionary leadership, and Bazargan was its functional, though not formal, leader.

The strategy that emerged from this group and that really bore Bazargan's imprimatur was to form a transitional government. Anthony Parsons, the British ambassador, and Brzezinski used the term "coalition government" to describe that plan, but that description reflects a misunderstanding of the revolutionary dynamics as Bazargan and his allies saw it.[19] The objective was regime change, not merely regime liberalization. The royal dictatorship had to be replaced by at the very least a constitutional monarchy, but more likely by a republic. The question was how this alteration could be accomplished. It was Bazargan's hope that violent revolutionary change could be avoided. Were a revolution to occur, the liberal leadership would have great difficulty maintaining control, and Bazargan from the beginning understood that.

The transitional schemes advanced conformed to a general model. The shah should appoint a regency council that would include a member of the court—Empress Farah, for example—a general or admiral, a conservative elder statesman such as Ali Amini, a major religio-political leader such as Ayatullah Mohammad Beheshti, who was respected by Khomeini, and a leading opposition figure such as Mehdi Bazargan. A new prime minister and cabinet would be appointed who would represent various opposition groups and government supporters who accepted the inevitability of regime change. The choice for prime minister was likely to be a secular National Frontist such as Karim Sanjabi. The shah would leave for an extended vacation, and while he was gone a free election for parliament would be held. Then a new government would be formed that almost certainly would call for a referendum on the institution of the monarchy. Ayatullah Khomeini would be invited to return to Iran with the expectation that he would go then to the religious center of Qom from where he could guide government policy into conformity with the holy law. In this role Khomeini would serve to give the regime legitimacy and would interfere little in day-to-day policy, with which he in any case had only a marginal concern. The optimal role for the U.S. government would be to encourage or pressure the shah to accept this plan.[20]

There were of course many obstacles facing such a plan. Approval by Khomeini, the shah, and the American government would be essential for success, and in the first half of 1978 only Khomeini's approval was at all possible. Ibrahim Yazdi as much as any opposition leader understood the weak bargaining position of those advancing the plan and the extraordinary strength of Khomeini's bargaining position. Quite simply, Bazargan and his allies had to have Khomeini's support because of his great popular appeal. They had little to offer him other than their personal leadership skills. The secular element in particular had virtually nothing to bargain with. But Bazargan was insistent on the unity of the democratic opposition, and Yazdi, despite his personal influence with Khomeini, acquiesced. Still, this was of little consequence since the shah, though frequently demoralized and depressed, evinced no intention during the first half of 1978 of even considering the surrender of any of his prerogatives. As for the U.S. government, Ambassador Sullivan was beginning to sense a serious malaise in the Iranian government, but Washington was largely unconcerned.[21]

Viewed retrospectively, the first half of 1978 was the last period in which the revolution, with its radical consequences, could have been avoided. Had a transitional strategy been presented to and endorsed by Khomeini, the shah, and Jimmy Carter, it conceivably could have been successful. On the other hand, so might a highly coercive strategy as advocated by some military leaders. But the shah was still Iran's preeminent decision maker and he persisted in a policy of alternating brutality with concessions.

## Accelerating Momentum

Following the Islamic custom of celebrating the dead forty days following a death, religious supporters of Khomeini staged demonstrations throughout Iran on the fortieth day anniversary of the January riots in Qom. Security forces in the important city of Tabriz handled demonstrations in that city particularly badly and lost control. Before the military was called in, religious-led mobs roamed the streets burning theaters, banks, restaurants, and bars. The shah responded angrily against SAVAK and other security organizations and replaced several security force leaders. He could hardly have made a worse move. The effectiveness of the regime's coercive arm depended on a perception among the dissatisfied of such omnipotence as to deny the option of overt opposition to it. The performance of the security force in Tabriz reduced this sense of omnipotence and the shah's behavior compounded this effect. There was increasingly a sense of the regime's vulnerability. The shah could not allow that sense of vulnerability to develop to the point where it could be perceived as fatal. But through this six-month period, the number of Iranians seeing a fatal vulnerability grew daily, largely because of the shah's policy.

In August 1977 the shah had replaced Amir Abbas Hoveida, his prime minister for twelve years, with a talented technocrat, Jamshid Amuzegar. Hoveida had been an ideal prime minister for the shah's golden years. He uncritically accepted his role as implementer of the shah's decisions. His skills in interpersonal relations were substantial and he was instrumental in producing a stable, even tranquil, atmosphere within the administration and good relations with important interest groups. But he was not the man to deal with a major crisis. The shah's purpose in appointing Amuzegar was to enlist his skills in dealing with the economic crisis. Not suprisingly, Amuzegar's policies were a textbook application of how to deal with excessive inflationary pressures. He advised cutting back on spending and restricting price and wage increases. However, in application, the government's policies did little to relieve some of the worst problems, such as the terrible price of housing. Yet prosecution of those charging excessive prices occurred frequently enough to cause a sense of unease among the elements favorable to the regime. Control of wages was more effective, but had the effect of increasing dissatisfaction among industrial workers and government employees—two of the major accommodating elements of the population. Amuzegar's concerns were essentially technical. His excellent reputation was gained as a technocrat who left political questions to the shah. Now as prime minister he had little to offer, since the crisis was by now primarily political, not economic.

By late summer 1978, the shah had come to the conclusion that he must seek some accommodation with those who stood at the margins of revolutionary activity. In May he had removed his longtime associate, General Nematollah Nasseri, as head of SAVAK and sent him to Pakistan as ambassador. In his place, the shah appointed

General Nasser Moqadam. Symbolically this amounted to the replacement of a tough hard-liner with a more sophisticated and subtle-minded manipulator. The signal was a strong one that the regime was prepared to compromise with opposition elements and, for the time being, had rejected proposals for a military solution. However, there was no sign that the shah was prepared to deal with those individuals who were at the center of the opposition and no sign that he would consider any proposal involving the diminution of his own authority. Since opposition leaders could only consider plans that incorporated an end to the shah's dictatorship, the shah's move toward accommodation had the effect of accelerating the revolutionary momentum. As this occurred, the options available to opposition leaders who hoped to avoid a revolution were narrowed.

The shah was following in 1977–1978 a pattern that was startlingly parallel to that which he had followed in the 1960–1963 crisis, which he barely survived. Then too he granted broader freedom of maneuver to the opposition, but never seriously addressed the question of sharing power with them. Most astonishing was his appointment in late August 1978 of Jafaar Sharif-Imami as prime minister. Sharif-Imami, who had been brought in as prime minister at a comparable moment in the 1960–1963 crisis and had failed totally, now was returning with exactly the same basic formula for coping with problems. That formula had worked in the pre–mass politics era when government authority was essentially oligarchic in structure. It required for its execution a leader with exceptional interpersonal skills, who understood implicitly the drives and aspirations of the competing oligarchs. With this understanding, the leader would attempt to satisfy, at something more than a minimal level, enough of the oligarchs to produce an operating consensus. This was in fact essentially the formula that had worked so well for Hoveida. But Hoveida was dealing only with individuals whose self-interest tied them to the shah's regime. Sharif-Imami was seeking to apply the same formula with individuals whose self-interest demanded the fundamental alteration of the regime.

Apparently, even in late 1978 the shah had not understood that political leaders who spoke for great popular constituencies were sharply restricted in their range of maneuverability by those constituencies. Before the mass politics era, religious leaders might well be mollified by a subsidy or an appointment to a lucrative position. But

Sharif-Imami's good relations with many prominent clerics in 1978 could not result in a comparably easy strategy. Now those leaders understood that their own political survival demanded that they do nothing to reduce their credibility with increasingly radical young clerics who were organizing mass demonstrations. The same was true for those who spoke for industrial workers and government employees who had suffered severely because of inflation. The *mullahs* demanded freedom to advance their demands particularly for Khomeini's return, and Sharif-Imami acquiesced. Spokesmen for workers and government employees had their wage demands granted. Leaders of organizations of journalists demanded and gained greater freedom of the press.

In early August, the shah had promised new parliamentary elections for the following year that would grant the electorate a free choice. This promise was the shah's most concrete manifestation of a willingness to share power. But by August 1978 the promise was suspect and in itself insufficient to produce an agreement with an opposition leadership still willing to negotiate one. The shah had two strategic options—accommodation or suppression. He had chosen the second, but was somehow unable to follow through with it. In failing, he turned to the first. Sharif-Imami's policies and his own conciliatory stance gave him the worst of both worlds. The momentum of the revolution continued to accelerate. The press was almost free. Demonstrations and strikes were daily occurrences and even the parliament had come to life with a minority of the deputies in full opposition. Yet there had been no serious effort to enter into dialogue with the opposition leadership, and short of this no real success for the accommodation strategy could be expected. As in the 1960–1963 period, the shah appeared to be trying to ride out the crisis. But in both cases, far from taking the wind out of the opposition sails, he turned the wind into a gale force.

## Brzezinski and American Policy

In January 1977 the Department of State's Bureau of Intelligence and Research issued a summary analysis of the regime's stability. It concluded, "Iran is likely to remain stable under the Shah's leadership over the next several years, and committed to its relationship with the US as long as the Shah rules. . . . The undercurrent of terroristic violence notwithstanding, the Shah rules Iran free from serious domestic threat."[22] On September 1, 1978, the INR disagreed with a CIA estimate that continued to see Iran as INR had seen it eighteen months earlier. Now the INR concluded,

We expect that violent dissent from the Shah's rule will continue to disrupt Iranian society despite his efforts at political liberalization and other reforms. We are dubious that the Shah, in the near term, can suppress urban violence without substantial use of force. . . . We see a basic unresolvable conflict between the Shah's liberalization program and the need to limit violent opposition; . . . we see some chance that the Shah will be forced to step down by 1985. At the moment we would rate that chance as less than fifty-fifty.[23]

Thus six months before the revolution's success, some awareness was beginning to develop in Washington that a regime-threatening crisis existed in Iran. But the possibility of salvaging even a modified version of the regime may already have passed by that time. The INR speaks of "violent opposition" as the problem, but violence was confined to the guerrilla forces of the secular and religious left. The mainstream of the revolution was nonviolent and expressed itself increasingly in public demonstrations. Long denied any access to the opposition, the U.S. bureaucracy concerned with Iran had no real picture of it. It follows that without even a rudimentary understanding of the force with which they must deal, any strategy and associated tactics that might have been devised would have missed the mark.

Within the U.S. embassy there was far more understanding of the seriousness of the situation. Both Ambassador William Sullivan and the United Kingdom's ambassador, Sir Anthony Parsons, have written accounts of their tours in Tehran. These are mutually confirming descriptions of an awareness of fundamental malaise. Indeed, comparing the two, one can see that Sullivan's understanding of the forces opposing the shah was more detailed and richer than that of Sir Anthony. Gary Sick, who bore the responsibility for Iran in the National Security Council, has challenged Sullivan's claim that he was aware of developing difficulties in Iran, and points to a far greater ambivalence in Sullivan's view at the time than Sullivan's book suggests. However, Sullivan, unlike his predecessors from 1967 on, encouraged contacts between his staff and opposition groups. One of his officers, John Stempel, later wrote of his experiences in *Inside the Iranian Revolution*. It is a most revealing account. Stempel was made aware of the transitional plan approach that preoccupied Bazargan and his associates. According to Stempel, the Freedom Movement "contacted" the American embassy in October 1978 to urge American consideration for the plan. Stempel was told, "For two years now we have tried to keep nationalist activity non-violent. Events are now reaching a certain point where the masses are leaving us for violent activity." In explaining his judgment that the plan was "unrealistic" and "deliberately designed for Western ears," Stempel contrasts the Freedom Movement's view of the United States with the growing hostility from Khomeini. He concludes, the Freedom Movement "did not consider a religious anti-American form of government and continued ties to the West incompatible."[24]

Stempel's account demonstrates that even this officer with good access to the opposition failed to understand that which was explicitly told him. Bazargan and his associates knew they were losing control of revolutionary momentum. In the early fall of 1978 schisms were appearing in the united front of the opposition. Ayatullah Taleqani was strongly in favor of a full association between the Mujahaddin and the front, even though their tactics were violent and their objectives fully revolutionary. On the other side, Ayatullah Beheshti, Ayatullah Mahdavi Kani, and Hojatolislam Hashemi Rafsenjani were somewhat restive with the continued tactics that Bazargan favored and were increasingly in control of the organization of the by now huge popular base for the religious opposition.[25] A transition scheme that would produce a parliament in the National Front–Freedom Movement mold was one implicitly designed to maintain liberal reformist control of the successor regime. The dynamics of the situation were such that success for such a scheme could only occur if Khomeini, the shah, and the Americans quickly endorsed it and put it into effect. Far from being designed simply for Western ears, it was the only accommodation strategy with even an outside hope of success. And of course Bazargan was hoping to avoid a "religious anti-American form of government."

Bazargan and his associates continued to advance transition plans into January 1979. But Stempel's judgment that they were "unrealistic" even four months earlier is confirmed by his own account and the accounts of the Iranian revolution by Jimmy Carter, Zbigniew Brzezinski, and Gary Sick. There simply was no real comprehension of the plan by the Americans, and thus U.S. support, essential for the plan, was never a possibility. Stempel notes that despite prodding from Ambassador Sullivan, Washington didn't even respond to the transition plan proposal.[26] Brzezinski's picture of revolutionary momentum in Iran makes clear why. Brzezinski lived in a world defined by the Soviet-American cold war.[27] The shah of Iran was America's ally in that conflict — in fact, an essential ally — and could not be permitted to fall. Brzezinski began to worry about Iran in the summer of 1978. Apparently none of the earlier signs of difficulties had made any impression on him. To brief himself on the problem, he chose to turn to Iran's ambassador to the United States, Ardeshir Zahedi. Zahedi, the son of Fazlullah Zahedi, the Anglo-American choice for dictator of Iran when Musaddiq was overthrown and a major actor in the coup in his own right, has never been accused of analytic acuity. But he did confirm Brzezinski's suspicions of a rapidly developing deterioration in Iran fed primarily by the shah's unwillingness to take decisive action.[28]

There is in Brzezinski's account not the slightest hint of an understanding of the impact of the human rights policy, of which he was a strong advocate, as a precipitator of Iranian events. Nor is there any indication of even a passing interest in the conglomerate makeup of the opposition. For Brzezinski, there was only one acceptable strategy and that was suppression. If the shah was incapable of executing such a strategy, then there must be a military coup d'état. He was supported in his thinking by Secretary of Defense Harold Brown and Secretary of Energy James Schlesinger.[29] Increasingly, as the crisis progressed, Brzezinski spoke for Jimmy Carter. Ambassador Sullivan's efforts to bring some awareness of the complexity of the situation were rebuffed — ultimately rebuffed contemptuously by Carter as well as Brzezinski.

A critical moment both for the revolution and for American relations with Iran occurred on September 8, 1978, a day known as "Black Friday." A series of demonstrations had taken place in Tehran before September 8 and were viewed, especially by the military, as potentially dangerous. Far from being violent, the demonstrators made a special effort to establish rapport with the soldiers who lined the demonstration area. Florists gave the demonstrators bunches of flowers and many were placed in the muzzles of guns held by bemused soldiers. A feeling of brotherhood and community pervaded the gatherings and many demonstrators brought along their children to enjoy the festivities. On September 7, at Sharif-Imami's suggestion, the shah agreed to impose martial law. The next morning, when crowds gathered, most participants were not even aware of the prohibition of assembly of more than three persons. Military officers ordered the crowd to disperse and when it did not, ordered their troops to fire. Many died, including children. Participants were so shocked at the contrast between the military's behavior of September 8 and that of preceding days that rumors spread that in fact the offending troops were Israeli.

When the events of the day became known in Washington, Carter was negotiating with Sadat and Begin at Camp David. With Brzezinski's endorsement, Carter telephoned the shah, encouraged him, and promised full and continuing support.[30] Thus Brzezinski and Carter, the men most responsible for the human rights policy which so exhilarated the Iranian opposition, now seemed to condone what Iranian oppositionists saw as a brutal massacre. Obviously the transition plan, which was given to the U.S. embassy some time after "Black Friday," was not designed for Brzezinski's ears. Iranian oppositionists were aware of differences within the Carter administration. Embassy officers were in contact with them, and some American visitors, members of the human rights section of the Department of State, seemed to understand to the point of being sympathetic. Ibrahim Yazdi, in particular, had a reasonably accurate view of differences within the Carter administration and continued to see some hope for a change of policy. But from both the left and from the revolutionary Islamic leaders, including Khomeini, there was a sharp intensification of anti-American sentiments expressed in their statements.[31]

The rhythm of official American awareness of the crisis in Iran had its parallel among Iran's population. That large section of the public described in the previous chapter as willing to accommodate themselves now saw a real possibility of an alteration of the regime, if not total change. A sense of vulnerability was growing among those called enthusiasts as well. The strikes of industrial workers and government employees that were spreading rapidly in September and October reflected the movement of accommodating elements into the revolution. Those elements that were closest to the regime lacked this alternative. Some among them, the most far-sighted, began to slip quietly out of the country, taking with them as much of their wealth as could easily be transferred. The technocrats who had tried to make the official party, Rastakhiz, a vehicle for their own career advancement found themselves abandoned when the shah canceled the party's official status. On September 30, 1978, it announced its dissolution. That announcement was preceded a few days earlier by the arrest of thirty-three senior SAVAK officers and followed by the recall from Pakistan of General Nematollah Nasseri, the former head of SAVAK. Nasseri would soon be placed under arrest and charged with sanctioning brutality by SAVAK. The shah seemed to be following a policy of staged disintegration of the institutional base of his own regime.

The speed of disintegration was more a consequence of official policy than a response to opposition pressures. But the results were the same. By late October, the regime was seen by much of Iran as fatally vulnerable. There was nervousness only over the possibilities of a military coup sanctioned by Britain and the United States. Sir Anthony Parsons, in his account makes emphatically clear his belief that the moment for success for a military option had long since passed.[32] William Sullivan seemed to agree, but unlike Sir Anthony had to deal with his government's unwillingness to accept this assessment. National Security Adviser Brzezinski, recognizing the shah's mental attitude as the primary obstacle to the kind of decisive policy of political suppression that alone—Brzezinski believed—could save the regime, wrote the shah that the United States would not oppose his establishing a military government.[33] In Washington Brzezinski continued to press for serious consideration of encouraging a military coup in Iran. In his book, however, Brzezinski gives no indication that there was a well-formulated contingency plan involving a military coup, and Jimmy Carter at one point commented to Brzezinski that he didn't even know who might lead such a coup.[34] In December 1978, copies of an alleged coup plan that was highly detailed were circulating freely in Tehran. But there is as yet no overt documentation indicating that the American government had actually authorized that or any other plan. But Brzezinski was able to have included in the instructions for General Robert Huyser in his visit to Tehran in January 1979 a provision that a military coup could be considered as a last resort if the military appeared to be disintegrating.[35]

The fact that Jimmy Carter and his administration would consider seriously executing a coup in Iran in the midst of this most popular revolution in history, tells much about American understanding of the situation. The coup of August 1953 had blundered into success at a very different stage of Iranian development. To be sure, the leader against whom the coup was executed, Mohammad Musaddiq, was the first charismatic leader in Iranian history. But the percentage of the Iranian population capable of political participation was still small. Now another charismatic leader had attracted the enthusiastic support of millions of Iranians and the acceptance of millions more. The institutional base of the shah's regime, including SAVAK, was disintegrating. Conscripted soldiers were responding to the revolutionary enthusiasm of their brothers, cousins, and friends. And Iran's economy was passing into paralysis. Furthermore, the shah's personal control of the military, based on an elaborate system of direct lines of authority from military commanders to the shah and the monarch's personal involvement in promotions of high-ranking officers, was still firm. Since presumably the coup would remove the shah from direct authority while retaining him as symbolic leader, officers who had not routinely coordinated their activities and were rivals for the shah's attention would have to find some way of uniting in conspiracy. Planning for the overthrow of Musaddiq consumed months and even so failed initially. Now the instructions for a far more difficult operation were advanced seemingly casually by the United States. It is difficult not to share Sir Anthony's flabbergasted disbelief that such an operation could even be considered.

## The Final Act

The support base of the revolution by late October 1978 had expanded to include all but the most enthusiastic regime supporters among the population. This meant that the proportion of revolutionary supporters looking to the clerics for leadership had declined. And by now the activities most destabilizing for the regime—the strikes of industrial workers, public utility employees, and bureaucrats—were led and supported by individuals closer to the secular left and center, or to the Mujahaddin, than to religious leaders such as Ayatullah Mohammad Beheshti. Indeed, few of them would even recognize the names of Beheshti, Mahdavi Kani, Motahari, and Rafsenjani, and others who would soon be recognized as the core clerical leaders of the revolution. Yet the preeminence of Khomeini in the revolution was now accepted by almost everyone. The organizational base that could orchestrate disciplined demonstrations and direct gangs of young men into the streets was that of the clergy and the mosque bureaucracy. Khomeini at the very least had a veto power over revolutionary strategy and did not hesitate to use it. As his power grew, Khomeini was less and less inclined to agree to anything less than total capitulation by the regime and its replacement with an Islamic republic.

This hardening of Khomeini's attitude reduced considerably the flexibility of the revolutionary leadership in Tehran. Their various transition plans were all premised on the assumption that, were one of the plans accepted, the dynamics would lead inexorably to a referendum on the monarchy that would result in a republic. But when a delegation consisting of Mehdi Bazargan, leader of the Freedom Movement, Karim Sanjabi, most prominent of National Front leaders, and Nasser Minatchi, the director of the Iranian Committee for Human Rights and Liberty went to Paris to gain Khomeini's support for a transition plan approach, they were rebuffed. By this time Khomeini was refusing to support any government appointed by the shah. When Sanjabi issued a statement on November 3, 1978, that he could not participate in a shah-appointed government, he was giving voice to Khomeini's hard-line stance and appeared to some observers, including John Stempel, to be closing the door to compromise.[36] But this was not the conclusion drawn by the revolutionary command in Tehran. As I have mentioned, it persisted in looking for a transitional formula into January 1979, and Minatchi, Bazargan, and Sanjabi were always active participants in the search. This persistence can be explained by the peculiar quality of Khomeini's contribution to the decisional process. Unconcerned with detail and unconcerned with tactical planning as he was, Khomeini was open to manipulation by those around him who did think in tactical terms. Yazdi, Qotbzadeh, and Bani Sadr thus had a critical role to play, and the personal ambitions of the three required that they be on good terms with the revolutionary leaders in Tehran. But any transitional plan now had to avoid any appearance of agreeing to an acceptance of a role for the shah as constitutional monarch.

Two days after Sanjabi's statement, severe riots broke out in Tehran that resulted in a great deal of property damage. These riots had the distinction of being led by groups that did not look to the organization in which Ayatullah Beheshti appeared to play the leading role. Beginning at the University of Tehran, the violence reflected both the broadening of support for revolutionary activism and the decisions of leftist leaders to serve a major catalytic role in the revolutionary process. Participants included the Mujahaddin, the Fadayan, the Tudeh party, and a number of other organizations. Functionally it involved a recognition of the fact that Khomeini's charismatic appeal was the central ingredient in producing this revolutionary moment. It was in addition a further signal to the essentially reformist opposition leaders that a revolution could not be denied. From this point on, the leftist revolutionaries would join religious-led youths in the streets and in all other overt activities.

These riots marked the end of the Sharif-Imami interlude. Indeed, the evidence is incontrovertible that the security forces had welcomed, if they did not play a role in stimulating, these riots.[37] They needed to prove to the shah that step-by-step capitulation to revolutionary demands could only lead to collapse. The shah did then appoint a military government led by General Gholam Reza Azhari. But in doing so he was not turning to the military option that so attracted Zbigniew Brzezinski which called for a crackdown on revolutionary organizations. There were some arrests, including that of Karim Sanjabi. But even that act was symbolic of weakness. Sanjabi represented a group of elderly gentlemen who in their youth had served Mohammad Musaddiq. The revolutionary organizations able to orchestrate demonstrations, and (if necessary) active combat, belonged to the religious and secular left and to those who directed the alliance of clergy and the mosque bureaucracy. The government had to be aware of the extraordinary importance for the latter organization of a handful of men, including in particular Ayatullah Beheshti. Troops with fixed bayonets stood outside Beheshti's house, but they did not impede systematically the steady flow of visitors. Nor did they do anything to halt on a permanent basis the vital communications operation taking place inside the house. Beheshti claimed that recordings of Khomeini's statements from Paris would be available on cassette in every mosque in Iran within twenty-four hours of their utterance. His house was a central transmission station and many of the visitors were in fact technical operators.[38] Beheshti was briefly incarcerated, but that did not indicate a decision to destroy the organization he presided over.

Overt revolutionary activity therefore persisted, as did the disintegration process. Strikes by oil workers cut deeply into government revenue and produced long gasoline lines. The airlines serving Tehran were crowded with the nouveau riche making permanent departures from Iran. And the process of desertion by enlisted, conscript personnel from the military gained force. The shah at last began to explore seriously transition formulas that a few months earlier might have had some chance of success. He found one National Front elder statesman, Dr. Gholam Hossein Sadeqi, who was prepared to cooperate in spite of Sanjabi's pronouncement.[39] The shah in making this proposal was finally accepting a leader who would insist on exercising independent authority. Sadeqi, unlike Ali Amini sixteen years earlier, had at least the possibility of attracting an independent base of support. But he did not accept as a given that the central feature of the revolution was Khomeini's charismatic appeal. He therefore was willing to run the risk—in fact, the certainty—that were he to accept the shah's appointment to the premiership, he would be declared a traitor by Khomeini. Sadeqi made an effort to find individuals to serve in his cabinet who would be both independent of the regime and willing to accept the opprobrium of Khomeini's denunciation. But there was at the time a serious transition plan under consideration by revolutionary leaders that had some real possibility—not of Khomeini's active approval, but at least of his acquiescence. Sadeqi's efforts therefore were seen as threatening the one real hope of avoiding a sudden collapse of the regime or a military coup that would lead inevitably to terrible violence and bloodshed. He therefore was rebuffed everywhere and gave up his efforts. This last serious transitional plan too, it is clear in retrospect, had no real possibility of success. Like its predecessors, this plan had to have the support of the U.S. government. Its authors believed Khomeini's acquiescence was likely and that the shah was prepared to accept it—including the requirement that he leave Iran if urged to do so by Ambassador Sullivan, speaking for the American government. But by now Brzezinski's control of American policy toward Iran was sufficiently complete and his lack of sympathy for any transitional scheme was so total as to make such an American role unthinkable.

Iranians in exile continue to believe years after the revolution that the British and/or the Americans were responsible for Khomeini's coming to power. But no aspect of the Iranian revolution is more clear than the absence of substantial external support for the revolution. The governments of Algeria, Libya, and Syria, and some of the PLO leadership were sympathetic to the revolution. But whatever aid these governments gave and whatever training the PLO provided for a few Iranians, the sum total of outside support was inconsequential. The shah, on the other hand, had the active sympathy of many of the world's leaders and acceptance by the rest. Eastern European governments went so far as to play down reports of revolutionary activities in Iran at the Iranian government's request — an attitude that surely would not have prevailed if there had been Soviet complicity in the revolution.

Judging from official, journalistic, and academic remarks in the Soviet Union regarding the Iranian revolution and from Soviet policy behavior, one can conclude that there was more bemusement than appreciation of the revolution.[40] Americans who viewed the world through cold war lenses, assumed without question that the Soviet Union, if not directly involved, certainly was deeply satisfied by the revolution. After all, an American surrogate regime was being ousted and replaced by a regime whose leader was fiercely anti-American. But the perception of Iran as a U.S. surrogate was an American, but not necessarily a Soviet, image. There was little in Soviet rhetoric regarding Iran to indicate that the Soviets viewed the American presence in Iran as a matter for serious alarm. Only the National Voice of Iran, a clandestine radio broadcasting from Baku and reflecting Iranian communist thinking, described the shah in terms that Americans of a cold war persuasion would anticipate.[41]

In fact, the role of Khomeini and his remarkable appeal to what could be described in Marxist terms as the Iranian proletariat and petty bourgeoisie was hardly mentioned by Soviet observers. Only when Khomeini's charismatic appeal was undeniably self-evident did official Soviet commentary begin to take note of him.[42] Even then, such notice was couched in terms that fit conventional Marxist expectations. In mid-November 1978, Leonid Brezhnev issued a warning to the United States government not to intervene in Iranian internal affairs.[43] The statement followed official American remarks made in answer to reporters' questions suggesting that the U.S. government would consider active support for the Iranian regime if it were requested to do so and if the situation appeared critical. And

Soviet intelligence may well have been aware of Brzezinski's advocacy of a coup, especially if there was some groundwork being done for it in Iran. But as yet no evidence has surfaced to indicate that Soviet support for the revolution went beyond routine assistance to the Tudeh party.

The revolution, in short, was an exclusively Iranian phenomenon. The only significant foreign involvement was American and that was on behalf of the regime. Sir Anthony Parsons's personal account is a testimonial to Britain's acceptance of the fact that it could not affect seriously the outcome of the crisis. Sir Anthony, while critical of the shah's leadership, was obviously personally friendly toward the shah and his regime. The best evidence of this, in fact, is his apparent lack of any real understanding of the revolutionary forces. There are in his book moving portraits of official Iranians, such as Prime Minister Hoveida; there is also a basic understanding of the regime's vulnerability. But had the British been involved operationally there would surely be some pictures of the opposition in Parsons's book, even stereotypical portraits, that would have been the primary negative target. In fact, there is nothing. Indeed, only two important groups appear not to have recognized implicitly that the Iranian revolution was ending the era of European dominance in Iran. These were the shah and his supporters and the Brzezinski wing of the Carter administration that had gained control over U.S. policy toward Iran in the final months of the shah's rule.

The last major transitional plan emanating from the Iranian Committee for Human Rights and Liberty had at best only a marginal chance for success, even if the American government had cooperated fully. But it was the last possibility for avoiding loss of control of the revolutionary forces by Bazargan and his associates. The shah made one last effort. He attempted to impose his own transitional plan, one with American support, that would incorporate most of the features of the plans he had been responding to with increasing interest. This included acceptance of the dissolution of SAVAK, an end to relations with Israel, and the shah's departure from Iran on indefinite vacation. What it could not include would be its acceptance by Khomeini. The shah found an individual, Dr. Shapur Bakhtiar, a veteran member of the Iran party and the National Front, who agreed to attempt to form such a government. Bakhtiar, a French-trained and intensely Francophile self-identified aristocrat, had an impeccable record. He had opposed the regime courageously and had accepted incarceration in good spirit. However, he viewed the Iranian revolution more as an aristocrat than as a nationalist. To him, the mass religious following was a rabble incapable of sustained political interest. His most telling remark came in response to a reporter's question asking him if the chants by huge crowds calling for his death bothered him. His response was, not at all; if the cinemas were open, the crowd would be there.[44]

In Bakhtiar's view, Bazargan, Sanjabi, and the mainstream of the revolutionary leadership were both unperceptive and weak. They failed to see the terrible danger of a fascist theocracy and they lacked the courage to stand up to those who, making full use of demagogic manipulation of an unlettered mass, would impose such a rule. Bazargan and his associates, in contrast, were in the first place fully aware of their relative weakness with the public. They had a large potential base of support, but one that could come only from the section of the population that had accommodated themselves to the regime and had joined the revolution late. The revolution was going to take place with or without their support, and the best they could do was to stay in its vanguard and thereby to exercise some influence over its tempo and its direction. They felt, in the second place, that they had an institutional base for gaining this kind of control. The polarization of revolutionary leaders had not occurred. In fact, Khomeini in Paris and Beheshti and other leading religious figures in Iran were surrounded by and in full cooperation with members directly or indirectly associated with the Freedom Movement. Bakhtiar, in their view, was a romantic who was allowing personal ambition and overweening vanity to prevent his recognizing the essential weakness of his and their position. They could only denounce Bakhtiar's agreeing to form a government without Khomeini's approval and to refuse to cooperate with it.[45]

In January 1979, the royal dictatorship had effectively disintegrated. What remained to collapse now were some illusions: those of Jimmy Carter and Zbigniew Brzezinski that somehow, magically, in a situation they understood not at all the Iranian officer corps, with American urging, could maintain Shapur Bakhtiar in power; those of Shapur Bakhtiar who believed that, while lacking any real base of support himself, by sheer will and courage plus the unequivocal backing of the military and the United States he could hold back a revolutionary force which momentarily had the support of the over-whelming majority of Iranians; and those of some in the Iranian military, proud of the fact that the officer corps had remained essentially loyal, that with American aid the situation could be saved.

Carter's decision to dispatch General Robert Huyser to Tehran reinforced all these illusions.[46] His mission was to encourage the Iranian officer corps to remain in Iran and to give their full support to Shapur Bakhtiar. If lingering resistance from the shah appeared to be preventing the military from playing its proper role, Huyser should explore the option of a military coup. Huyser followed his instructions closely, although there is as yet no evidence he seriously explored the coup option. But he certainly did raise both Bakhtiar's and the military's expectations and thereby strengthened an illusory belief in their survivability. However, the disintegration process was inexorable. The focus of attention came to be Khomeini's return to Iran after the shah—who by now suffered few if any illusions—had left. Both Bakhtiar and the military understood that, should Khomeini return, Bakhtiar and certainly the top command structure of the military must soon leave. But after some public blustering by Bakhtiar that Khomeini would not be allowed back, on February 1, 1979, he did return. Within days, the revolution was an accomplished fact. Officers who had followed Huyser's advice to remain in Iran were among the first sentenced to death by the revolutionary courts. Bakhtiar fled to his beloved Paris. Brzezinski turned his attention elsewhere.

The logic of the situation months before the regime's collapse called for an alliance of the military and the *mullah*s. Indeed, years before the crisis, the growing power of both military officers and religious leaders was apparent. But by early 1978 the more prescient military officers had come to see that the shah for whatever reason was not going to be able to preside over the forcible suppression of the revolutionary forces. The option of a military coup that would remove the shah as dictator but save the regime was considered, although apparently not seriously. But the option of a religious-military alliance could have produced a powerful and popular regime and would have served well the interests of both groups. Yet apparently so obvious an option was not seriously explored. Evidence for that conclusion is persuasive. After the success of the revolution, many observers expected to see emerge a contingent of military officers who had been covertly associated with the revolutionary forces for months and even years. But no such group appeared. Both Bakhtiar and the successor Bazargan government looked with favor on General Feridun Jam to take a major military post. Jam had been married to one of the shah's sisters and, though bitterly disappointed with his treatment by a monarch who seemed to take pleasure in humiliating him, remained a loyalist. Bazargan then turned to General Valiollah Qarani to lead the military. Qarani had been jailed after his involvement in a coup plan in 1958 was revealed. But in that plot both the nationalist and religious opposition were notably absent. He was obviously against the shah and ambitious — a would-be Iranian Nasser. His choice by the revolutionary regime was strong evidence that they had no one of their own at Qarani's level to take the leadership. Furthermore, the actions of two leading military officers, both close friends of the shah, in the last weeks of the regime suggests that there was receptivity for religious-military cooperation. General Abbas Qarabaghi, in the final days chief of staff, fully understood the strength of the revolutionary force and argued strongly for military association with it.[47] Personally devastating to the shah was the defection of his boyhood friend, General Hossein Fardust, who headed the Imperial Inspectorate, to the revolution well before its final triumph. But the revolutionary leadership apparently had not made the military officer corps a serious target.

The conclusion is impossible to avoid that the Iranian revolution, one of the most extraordinary events in human history, would not have occurred in early 1979 or would not have taken the form it did had it not been for the regime's entirely avoidable failure to maintain coercive control. To be sure, the shah's regime was seriously vulnerable both on the grounds of its lack of nationalist legitimacy and its unconcern with the material needs and demands for dignity of the majority of its population. The regime was despised by much of the intelligentsia, both liberal and left, and by a high proportion of young political activists. It was seen as corrupt, indulgent of the wealthy, vainglorious, brutal, and insensitive by the large urban lower and lower-middle classes, who were increasingly aware of their potential for political participation, and by the most respected of religious leaders. There was little question that it would have had difficulty surviving a truly severe economic crisis. But the crisis that did develop, though serious, should not have been fatal.

Much is made of the shah's failure to provide an institutional base for his regime. And it is true that he was unwilling to grant any institution that could mobilize political support and articulate the demands of interest groups enough authority to achieve viability. But he did construct a military/internal security force that was both highly effective and, as events would prove, loyal. The story of his last two years is preeminently a story of not merely a failure to make effective use of that force but also a weakening of the force that could hardly have been more successful had it been consciously planned. The extent to which the shah's illness contributed to his behavior can never be known. But the striking parallels in his behavior in the two crises, 1962–1963 and 1977–1979, suggest that the behavior was a manifestation of fundamental temperamental characteristics.

The case is equally strong that Carter's human rights policy was a major, if inadvertent, factor in determining the form and rhythm of the revolution. I have developed earlier the case that the effectiveness of the shah's coercive control of his country rested on twin pillars. One, the internal dimension, was his strong institutional base of support in the military and the security forces. The other, the external dimension, was the belief of the Iranian people—including the shah, his security forces, and those predisposed to oppose the regime—that the U.S. government was determined to maintain the royal dictatorship in power. Furthermore, by this view the United States had in the CIA an institutional instrument fully capable of achieving that objective. However, Carter's pronouncements that a concern for human rights would be central to his foreign policy raised serious doubts inside Iran about American determination to support the shah's dictatorial control. Evidence suggests that this Iranian interpretation was never understood even at the working bureaucratic level in the Carter administration. There was simply no awareness within the government of the exceptional importance of the human rights policy as interpreted in Iran in providing momentum for the revolution. Therefore there was no awareness of the need to correct Iranian misinterpretations of U.S. policy. The case is overwhelmingly strong that despite its human rights stance the Carter administration did not waver in its support for the regime until its disintegration was almost complete. But it is also undeniable that the shah was never sure of that support.

Had coercion been applied effectively in 1977 when the opposition was exploring its options, the revolutionary force may well have developed so slowly that revolutionary activity would have remained at the urban guerrilla level, and U.S. government projections would have been realized. Had coercion been applied strongly in 1978 when the revolutionary dynamic already was accelerating and difficult to halt, the opposition leadership would have had to adopt a different strategy. In all likelihood this would have led to tactics of violence along with civil disobedience. This in turn would have taken revolutionary centrality away from men who thought in terms of transitional schemes and away from mosque bureaucrats who planned and orchestrated what were in effect officially tolerated demonstrations. Elements such as the Mujahaddin and the Fadayan with disciplined organizations would have had a much more central role to play and their leaders would have had a stronger claim to primary influence within the top command. However, the rhythm the revolution was able to follow, thanks largely to the shah's behavior, was ideally suited to the emergence of Khomeini as its unchallengeable leader.

# 6

## THE RHYTHM OF THE REVOLUTION

On February 1, 1979, Ayatullah Khomeini returned to Iran to one of the most tumultuous public demonstrations in human history. Four days later he named Mehdi Bazargan head of a provisional government, and for the next week both Bazargan and Bakhtiar claimed to be prime minister of Iran. On February 10 a battle broke out between noncommissioned officers of the air force who had gone over to the revolution and some of the shah's imperial guard. It became apparent quickly to the military that the revolution had triumphed, and the top command indicated it would no longer support Bakhtiar. On February 12, Bakhtiar slipped out of view, and the revolution was an accomplished fact.

The shah's regime had disintegrated with a totality not seen since the collapse of the Russian government in November 1917. Now there was a government, but it had no coercive arm; the economy was paralyzed; and the normative structure of authority was in such disarray that the citizenry had no idea what rules continued to prevail. Control rested exclusively on the overwhelming consensus of the public regarding the right of Ayatullah Khomeini to establish a new basis for governmental authority. But Khomeini's thinking on that subject was at such a high level of abstraction that the public, even the most attentive section of it, was mystified. An Islamic republic was to be formed in which he and others with a profound comprehension of the divine plan would serve as guides. Just how this guidance would be institutionalized and how it would relate to other governmental and social institutions was completely unclear.

Bazargan named a cabinet along established departmental lines. His appointees were chosen from among individuals who had supported the revolution mainly in association with the Freedom Movement and the National Front. They were generally well qualified for their positions and conformed well to Bazargan's desire to establish a new government that would quickly establish and then defend the

189

rule of law. But the new government was confronted with an immediate problem of establishing law and order. The internal security forces had melted away and some immediate replacements had to be recruited if anarchy was not to prevail. An equally, if not more, urgent concern for the new regime was the possibility they saw of a move by SAVAK and military officers, probably with CIA orchestration, to seize political control of the country. Not even the leaders of the revolution comprehended the totality of the disintegration of the old regime.

Bazargan and his cabinet could not cope with the task of restructuring control in the critical short run. Time would be required for departmental restructuring and selection of personnel. In the meantime, new institutions had to be created to deal at least temporarily with the immediate crisis of authority. The process by which these institutions emerged was one that developed naturally within the organizational base that so successfully had mobilized and orchestrated revolutionary activities. Since technical competence for running a complex government was to be found among the liberal professionals associated with the National Front and the Freedom Movement, departmental administration was chosen from their ranks. But the revolution had been managed in the streets, essentially from the mosques. The discipline and effectiveness of the great mass demonstrations of December 1978, and the impressive administration by religious authorities of aid to earthquake victims in eastern Iran earlier that year, reflected the existence of a bureaucratic force fully capable of providing order after the collapse of the royal regime.

Presiding over the creation of a new institutional structure for the emerging Islamic republic was Ayatullah Khomeini. But there is no real evidence for concluding that Khomeini had a blueprint of any specific kind for this task. His role from the outset was that of supreme guide. Others could propose institutional structures and the personnel to man them. Khomeini would judge their appropriateness in terms of conformity to the divine plan for society. Lacking interest in the administrative process and having long been absent from Iran, knowing few individuals who could serve as government officials, Khomeini had few specific suggestions to make. Just how these choices were made remains something of a mystery. But the leading governmental authorities were chosen from among individuals who had played prominent and visible roles in the revolution.

Noticeable by their absence were representatives of the left. Neither the Mujahaddin nor the Fadayan were granted any real recognition for their significant contribution to the success of the revolution. Bazargan identifies the thirty leading government officials in terms of group affiliations. He lists 36.6 percent as Freedom Movement, 36.6 percent as National Front, 13.3 percent as Society of Islamic Engineers, and 13.3 percent as clerical members of the revolutionary council.[1] The latter served as assistant ministers of the most important cabinet departments.

There emerged, apparently naturally, alongside the government a set of revolutionary institutions. At the apex was a revolutionary council the membership of which was at the time kept secret. According to a list since published by Bazargan, there were in these early months seventeen members, eight of whom were prominent clerics. The other nine had a history of membership in or close association with the Freedom Movement.[2] The National Front was not represented. The apparent function of this council was to assure that the government operated in day-to-day concerns in accordance with the holy law. Because its membership was kept secret, there was uncertainty in Tehran as to how important the revolutionary council was. The tendency was to ascribe a far greater role to it than was in fact the case. On the surface, its composition would suggest that it would be at least as liberal as the cabinet. But in fact there was a built-in dynamic in the creation of the revolutionary council. It was composed of individuals several of whom were highly ambitious and who understood full well that only one man, Ayatullah Khomeini, had a significant constituency and that this constituency was truly massive. Since their position offered them access to Khomeini, direct or indirect, they had the potential to achieve great influence in the soon-to-emerge Islamic Republic. A struggle for control between Bazargan and his cabinet and some combinations of these individuals was inevitable.

Three institutions quickly emerged that would provide the basis for order in the new regime. The revolutionary organizations, decentralized as they had been around local mosques, were now formally institutionalized as *komitehs* which quickly took over the function of the local police and the local administration of justice. Inevitably the competence and the philosophy dominating local *komitehs* varied enormously and reflected the talents and thinking of local clerics as well as their bureaucratic and lay associates. Coordination in the short run was impossible; hence, security was functionally decentralized. In some jurisdictions brutality and arbitrariness of enforcement were characteristic features. In others there was a far greater concern with equity and fairness. Each one reflected the emerging power structure of the jurisdictional area.

Also appearing naturally from the organizations of youths who had been engaging in such acts as burning tires in the streets and disrupting communications and governmental routine were the *pasdaran* or revolutionary guards. One revolutionary leader described the composition of the revolutionary guard contingents he knew as 10 percent city thugs, 60 percent poor youths who needed a job, and 30 percent ideologically dedicated youth.[3] They were supplemented by bands of armed individuals, some representing the leftist organizations and others loosely described as *hezbollahi* or members of the Party of God. The *pasdaran* were at first a paramilitary force; contingents of them, occasionally as many as a few hundred, were assigned to particular revolutionary leaders. Later a military revolutionary guard, the *pasdaran sepah,* developed that increasingly paralleled the regular military forces.

There developed also revolutionary courts designed to secure the function of a judiciary, which was as best loosely coordinated and virtually independent of the cabinet. Some Islamic judges quickly achieved international notoriety for the lack of any due process in their trials of individuals who had served the shah, especially in his security forces.[4] Summary executions soon began to take place in an atmosphere of arbitrariness and lack of control. Mehdi Bazargan, the provisional prime minister, was powerless to do anything more than protest. One cleric, Sadeq Khalkhali, obviously relished his reputation as the "hanging judge." But he had many competitors. Among the several hundred executed were former Prime Minister Hoveida, former head of SAVAK Nasseri, his successor General Nasser Moqadam, and almost all of the leading military officers who remained in Iran.

The stage was now set for a major struggle for direction of the postrevolutionary government. Policy positions at first were not at all crystallized. The all-consuming objective had been to overthrow the hated dictatorship of the shah. The individuals involved had worked in substantial cooperation. Many of them were old friends whose common struggles, common sacrifices, and constantly shared dangers created strong bonds of cameraderie. All could agree that the succesor regime should abolish tyranny and restore the rule of law, eliminate corruption, reduce the income gap, advance social justice, end all subservience to the imperial powers, and accept the moral guidance of Ayatullah Khomeini. In the months before achieving power, this sounded more programmatic than it in fact was. Many of those who would soon fight for power had had little to do with politics or policy and held few concrete positions on any subject. Then sitting above them all was Ayatullah Khomeini, whose notions of governmental authority were ethereal.[5]

But almost immediately following the revolution it was apparent that a struggle for power would occur around this institutional duality. One set, the formal governmental institutions, were under the control of individuals who were best characterized, and self-characterized, as reformists. The other, the revolutionary institutions, were under the control of individuals who favored radical cultural and normative change. The implicit strategy of the first group, under Mehdi Bazargan and his governmental associates, was to return the government and the economy to normalcy as soon as possible. They had no major institutional changes to propose. They had stood for a return to the rule of law and this remained a primary objective. To achieve it, the government had to gain control over the revolutionary institutions as quickly as possible. Executions following trials marked by an absence of due process, the seizure of property, and acts of violence, especially against Bahais, had to be stopped. In its foreign policy Iran's sovereign equality had to be recognized and a policy of independence from any blocs established. But there was no thought of exporting the revolution. Bazargan and his foreign minister, Karim Sanjabi, favored a restoration of good relations with the shah's former friends, including the Soviet Union and the United States, but excluding Israel and South Africa.

There quickly appeared on the scene a second group of leaders who favored genuinely radical change. In their view, Bazargan and his associates were merely advocates, as the shah had been, of what Westerners meant by "modernization" and "development." They had in effect accepted—even welcomed—acculturation. What was called for now, said the revolutionary radicals, was nothing less than a return to an authentic Islamic value system. Liberal and national values, to which the Freedom Movement was so deeply attached, were aspects of a Western value system. The community this radical group was concerned with was the community of believers in Islam. Tolerance and freedom for the individual personality could be viewed only in the context of a holistic Islamic view of society. Admittedly, it would take much time and thought to translate an Islamic value system into concrete programs. There was, after all, no existing model to refer to. But in the meantime, the price for true change must be paid. Programs could not be left in the hands of those who had accepted Western values, and Bazargan's drive for normalcy was designed to do just that. Such individuals must be purged from positions of authority, from education, and from communications. The revolutionary institutions for preserving law and order would have a major function to perform for many months to come. Inevitably there would be acts of arbitrariness, brutality, and injustice. But because these are contrary to Islam, this extraordinary revolution would be, in comparison with other great revolutions, remarkably free of such crimes.

This radical line was advanced particularly by young clerics and theological students. But the line was actually a purist version of what many of the clerical leaders of the revolution believed. They were therefore attracted to it, and not just incidentally, because advancing it would serve their interests: a drive for power of some exceptionally ambitious individuals. The polarization process was under way.

From the beginning the revolutionaries had a major advantage over the reformists: Ayatullah Khomeini was fully in accord with their basic objectives. "The rule of law," an objective so dear to Bazargan and his associates, had no meaning for Khomeini. Such a concept was grounded entirely in the individualistic liberalism of another tradition and had no place in the divinely ordained order as Khomeini interpreted it.

Iranians in exile draw a common interpretation of Khomeini's leadership. They share a view that Khomeini intended from the beginning to isolate, purge, and ultimately destroy reformist leaders such as Bazargan who saw Islamic values as embracing tolerance and respect for the dignity of the individual personality. In this view, the two-and-a-half-year alliance of the Khomeini regime and such Islamic liberals as Bazargan, Yazdi, and Bani Sadr was purely tactical in intent. The ultimate objective was to isolate and destroy them.

The problem with this interpretation is that Khomeini had little need after the triumph of the revolution for an alliance with religious liberals. He, not they, was the object of massive public support. What they had to offer was experience in government and technical competence. For the genuine revolutionary, these counted for little. The intent of the revolutionaries was nothing less than fundamental cultural change, a true cultural revolution. The devil theory of Khomeini, so appealing to so many exiled Iranians, is premised on the assumptions that the new regime was born in a polarized situation and that Khomeini, far from being essentially a disinterested observer of factional politics and specific policy conflict, viewed the situation in all its concreteness. To those holding the devil image, Khomeini was a tactician of inordinate brilliance, capable of orchestrating complex maneuvers involving hundreds of actors and occurring over many months and even years.

But the weight of evidence is that the process of polarization, although clearly under way before the revolution was an accomplished fact, did not fully crystallize for many months and does not appear to have been the product of anyone's conscious manipulation. Bazargan's association with radical clerics such as Beheshti, Rafsenjani, Montezari, and Khamenei, who would become preeminent at the revolutionary pole, was of long duration; sometimes they were in close collaboration. They had been allies in a consuming struggle to overturn the ancient regime. Programmatic conflict that occurred after the revolution eventually revealed the breadth of the philosophical chasm separating them. But this was a slow process and the two groups were more frequently than not in agreement concerning important policy objectives, especially those related to establishing the authority of a new regime.

Bazargan's published accounts of the period, and Oriana Fallaci's interviews of him confirm the picture of Khomeini that had early begun to take shape — as a man with only an abstract grasp of politics and one neither interested in nor informed about lower-level concerns.[6] Such a view of Khomeini would encourage hopes that the reformists' ideals for Iran could be achieved. During the revolution and for years to come, Khomeini gave every indication that he fully accepted Bazargan as a true and devoted Moslem who wished to see Islamic values prevail. Since this was Bazargan's self-conception as well, he, as prime minister, couched his arguments for his policy preferences in terms that would appeal to Khomeini. Given Khomeini's respect and affection for Bazargan, the more revolutionary-minded clerics with access to Khomeini would have been ill-advised to counter Bazargan with ad hominem attacks. Nevertheless, the revolutionaries had a clear advantage since their view of the desired direction of change was far closer to Khomeini's than was Bazargan's. The focus of the policy conflict came to be Bazargan's desire to gain institutional control over judicial procedures and the exercise of authority at the national and local levels. Bazargan's views in these matters sometimes prevailed, but the trend over the course of a year was clearly in the revolutionary direction.

In his struggle to prevent the development of a radical clerical dictatorship in Iran, Bazargan received little support from secular liberals. Over a third of his cabinet was drawn from this group and Bazargan made every effort to maintain his close alliance with them. But from the beginning a significant percentage of this group refused to recognize the weakness of their position. They viewed with deep alarm the prospects of clerical rule and believed that it could be prevented by taking forceful action. To them Bazargan was allowing himself to become Khomeini's Hoveida, a prime minister shorn of all dignity, abjectly executing his master's every order. In retrospect they saw Shapur Bakhtiar as a heroic and prescient figure who had understood early that, as bad as the royal dictatorship had been, a Khomeini dictatorship would be infinitely worse. One of Musaddiq's grandsons, Hedayatullah Matin-Daftari, an energetic opponent of the shah, exemplified this group. He was instrumental in forming the National Democratic Front, which quickly moved into open opposition to the regime.

The effect of defections from this element seriously damaged the prospects for success of the reformist section of the regime. The rhythm of the revolution had granted the revolutionary section an enormous advantage. Since the element of the mass public that first joined the revolutionary process was the religious urban lower and lower-middle classes who had only recently begun to participate politically, revolutionary-minded clerics were in position to provide the initial organizational basis for mobilizing mass support. As the revolution progressed, an organizational dichotomy had developed. Its central leadership was dominated by reformist liberals, secular and religious, and the mass organization was dominated by the revolutionary clergy.

The liberals' natural base of support was that large and important section of the population described in the previous chapters as the accommodators. In the final six months before the revolution, this element joined the revolution in great numbers, and the strikes and governmental slowdowns they initiated were critical for the success of the revolution. But like the religious and secular left, they in effect acknowledged Khomeini's leadership and cooperated with the existing largely mosque-based revolutionary organization. After the revolution, this organization became the basis for new revolutionary institutions. But there was no place in these institutions for either the leftists or the former accommodators. Since the formal government established on a provisional basis was overwhelmingly liberal in composition, presumably it had the potential for serving as a rallying point, possibly even as a core organizational base. However, it failed completely to play this role.

Ayatullah Beheshti turned his attention soon after the revolution to forming a supporting party for the revolutionary-minded, the Islamic Republic party. Logic would argue that, if the revolutionaries had a party through which popular support could be mobilized, so should the reformists. Indeed, a National Front–Freedom Movement coalition with the full legitimizing force of their dedication to Musaddiq's path would seem to be an ideal vehicle for the reformist purpose. Dariush Foruhar, a minister in Bazargan's cabinet and once the leader of the Pan-Iran party, led the kind of party that could have furnished a vehicle for the reformists, the Mellat party. Its appeal was national and religious, social democratic and liberal. It accepted Khomeini's leadership but was in the reformist mold. Foruhar had an established base of support and thus a ready-made constituency for his party. But it did not attract support beyond that constituency. The liberal and secular element of the public very quickly rejected the leadership of the reformists. Karim Sanjabi, the foreign minister and the most prominent of National Front leaders, fared particularly badly. He was excoriated by former colleagues and, far more seriously, by spokesmen for the element of the population the National Front had to attract in order to play a significant role in politics. Bazargan was treated with more generosity by members of the Freedom Movement, but fairly quickly the reputation and appeal of the Freedom Movement began to fade.

The dilemma of Bazargan, Sanjabi, and other liberals in the provisional government was ultimately insoluble. Recognizing as they did the enormous bargaining advantage of Khomeini's massive popular appeal, the liberal leaders understood the impossibility of emerging victorious in any open conflict with the charismatic leader. In order to prevail, they had to maintain their close relations with Khomeini and to convince him to grant their demand for governmental control of the revolutionary institutions. This meant they must accept policies that Khomeini directly sanctioned even though those policies, in some important cases, would be anathema to them. But since Khomeini was involved only occasionally in decision making and since reformist-revolutionary polarization was not yet irrevocable, they could and often did prevail in important decisions. To continue to do so, however, they had to attract a large and supportive constituency. That natural constituency was the professional and progressive commercial communities. The prospects for success were reasonably good. Unfortunately, however, some of the early policies that Khomeini clearly sanctioned made attracting this constituency impossibly difficult. Bazargan, Sanjabi, and the others had focused their attacks on the shah for his failure to abide by the rule of law. Yet only a few days after the success of the revolution, trials were being held of former government officials that violated that very rule of law. The treatment of General Nematollah Nasseri, for example, probably the most feared and hated of the shah's lieutenants, was so grossly unfair that it generated a wave of sympathy for Nasseri and a shocked revulsion toward the regime. As executions extended to such inoffensive individuals as former Foreign Minister Abbas Khalatbari, disgust toward the new regime deepened. Policy toward women, as it began to take shape, appeared to be a direct assault on women's rights — one that would lead to a status for women even worse than that of traditional Iran. And for Bazargan's and Sanjabi's constituencies, this policy was as negative symbolically as was the disregard of due process. Within these constituencies there emerged a view that Iran was already in the grip of an utterly intolerant theocracy. The contention of liberals in government that this process could be reversed appeared not only naive but pathetically weak. This formerly accommodating element of the country had been oblivious to the emergence of a huge mass public insisting on the right to political participation. Now, when enormous demonstrations made impossible a continued denial of the fact of mass politics in Iran, they persisted in viewing the newly participant masses with contempt. Implicitly they agreed with Bakhtiar in seeing a rabble that could easily be controlled by strong leaders who had the courage and determination to do so.

The decay in the political fortunes of the liberals was hence almost impossible to avoid. Believing as they did that access to Khomeini was the sine qua non for success for their strategy, Bazargan and his cabinet made frequent trips to Khomeini's residence in the religious center of Qom, ninety miles south of Tehran. They did have some success; Khomeini was prevailed on to make periodic calls for the unity of revolutionary forces—which meant, in effect, that Bazargan should be supported and the drift toward polarization halted. But in the crucial matter of gaining control over revolutionary institutions, Bazargan and his cohorts were unsuccessful. Thus the policies their constituencies found so appalling from revolutionary courts and *komiteh*s continued. Because a purge of secularists gained momentum in all aspects of society and government, more and more Iranians of this persuasion left Iran. As their potential constituency moved into sullen opposition or left the country, the liberal reformists inside the government suffered a steady decline in their bargaining position. To compete with the revolutionary clerics at the local level, the reformists had to be able to make obvious their support in the form of impressively large public demonstrations opposing the arbitrariness of the courts and the *komitehs*. The demonstrations that did occur, such as those denouncing the treatment of women, were clearly antiregime and hence more damaging than helpful to Bazargan. Within six months, Bazargan was in the humiliating position of being totally dependent on Khomeini's beneficence for his continuation in office.

The three men who had been closely associated with Khomeini in Paris—Ibrahim Yazdi, Sadeq Qotbzadeh and Abul Hassan Bani Sadr—played an important, possibly critical, role in this disintegrative process. The three understood Khomeini's enormous charismatic attraction. They also saw in Khomeini's abstractness and lack of programmatic direction a great potential for their personal manipulation of his appeal. But they saw more clearly than did Bazargan, and possibly even such clerical leaders as Beheshti, how strongly revolutionary Khomeini's thinking ultimately was. Their strategy was to present the appearance of being highly revolutionary, and thereby to retain Khomeini's confidence, but to carry out policies that were far more pragmatic. Having spent their entire lives in pursuit of the revolution, they held those who had accommodated themselves to the shah's rule in some contempt. Therefore they saw only one vital requirement for achieving personal power: Khomeini's favor. None of the three saw, as Beheshti did, the need for constructing an organizational base of support. Indeed, within a few weeks of the success of the revolution, the three became a focus of intense dislike within their natural constituency, the liberal reformists.

As deputy prime minister after the revolution, Yazdi affected a new and revolutionary demeanor. Qotbzadeh, in control of radio and television, proved to be a master of revolutionary rhetoric and seemed to revel in his task of manipulating mass opinion. Bani Sadr moved most directly toward achieving personal power by establishing literally hundreds of alliances with leaders of local *komiteh*s, an activity that would result in his winning the first presidential election in 1980. The activities of the three were thus entirely counterproductive to the purpose of attracting a major constituency to Bazargan. None of the three appeared to be interested in strengthening Bazargan in his increasingly desperate struggle to retain power. In fact, on occasion Bani Sadr directly weakened him. Yazdi became foreign minister when the frustrated and heartsick Sanjabi resigned, and from that time on did what he could to strengthen the Bazargan government. The other two and especially Bani Sadr, however, contributed to its collapse in November 1979.

Illustrative of both the situation and the potential for success that men such as Bazargan perceived in it was the sequence of draft constitutions proposed for the Islamic Republic. The first draft constitution was in tune with the liberal-reformist thinking of the Freedom Movement. In expression it was heavily Islamic. But it was a liberal constitution with safeguards for individual freedom. Separation of powers was accepted and the government it outlined was a parliamentary democracy. There would be an Islamic institution to review legislation to ensure its conformity to the holy law. The constitution of 1906 had provided for such an institution, a board of *ulema,* but it was never really implemented. The new institution surely, in the atmosphere of 1979, would not have been ignored. But what was remarkable about this first draft was that the constitutional powers granted the *ulema* were not broad. There was in addition no obvious role for Khomeini; yet he was willing to endorse it and to submit it for popular approval. It was opposed, however, from two fronts: a by now vehemently revolutionary group of clerics, the secular liberals, and the secular left. Had the latter two groups been willing to accept the Islamic veneer of the document, there was a real possibility the Islamic Republic would have had a constitution that conformed to liberal democratic norms. But instead, because of strong criticism, an election was held for a constituent assembly, although it was clearly predictable that the election would be won by the radical fundamentalists.[7] The constitution that emerged from the assembly was entirely different. Its most important provision was for the formation of the *vilayet e faqih,* an institution ready-made for Khomeini, who was designated its first occupant as *faqih.* But his successor could be a plurality of learned clergy. The occupant of the position was given powers of appointment and dismissal of officials that added up to what could be the most powerful institution in constitutional history and the basis for absolute dictatorship if the occupant of the office, the *faqih,* chose so to interpret it.

The left, of course, favored change at a revolutionary rate. But, exactly parallel to the liberal reformists, they quickly polarized into two camps based on their diagnoses of the Khomeini phenomenon. The Tudeh party, under the leadership of the brilliant Dr. Nuraddin Kianuri, accepted a view of Khomeini that was remarkably close to that of Bazargan.[8] Kianuri too saw Khomeini's charismatic appeal as the central fact of the revolution and the basis for an overwhelmingly strong bargaining position. His speeches reflect as well an assessment of Khomeini as irremediably nonprogrammatic and hence manipulable. With this view it follows that access to Khomeini would be the key to success. If this hurdle could be crossed, the prospects for the pro-Soviet Marxist left, even in the short run, could be good. Obviously they would have to conceal both the Marxist view of religion and their close relationship with one of the two great oppressor states—the Soviet Union. But there was much in Khomeini's social philosophy that paralleled theirs. His views on social justice, egalitarianism, materialism, and many aspects of capitalism were easily reconciled with those of the Marxists. So were his notions that individual self-realization could only be achieved within a just society. Clerical followers of Khomeini and others who placed a high value on a society based on this image of social justice could be the allies and the channel of access for the Tudeh. Kianuri, in addition, and fortuitously, had a considerable personal advantage in being a direct decendant of Sheikh Fazlullah Nuri, whose views Khomeini deeply respected.

Kianuri's strategy, like that of Bazargan, called for resisting the strong trend toward clerical authoritarianism. Success for the Tudeh required freedom to maneuver while establishing close ties with regime leaders who had similar programmatic preferences. The first draft constitution was fully acceptable to Kianuri. He saw its early approval by Khomeini as confirming his view that Khomeini lacked any concrete model for a clerical dictatorship.[9] In this regard he was the natural ally of Bazargan. But Kianuri welcomed the steadily progressing purge of those who had accommodated themselves to the shah's rule, Bazargan's natural constituency. Indeed, he early concluded that liberal reformists like Bazargan, Yazdi, Qotbzadeh, and Mustafa Chamran were his enemies, since their objective really was to preserve the old elite structure of Iran. The clandestine National Voice of Iran, broadcasting from Baku and always an excellent reflection of Tudeh thinking, consistently pinpointed these individuals as traitorous members of a CIA conspiracy to subvert the revolution.[10] However, by opposing Bazargan, the only regime leader with any hope of reversing the trend toward clerical dictatorship, Kianuri was caught in what proved to be a fatal dilemma. His allies among the clergy were too few and too weak to protect the Tudeh once that last remnant of liberalism was eliminated.

Kianuri also paid a price similar to that of Bazargan by associating the Tudeh party so closely with Khomeini's regime. The appeal of the Tudeh had for years been badly muted by virtue of the good relations its external ally and mentor, the Soviet Union, maintained with the shah. The Tudeh's natural constituency, therefore, had turned overwhelmingly to the anti-Soviet left, in particular to the Fadayan. But those who remained were individuals prepared to accept party discipline and who were generally politically sophisticated. By associating the Tudeh with a regime that increasingly reflected the views of a clerical elite who were anathema to the secular left, Kianuri accepted the price of failing to broaden the Tudeh's mass base of support. But the logic of his position was strong and compelling, and apparently acceptable to his colleagues. Kianuri was seeking to associate the Tudeh party, whose name is translated as the Masses party, with a tremendous mass movement. In the long run, with the inevitable failure of clerical leadership, this could be the means for attracting to the Tudeh its long-sought mass base of support.

The role of the Soviet Union in all this can only be deduced. For those who see an aggressive Soviet Union that orchestrates the policies of its local instruments, of which the Tudeh party is the major one in Iran, this adds up to a strategy of infiltration with the ultimate objective of a subversive takeover. This was the conclusion of liberal reformists and of conservative clergy within the regime and of almost the entire nonleft opposition in Iran. Conservative Iranian exiles were inclined to accept the conclusion that the infiltration had been successful to the point of giving the Tudeh functional control of the government.[11] They persisted in this view even after 1983 when the regime cracked down on the Tudeh.

However, Soviet policy toward Iran has generally been clumsy, heavy-handed, ill-informed, and inconsistent. A counter view therefore would be that Kianuri's strategy, subtle and sophisticated as it was, had been acceptable to the Soviet Union but not suggested by it. More recognizable as obviously Soviet-inspired was the defense of the invasion and occupation of Afghanistan in Tudeh outlets.[12] Since that Soviet policy was almost universally unpopular among Iranians, defending it could only hurt the Tudeh and surely was damaging to Kianuri's strategy.

The anti-Soviet left in Iran at the time of the revolution had one great advantage over the liberal reformists. Its various components had disciplined organizations that could serve as cores around which a broader mass base could be attracted. The two major organizations, the Fadayan and the Mujahaddin, took advantage of the disintegration of the military to gather a supply of arms that would put them in a good position to compete for power. Both they and the Tudeh had in the final months of the shah's regime cooperated fully with the mosque-based revolutionary organizations, although the religious leaders were not always aware of the extent of the left's involvement. After the revolution the Fadayan and the Mujahaddin moved quickly to rally their natural constituencies, which were to be found primarily among well-educated and revolutionary-minded youths. Both, the Fadayan in particular, were active within ethnic groups that hoped to gain a good measure of autonomy in Iran. Their influence among the Turkomen, the Kurds, Arabs, and Baluchis was noticeable.[13] But in the Farsi-speaking areas and in Azerbaijan, like the Tudeh and the liberal reformists, the Mujahaddin and the Fadayan had to deal with the fact of Khomeini's enormous appeal. Like the Tudeh, they were anxious to retain their freedom to maneuver and also were fully in harmony with the ongoing purge of former government officials and educators who had accommodated themselves to the shah's rule. But, like the liberal-reformists, their constituencies were increasingly appalled at the movement toward a clerical dictatorship. Almost from the beginning, therefore, they faced the same terrible dilemma that Bazargan could not surmount.

The Mujahaddin apparently settled on their overall strategy early and easily. They would support and encourage the purging process and the efforts to incorporate Islamic values as governing norms, but they would resist any drift toward a dictatorship of the *mullah*s. Their organization had been badly mauled by SAVAK, but it had survived and was fully capable of mobilizing support for their program. They had attracted a significant percentage of intellectually talented youth and were in a good position to compete with revolutionary clerics for the best-informed and most activist of religious young people. Masud Rajavi, their leader, emerged within a year as possibly the revolutionary leader with the greatest popularity not derived from association with Khomeini. However, the Mujahaddin could not compete with Khomeini in terms of appeal to the large urban lower and lower-middle classes. Relations with the Khomeini regime steadily deteriorated, until by 1981 the contest had reached the level of violence.

The third of the important leftist organizations, the Fadayan, was literally torn apart by the question of the appropriate tactics to be followed. Initially their tactics seemed to resemble those of the Mujahaddin. Like the Mujahaddin, they had been a primary negative target of SAVAK and had suffered badly in the ensuing struggle. But also like the Mujahaddin, they retained a sufficient organizational base to make a major campaign to attract their constituency—for them, activist and well-educated secular youth. As the trends toward authoritarian control under a clerical leadership gathered strength, Fadayan leaders became painfully aware of their dilemma. To be optimally attractive to their constituents, they had to oppose openly and vigorously the imposition of the Islamic norms their constituents found suffocating — in particular those relating to the treatment of women. But if they moved into direct opposition, they would be in effect cutting themselves off from the revolutionary mass which was looking so uncritically and adoringly to Khomeini.

A split eventually developed, with a majority of leaders choosing to adopt essentially the Kianuri strategy. A minority opted to follow the confrontational tactics of the Mujahaddin. However, the terms "majority" and "minority" are misleading. The probability is that the majority of the Fadayan constituency followed the "minority" position. But the overall effect of the split was to diminish substantially the influence of the Fadayan among the revolutionary left. Presumably, though, that large element of Iranian youth that was secular and viewed favorably the purge of accommodators from governmental positions still remains receptive to the appeal of the Fadayan, which may well prove to be, therefore, a major factor in future Iranian developments.

The only major national party that emerged to compete with the Islamic Republic party for the support of the religious urban masses was the Moslem Peoples Republican party, which looked for inspiration to Ayatullah Kazem Shariatmaderi, one of the five great *ayatullah*s. The party began with many disadvantages. It would compete with, rather than incorporate, part of the great mosque-based organization that managed the revolutionary demonstrations. That organization was fully incorporated into the Islamic Republic party. Then Shariatmaderi had been more than a little equivocal about the revolution and lacked the strong, uncompromising, and utterly courageous image of Khomeini. He was unconcerned with organizational matters and had few of the instincts of a politician outside the theological community. In addition, he was from Azerbaijan and was far better known and more popular among Azerbaijanis than he was with the remainder of the populace. Rahmatollah Moqadam Maragheii, a member of an old Azerbaijani family and a popular political figure especially in Azerbaijan, gave the Moslem Peoples Republican party some badly needed organizational and strategic-tactical advice. But Moqadam Maragheii's Radical Movement remained an independent political force on the periphery of the regime. Moqadam Maragheii was elected to the constituent assembly from Azerbaijan, clearly with the blessing of the Shariatmaderi organization, and became the one really strong opponent of the article of the constitution that provided a major role for Khomeini, the *vilayet e faqih*.

Although poorly organized and largely regional in appeal, the Moslem Peoples' Republican party seemed to Khomeini and his lieutenants their most serious threat. That it should become a focus of the regime's enmity was only to be expected. Otherworldly and unconcerned with detail though he may have been, Khomeini, like any other of the great *ayatullah*s, had engaged in an esoteric political game to achieve his eminent position. He and the other important Islamic teachers attracted around themselves student followers whose personal achievement in the religious world depended heavily on the success of their mentor. Khomeini thus understood well the game of politics fought largely among coalitions of followers of great mentors. The Moslem Peoples' Republican party to him was easily recognizable as a continuance of Khomeini's personal struggle with Shariatmaderi. In late 1979 and 1980, the party's leaders and Moqadam Maragheii were forced to flee Iran.

The last major political force in Iran was the Democratic party of Kurdistan, an umbrella Kurdish party whose most prominent leaders were Abdul Rahman Qassemlu and Ezzedin Hosseini. The coalition members of the party included Marxist sections that were allied with the Tudeh, the Fadayan, and the Mujahaddin. Initially, revolutionary leaders had assured the Kurds of significant autonomy within revolutionary Iran. But suspicions developed that the party was really an instrument in a plot to play on Sunni-Shia differences. Khomeini, who had minimal sensitivity to nationalistic attitudes, saw the Kurdish movement very much in these terms. He therefore reinforced such men as Ayatullah Sadeq Khalkhali who were determined to suppress the Kurdish movement.[14] By late 1979 it was already clear that the Kurds, the Mujahaddin, and the minority Fadayan would be part of an antiregime political alliance.

## The American Adjustment

In February 1979 a group of youths took over the U.S. embassy in Tehran and briefly made prisoners of Ambassador William Sullivan and his staff. This act symbolized strikingly the collapse of American influence in Iran. General Huyser only a few days earlier had left Iran, still with the option of engineering a military coup figuratively in his pocket. Deputy Prime Minister Yazdi and others, such as Ayatullah Mohammad Beheshti, moved quickly to secure the release of the embassy personnel. But the United States had been placed on notice that the revolution would not tolerate and had the means to prevent any effort to overturn the Khomeini regime.

Thus the takeover symbolized as well the persistence of the illusion of American power in Iran. The CIA had, after all, orchestrated the overturn of another enormously popular Iranian a generation earlier. The new regime had to move quickly, it felt, to preclude any attempt by the CIA and SAVAK to restore the old regime. This was one rationale for the revolutionary courts that moved so quickly to execute past participants in the conspiracy they saw.[15]

But U.S. policy between the two embassy takeovers of 1979 was premised on the assumption that the emerging Islamic Republic was an established fact. Whatever suspicions there had been from Brzezinski and others that the revolution was at least to some degree Soviet-orchestrated now had largely evaporated. The United States may have lost a major regional ally, but the Soviet Union was not yet, at least, a beneficiary. The Department of State clearly was prepared to establish correct formal relations with the new regime. Embassy dispatches published by Iranians who took over the embassy in November 1979 paint a clear picture of diplomatic caution and good political reporting. That reporting indicated an understanding of developing trends in Iran that were deleterious to Bazargan and favorable to the revolutionary clerical leaders. They do not suggest any real sense that American policy could seriously affect this trend.

Nevertheless, the case can easily be made that American policy in this nine-month period was implicitly favorable to Bazargan and his cabinet. Evidence of American hostility and any hint of an inclination to think in terms of a coup would have confirmed the expectations of the revolutionaries, both secular and religious. The lack of overt evidence to this effect obviously did not prove those who expected a CIA move were wrong. But it did make arguing the case somewhat more difficult. Charges, particularly from Tudeh outlets, that the liberal-reformists were playing an American role were only to be expected. Embassy officers clearly understood that, and did nothing that could give substance to the charges.

Bazargan's strategy called for the rapid restoration of the health of the economy and the reestablishment of law and order through governmental, not ad hoc revolutionary, agencies. American policy was to encourage the rebuilding of Iranian-American commercial in-

terchanges and a return of U.S. corporations to Iran. But this coinci-
dence of strategies was never commented on. American officials from
time to time did lament the executions in Iran, but in a pro-forma
manner and never with a reference to the internal struggle for power.

The best indication of the direction of American thinking came
from the choice of an ambassador-designate to replace Ambassador
Sullivan. Sullivan's own appointment in 1977 had symbolized to Iranians a continuing policy of full support for the shah. The man chosen
in 1979, Robert Cutler, was a career officer not identified with any
ideological or policy proclivities. His appointment therefore should
have signaled the United States' acceptance of exactly what the Iranians had said they wanted: relationships based on full sovereign
equality. There had been some support for appointing William G.
Miller, a former foreign service officer who had served in Iran and
was well known to many members of the new regime for his empathetic abilities. But his acquaintances were drawn more from the
liberal-reformist group than from among the revolutionaries, and
therefore his appointment could have plausibly been interpreted as
an effort to reinforce Bazargan. In any event, the Cutler choice seemed
to be acceptable to Tehran.

American public opinion regarding Iran resembled very little the
official U.S. reaction. The public found events in Iran fascinating,
exotic, and—especially regarding the highly publicized executions
—appalling. U.S. television viewers could expect an execution body
count as part of their evening news routine much as the Vietnam
body count had been a decade earlier. Journalistic accounts focused
on the bizarre and excessive. Only rarely did an article discuss the
historic struggle among competing political philosophies in Iran.

In May 1979, as Robert Cutler was being briefed for his term as
ambassador, an Iranian court sentenced Habib Elghanian to death
for corruption and for having served as an Israeli agent. Elghanian
was a wealthy Jewish merchant who had been arrested on charges
of corruption by the shah's regime. From the Iranian point of view,
his execution was in no way exceptional. Elghanian had entertained
Israeli officials and had made frequent trips to Israel. The regime's
policy toward Jews had been explicated by Khomeini: as "people of
the book," those who, like the Moslems, accepted the canons of the
Old Testament, they were to receive the full protection of the Islamic Republic. But tolerance did not extend to political activities,

and Zionism was classified as proscribed political activity. The Jewish community of Iran therefore was vulnerable, and both Israelis and the world Jewish community were nervous about its fate. Thus when Elghanian was executed, a resolution was introduced into and easily passed in the United States Senate condemning Iran.[16]

The Department of State did its best to dissuade the Senate from acting on the resolution, arguing that the impact on Iran would be the opposite of that intended. But there was little more understanding of Iran in the Senate than among the public at large. The resolution was taken in Iran, as the Department of State knew it would be, as proof of a continuing Zionist-imperialist alliance and of American determination to persist, after the revolution as before, in interfering in Iran's affairs. Bazargan's and Foreign Minister Yazdi's efforts to normalize relations with the United States received a lethal setback. The Iranian government issued a fiercely worded protest and declared it would not receive the ambassador-designate. Thus the U.S. government was denied the opportunity to send an ambassador to Iran whose task would have been to begin the long process of bringing a better perspective to Iranian-American relations. And the United States' quietly correct efforts to normalize relations, with the possibility of reinforcing Bazargan and his colleagues, were largely counterbalanced. It of course can never be known if sending an ambassador to Iran could have made a difference in U.S.-Iranian relations. Establishing rapport with Khomeini in the short term was surely not possible, but some progress could have been made in combating the stereotypical view of the United States held by some influential religio-political figures.

However, as the Elghanian case well illustrated, the exaggerated opinions of Iranians regarding U.S. power in Iran had their exact parallel among Americans at home. The irony was exquisite. The Senate believed its resolution might carry such an impact as to reverse an Iranian policy of executing Iranians imagined to be agents of an all-powerful Zionist-American imperialism. Similarly misguided was Brzezinski's blithe assumption that even at a moment of extreme duress the United States could order and execute a coup in Iran. So was the view of Carter's critics that he could easily have saved the shah of Iran from the fate that befell him. So obvious is the point to those holding this view of American power even today that it does not occur to them to address the question of just how the shah could have been saved through American auspices or how a coup could have been executed.

## The Hostage Crisis

The above point is important if the context of the Carter administration's decision to admit the shah to the United States for medical treatment is to be understood. Individuals such as Henry Kissinger and David Rockefeller were among those who simply assumed the shah could have been kept on his throne. Kissinger's anger and distress at his fall, the "immorality" of the U.S. failure to keep the shah in power, is made abundantly clear in his memoirs. It follows that for Kissinger and Rockefeller, when it finally became known that the shah was suffering from cancer and wanted to be treated in the United States, to deny him access to the best facilities the United States had to offer would be to compound the injury inflicted on this true friend and ally. Jimmy Carter, with polls showing him at an all-time low in public favor, really had little choice but to grant this request. The embassy in Tehran opposed the decision and warned of a possible takeover of the embassy by hostile forces. But Bazargan and Yazdi promised to do all they could to protect the embassy and other American offices should Carter take this ill-advised action.[17]

On November 1, 1979, a week after the shah entered a New York hospital, Bazargan and Yazdi met National Security Adviser Brzezinski in Algiers. The meeting was amicable and Brzezinski indicated, according to Bazargan, that Ayatullah Khomeini was viewed favorably by the American public. His determination to keep Iran out of the communist grasp made him a positive factor in this critical Soviet-American battleground. But this meeting alarmed the more revolutionary elements in Khomeini's entourage who saw it as a manifestation of a U.S. resolve to return to a position of influence in Iran.

On November 4, 1979, the embassy for a second time was overrun. But this time the young people involved in the takeover were militant supporters of Khomeini, calling themselves the "Followers of the Line of the Imam." Still, the seriousness of the takeover was not apparent to top governmental and revolutionary council leaders. Ayatullah Beheshti, the organizational genius of the revolution, remarked that the Americans would be released in twenty-four hours.[18] But instead within hours Ahmad Khomeini, the son of Ayatullah Khomeini, held a news conference to announce his father's support of the takeover. One of the strangest episodes in the annals of diplomacy had begun.

On the surface, there was a somewhat plausible explanation for Khomeini's actions. The shah's arrival in the United States was part of a larger pattern. Much of the royal family and the entourage of the court now was in the United States; so were a large number of leading officials of the royal dictatorship. Add to this the efforts of the American government to normalize relations with Iran, culminating in the Brzezinski-Bazargan meeting. In sum, it could have been seen as an American bid for preeminence in Iran. Taking hostage American diplomats could signal to Washington Iran's awareness of the United States' none-too-subtle efforts to restore its lost position in Iran. Returning by reestablishing good relations with Bazargan was one path. A restoration of the monarchy was another, and far more adventurous path.

However, Khomeini's speeches and his remarks to confidants such as Sadeq Qotbzadeh suggest the explanation for Khomeini's behavior was much different and more in tune with the abstract quality of Khomeini's thinking.[19] As I have described earlier, Khomeini's explanation of the reason for his selection as the God-ordained leader of Iran and Islam was that his determination to make evident the declining power of oppressor states and the ascending power of the oppressed was in harmony with divine will. The United States government had suffered one great shock in being unable to maintain the shah on his throne. But in Khomeini's view a series of shocks would be necessary before the American oppressor and the oppressed people of Iran would understand that a fundamental power shift had occurred. Khomeini had given a strong speech attacking the United States' arrogance in offending the Islamic Republic by receiving the shah ostensibly for reasons of health. When he heard that his young followers, partly in response to his speech, had overrun the American embassy and had taken embassy personnel hostage, he concluded that their action was in harmony with divine intent and therefore should be endorsed. He told Qotbzadeh that the Americans would be kept hostage until the full lesson in terms of power realities had been learned. At that point, the hostages would serve no further purpose and hence could be released. According to Qotbzadeh, he understood very well that Jimmy Carter could not extradite the shah to

Iran as demanded and therefore that this was not a real condition for the release of the hostages.

The seizure of the hostages thus was, given Khomeini's world view, a rational act. But even his closest lieutenants found Khomeini's stand bewildering and some, such as Prime Minister Bazargan, found it mortifying.[20] Bazargan resigned and with his resignation the effort to bring revolutionary institutions under the control of the cabinet collapsed. Now the Revolutionary Council was in effect a collective executive. Bazargan remained a member of that council, but the focal point of governmental power shifted away from the Freedom Movement and toward the more revolutionary-minded. For the next several months, the primary personal beneficiaries of the shift were Sadeq Qotbzadeh and Abul Hassan Bani Sadr. Neither man had a significant personal constituency in Iran independent of Khomeini. Their moment of great importance apparently came entirely as the consequence of Khomeini's trust, respect, and affection for them. Those who accept a devil theory of Khomeini, and within two years Bani Sadr would be among those who did,[21] saw Khomeini as having followed a devious and infinitely clever strategy of destroying the individuals and groups that stood in the path of his insatiable drive for absolute power. Bani Sadr was to receive 76 percent of the vote for president in January 1980; in his view this proved that he was personally popular—perhaps even more so than Khomeini—and therefore Khomeini saw him as a major threat. But there is every reason to believe that in fact Bani Sadr's popularity was a derivative of Khomeini's charismatic appeal and that he could not have won the presidency had it not been for a widely perceived notion that Bani Sadr was the officially favored candidate.[22]

If Khomeini's own entourage found his behavior bewildering, the reaction of the American government and people to this studied affront to U.S. national dignity was one of bafflement mixed with outrage. Yet the American policy response did in fact conform to Khomeini's expectations, based on his assumption of American powerlessness. Just what could the United States do to compel an Iranian government, led by a man who honored martyrdom, to release the imprisoned Americans? During the first phase of the crisis, from the takeover until the Soviet occupation of Afghanistan, the policy adopted was to punish Iran by all means short of violence. Assets were frozen, purchases of oil and other commercial transactions were halted, and serious restrictions were placed on Iranians, many of them vigorous opponents of the regime, living in the United States. Actions such as a blockade of Iranian commerce in the Persian Gulf and selected bombing of Iran were considered and rejected. Relations with the Soviet Union were deteriorating, and the Carter administration did not wish to take actions that would push Iran toward the Soviets.[23] Nor was there any desire to offend the Islamic world by taking precipitous and forceful measures against Iran. Such actions could result in a weakening of friendly governments because of a still strong sympathy for what Khomeini wanted to do. Iran's bargaining position was a strong one.

After Soviet forces moved into Afghanistan and after the Iranian government made clear its complete abhorrence of that act,[24] the absurdity of the hostage crisis became even more apparent to the administration. Why, given the emphatic denunciation of the Soviet action in Afghanistan, should a crisis that appeared to have its roots in a long-past period in Iranian-American relations prevent a coordination of Iranian and American opposition to the Soviet Union? Sadeq Qotbzadeh, now Iran's foreign minister, communicated to Washington his view that the hostage crisis indeed was terribly damaging to Iran both internally and in its international aspirations. He indicated further that he believed a formula could be found for resolving the crisis in a reasonably short period of time. The Carter administration, lacking any clear ideas of how to resolve the crisis, decided to go along. From January until April 1980, the administration essentially followed Qotbzadeh's strategy — a strategy, it is now clear, the administration never fully understood.[25] For three months the United States government caught up in a serious dispute with the government of Iran, followed a strategy that was devised by Khomeini's foreign minister and whose primary target was Khomeini, the charismatic leader of Iran. Qotbzadeh wanted to demonstrate to Khomeini that the taking of the hostages had already accomplished its primary purpose, diminishing the Americans' image of the power they could exercise in Iran.

Sadeq Qotbzadeh had spent his entire adult life as a revolutionary opponent of the shah's regime. He was to all appearances a good Moslem. But he valued above all else the Iranian nation and his own personal influence. In temperament he was a man of reckless courage, flamboyance, audacity, and an almost limitless sense of personal efficacy. He treated the royal agents sent to monitor his activities, and in more than one case to dispose of him, with casual contempt. As a political strategist he was adventurous and daring, but rarely systematic. It was Qotbzadeh who came to know and enlist the support of Yasir Arafat, Hafez Assad, and many other Middle Eastern leaders who regarded themselves as anti-imperialists. He was among the earliest Iranian revolutionaries to recognize the extraordinary popular appeal of Ayatullah Khomeini and made a number of trips to Iraq to visit Khomeini during his long exile there. When Khomeini went to Paris, Qotbzadeh, like Yazdi and Bani Sadr, became a close political adviser and strategist.

After accompanying Khomeini to Iran from Paris, Qotbzadeh became a member of the Revolutionary Council and the director of the National Iranian Radio and Television. In that post he demonstrated how well he understood Khomeini's view of reality. The themes Qotbzadeh advanced were themes he knew Khomeini would approve of. He demonstrated as well an ability to manipulate popular attitudes. Liberal intellectuals began to see him as a potential Iranian Mussolini. But Qotbzadeh, for all his skill in manipulating symbols, failed to generate a personal following of any magnitude. Far more than Bani Sadr, his influence was the product of his relationship with Khomeini.

Qotbzadeh claimed that of the men closest to Khomeini, only he and Hojatolislam Mohammad Musavi Khoiniha understood how Khomeini would respond to the embassy takeover. From the beginning of the crisis, Qotbzadeh felt there was only one key to solving it—and that was to convince Khomeini that the hostage-taking had served its optimal purpose. Since that purpose was to demonstrate to the United States the clear limits of its ability to exercise influence in Iran, Qotbzadeh needed to be able to show Khomeini that indeed the United States government had learned something to this effect from the crisis and that it was unlikely to learn more from this particular shock.

For Qotbzadeh personally, the need was an urgent one to settle the hostage crisis in the shortest possible time. This was his moment in Iranian history and he fully recognized that fact. Unlike Bani Sadr, he understood his total dependence on Khomeini's favor. His view of Khomeini led him to believe that he might be able to manipulate Khomeini in such a way as to achieve for himself and for Iran extraordinary regional influence. Khomeini's vast appeal in Iran could be extended to the entire Islamic world, and indeed to the entire Third World—the oppressed world as Khomeini saw it—if Qotbzadeh were permitted to translate Khomeini's vision into a practical foreign policy. The hostage crisis, if it could be terminated quickly and on Qotbzadeh's terms, could serve Qotbzadeh's purpose exceptionally well. It could be portrayed as a dramatic victory for Iran which should indicate to the entire Third World the limits of American power. Together with the United States' inability to keep America's dearest friend in the area, the shah, in power, it would be a negative signal to all those Third World leaders who saw U.S. support as essential for their personal survival. Even more, it would demonstrate to their publics that they could dispose of such leaders without fear of retribution from the United States.

Qotbzadeh, with his long experience in the conspiratorial world of exile politics, had come to view the Soviet Union as an exceptionally adept player in the world of clandestine politics. He saw the same byzantine plots orchestrated by Soviet agents in Iran after the revolution that he had seen among Iranians in Europe before the revolution. After the Soviet occupation of Afghanistan, Qotbzadeh argued strongly in the Revolutionary Council that Iran should take the lead, especially among Islamic states, in condemning the Soviet action. He saw those in Iran who opposed him—and many did—as probable participants in the Soviet conspiracy. But in this policy area Khomeini and Qotbzadeh saw eye-to-eye. Therefore Qotbzadeh was entirely successful in gaining the Revolutionary Council's endorsement for his anti-Soviet stance. He was able to play a major role in the Islamabad conference of early 1980 in gaining a strong condemnation of the Soviet action.[26] In so doing, Iran demonstrated to the world that even though it was caught up in an intense conflict with one superpower, it had no policy qualms about opposing and offending the other superpower, one with which it shared a 1,200-mile border.

Qotbzadeh shared with Khomeini as well a view of Israel as a projection of Western imperialism in the Islamic world and as the usurper of the rights of the Arab people of Palestine. Iran's defection from the ranks of supporters of U.S. policy already had sharply altered the balance of power in the Middle East. But Qotbzadeh saw in this situation a role for the Islamic Republic that would quickly give it preeminence in the area. Iran, once freed of the restraints imposed by the hostage crisis, could take the lead in mobilizing a vastly invigorated anti-Israeli front to force a resolution of the Arab-Israeli conflict in the Arabs' favor. He assumed that the pragmatic leaders of the Arabian peninsula would quickly adjust to these changed circumstances and cooperate with financial support, and ultimately by agreeing to use their oil and petrodollar leverage, to compel a change in American policy. However, Saddam Hossein, the president of Iraq, was a major obstacle to the implementation of this strategy. The 1975 agreement between the shah and Saddam Hossein had been at the direct expense of Iranian opponents of the shah who had operated in Iraq with implicit and often explicit government support. When that support was withdrawn, Iranian opposition activities in Iraq were severely curtailed. Khomeini, living in Najaf, Iraq, at the time, would henceforth be limited in the activities in which he could engage.

Too much could easily be made of this personal affront to Khomeini in terms of explaining his later enmity toward Saddam Hossein. But it did push the Iranian non-Marxist opposition toward the Arab rivals of Saddam Hossein—in particular, President Hafez Assad of Syria. Thus when the Iranian revolution occurred, it was welcomed with enthusiasm by Syria but with restraint by Iraq. More important by far was the fact that the majority of the Arab population of Iraq was Shia and that some (although no one could estimate what) percentage of that population was intensely pro-Khomeini. Saddam Hossein dealt with this problem in two ways. He crushed any open manifestation of sympathy with Khomeini. He executed Ayatullah Baqr Sadr, the most prominent of Iraqi Shia clerics and a man widely respected throughout the Shia world, and, for good measure, the *ayatullah*'s sister. But he also built new mosques and granted other favors to those in the Shia community who were willing to accommodate themselves to his regime.[27] Iranian radio broadcasts and other propaganda efforts targeting this community in Iraq were bitterly resented in Iraq. Relations between the two regimes quickly deteriorated. Qotbzadeh was too preoccupied with the hostage issue to deal with these obstacles to good relations, but his hope was to isolate Iraq and then, with his superior leverage, to bring it into line.

There were few indications in any of his policies that Qotbzadeh saw the spreading of the Islamic revolution as his primary foreign policy objective. Far more apparent is an interest in achieving for Iran foreign policy prominence in the Islamic world and in the Third World generally. However, to do this the hostage crisis could not be prolonged and this for both internal and external reasons.

External, the more prolonged the hostage crisis, the greater was the erosion of support from the very public elements, those in the Third World, whose support was essential to the realization of Iran's strategic objectives. To the Third World, the appearance of American impotence in the face of so humiliating a challenge—the immediate consequence of the taking of the hostages—had to be an appealing development, since much of the Third World saw itself as the victim of Western imperialism. As the weeks passed, however, sympathy for the hostages would inevitably spread and with it a grudging respect for American restraint in the face of so brutal a provocation. Iran began losing the moral edge it required to best the American government in the world opinion arena.

Internally, the taking of hostages tended to divide the supporters of the regime into factions. Opponents almost universally saw in the taking of the hostages an Iranian, not an American, humiliation. That opinion was shared by many governmental officials, including some clerical leaders. But among the urban lower and lower-middle classes, the revolution's core support group, the taking of the hostages was a declaration of independence. Younger, radicalized clerics and students in religious institutes agreed. Older clergy, including members of the Revolutionary Council, recognized the growing popularity of this view and tended increasingly to move toward it themselves. An early unity of purpose within the Revolutionary Council in support of a quick settlement of the issue began to fall apart. Powerful men, such as Ayatullah Beheshti, who had been prominent clerics in the era of the shah's stability, had often been the indirect recipients of state funds given for religious activities. Therefore, even though most had spent some time in jail, they were vulnerable to the charge of collusion and naturally sought to restore their lost credibility by adopting radical positions. The dynamics of public opinion were such that it was quickly apparent that support for a settlement on terms envisioned by Qotbzadeh would soon dissipate.

The theoretical underlay of Qotbzadeh's strategy reflected his basic assumptions regarding the situation in Iran. Khomeini by virtue of his enormous personal appeal was all-powerful in the country. It follows that whenever Khomeini took an adamant policy position, that policy would prevail in his government. Because of Khomeini's unconcern with day-to-day events, the number of fixed policy positions was small and the area of decisional freedom for his lieutenants extensive. Thus Qotbzadeh would have a free hand to negotiate with most Arab governments. He would have Khomeini's sanction for opposing the Soviet Union in Afghanistan and full freedom in developing the tactical responses to that move. However, with regard to the taking of hostages, Khomeini's policy directive was fixed — albeit at a highly abstract level. The hostages could be released only when Khomeini was convinced that the American government had gained some understanding of the limitations of its power.

Qotbzadeh took on the task of convincing the Carter administration to agree to acquiesce in a number of tactical schemes that could, in sum, give the impression to Khomeini of a changed U.S. attitude in the desired direction. But this was if anything the easier part of his strategy; at the same time, he had to produce a consensus in the Revolutionary Council for his tactics. The task of orchestrating both the internal and external political environments was obviously enormously demanding, and ultimately Qotbzadeh would fail to achieve it. But the amazing fact is that he came on two or three occasions remarkably close to succeeding.[28]

The Carter administration went along with Qotbzadeh's schemes, regardless of their otherworldly premises, simply because at the time no other approach seemed to have any real potential for success. This involved acquiescing in three of Qotbzadeh's approaches. The Carter administration agreed not to oppose publicly a move by United Nations Secretary-General Kurt Waldheim to inaugurate a procedure by which an international tribunal might be set up to listen to the Iranian government's presentation of the crimes of the shah. In fact, the administration privately did a great deal to facilitate Waldheim's mission. Second, the administration was willing to make public a statement that would indicate an American agreement not to interfere in Iran's internal affairs and a willingness to conduct relations with Iran in a manner fully in harmony with its sovereign equality. Qotbzadeh hoped such a communication could be depicted in Iran as an apology for past crimes without being seen by the American public as damaging to national dignity. Third, after the shah left the United States for Panama, Qotbzadeh attempted to orchestrate a charade, with the cooperation of the Panamanian government, in which the latter would appear to be giving serious consideration to an Iranian request for extradition, although in fact it had no intention of doing so. The Carter administration's role here would be to remain silent while privately endorsing the scheme with the Panamanians. Understandably, this maneuver led to a considerable nervousness in the shah's entourage and was a major reason for his leaving Panama for Egypt. It was an uncomfortable maneuver for the Americans as well, but they, mainly through Hamilton Jordan, played their passive role seriously.

As described by then Assistant Secretary of State Hal Saunders, American policy followed two tracks.[29] The one—premised on the "this-worldly" assumption that Khomeini would respond to bargaining in the form of threats to damage Iran economically and to isolate it diplomatically—involved some vigorous attempts to rally support from America's friends and allies. The second, which Saunders described as efforts to change the atmosphere in Tehran, was in fact premised on the "otherworldly" assumptions described above. But the implicit contradiction of these two approaches, strangely, did not damage Qotbzadeh's efforts too seriously. Khomeini apparently paid little or no attention to the first-track efforts, and it was certainly not in Qotbzadeh's interests to dwell on them. For three months, the U.S. administration's persistence in following Qotbzadeh's strategy is even more surprising, since it is abundantly clear from Hamilton Jordan's account of the crisis that Jimmy Carter did not understand the premises. When Jordan at one point, after a serious setback in the Qotbzadeh effort, appealed to Carter to help "get the scenario back on track," Carter replied, "It's beginning to seem like a deal that we made with ourselves. Everybody's on board except the one person who can free the hostages—Khomeini!"[30] Obviously, Carter had not understood that Khomeini's attitudes were the target of the approach.

The real problem for Qotbzadeh was internal. It was well symbolized by the fact that Qotbzadeh, the foreign minister of Iran, did not know and could not learn from their captors the exact number of hostages being held. The student "Followers of the Line of the Imam" were the vanguard of the most revolutionary element of Khomeini's support. They regarded Qotbzadeh and Bani Sadr, as they regarded Bazargan, as nonrevolutionary reformists who could not be relied on to achieve Khomeini's vision for Islam. The Revolutionary Council placed full authority on Qotbzadeh for dealing with the hostage crisis, but everyone in the council understood that Khomeini's attitude was in full harmony with that of his student followers. They understood further that the dynamics of the situation were in the students' favor. To be successful, therefore, Qotbzadeh had to move quickly; he had to gain from Khomeini an order to his student followers to turn the hostages over to the government. Once in government hands, Qotbzadeh and the newly elected president, Bani Sadr, almost certainly could maneuver their release. It soon became apparent that Khomeini would issue such an order only if the Revolutionary Council would recommend unanimously that this be done. Each time Qotbzadeh came close to achieving this goal, the unanimity of the council evaporated. The clerics in the council, in particular, could not afford to offend the fervent support base of the regime and thereby risk losing their claim to lead it. By April 1980 there were no longer any prospects that Qotbzadeh would be able again to produce a consensus in the council. This phase of the hostage crisis had come to an end. Khomeini announced that the soon-to-be-elected parliament could dispose of the hostage crisis. It was becoming more apparent each day that the Islamic Republic party, even though it had not been able to elect a president, would win a major parliamentary election victory. The party leaders therefore would soon have no choice but to assume responsibility for the crisis.

Having given up on the Qotbzadeh approach, Carter administration statements began sounding seriously threatening. It appeared in fact that tactically the administration was about to test in Iran an approach that had failed in Vietnam. Thomas Schelling in his book, *Arms and Influence,* had advanced the bargaining strategy called "graduated compellence." This "strategy" called for signaling a desired objective, in this case the safe release of the hostages from a target government. Then a signal is given with some clarity indicating the punishment that will be inflicted if the target government fails to meet the objective. A blockade of Iranian oil shipments through the Persian Gulf was the most frequently signaled punishment. If the target government fails to comply, signals of additional acts of punishment could be suggested, but here a certain ambiguity is desirable. If the target persists in noncompliance, the initially signaled punishment must be carried out—otherwise, there will be a loss of credibility—and new, increasingly clear signals given as to what the target can expect next. This tactical bargaining approach is a natural one, and there is no reason to believe the Carter administration was following explicitly Schelling's model. But the premise nevertheless is that the situation lends itself to bargaining. And if the Qotbzadeh picture of Khomeini is valid, the Iranians simply would not have bargained. Martyrdom would be accepted by Khomeini in the serene confidence of his belief that the course he was following was divinely ordained. Since implicit in the graduated compellence bargaining approach is the assumption that a failure to execute a signaled punishment in the face of noncompliance would destroy the credibility of the entire process, the U.S. administration would have been compelled to climb the escalatory ladder to an uncertain end.

In fact, whatever the seriousness of purpose of this new threatening stance, there was another agenda that called for the rescue of the hostages.[31] Cyrus Vance had always understood that the Khomeini regime bore little resemblance to most other world regimes. The otherworldly quality of official Iranian thinking was recognized although surely not understood. It follows therefore that the kinds of expectations that could guide policy in dealing with "this-worldly" aggression on the part of most nations could not be held regarding Iran. Punishing Iran as a bargaining technique was not likely to succeed, and Vance strongly preferred not to follow that course of action. It follows as well that if Iran was seeking to demonstrate American impotence and a rescue operation succeeded, then the Iranians would look to another avenue for humiliating the United States. Vance's fears that this might involve imprisoning nonofficial Americans in Iran, many of them married to Iranians, were hence reasonable. So also, given his premises, was his preference for continuing to search for a diplomatic solution. But Vance's deeply held reservations were disregarded by the Carter administration.

On April 24, 1980, a rescue operation was initiated. It was at best a long shot. Involving as it did several difficult stages, culminating in a drive by trucks from the outskirts of Tehran to the embassy walls, the operation could have failed at any point. In fact, it failed in its initial stage, a flight by helicopters into the central Iranian desert.

The aborted rescue attempt, and in particular the manner of its failure, was entirely in accord with Khomeini's expectations. A divine pattern was easily inferred. The painstakingly trained and superbly equipped American force was defeated by weather, mechanical failures, and human error. The incineration of the men in one of the helicopters, described as agents of the great oppressor, was particularly symbolic. It was a fate to be expected for agents of Satan. Khomeini has never tired of pointing to the failure as final evidence of God's favor for the Islamic Republic.[32]

Cyrus Vance's decision to resign as a consequence of Carter's following this course of action may well have contributed to a shift in U.S. policy. Following the failure of the rescue attempt, Edmund Muskie, the new secretary of state, was determined to maintain control of American foreign policy and not to share it with Zbigniew Brzezinski. Thus the main proponent of a tough line toward Iran lost his influence with Muskie, who supported his departmental officers' preference for diplomacy.

In retrospect, it appears likely that when Khomeini issued the statement that the soon-to-be-elected parliament should deal with the hostage issue, he was losing interest in that most important of foreign policy concerns. He may already have concluded that the taking of hostages had served its limited purpose, that is, as one of many shocks that must be administered to the great American oppressor in order to bring the U.S. government to an awareness of its limited influence in the oppressed world. In any event, after several months of little activity by the American government concerning Iran following the failed rescue attempt, Khomeini made a basic policy statement. On September 12, 1980, Khomeini effectively indicated that the hostage crisis was no longer his concern and that his government could settle it according to guidelines that he understood could be the basis for serious negotiations.

### The Iraqi Invasion

However, Khomeini on countless occasions before and after September 12, 1980, articulated his expectation that Iran would be confronted with a major challenge from the two oppressor nations. He accepted as real the mutual antagonisms of the two great superpowers. But he argued that, faced with a serious challenge from one of the oppressed peoples, the oppressors would recognize their mutual danger and would unite to deal with the threat. The challenge from the Islamic Republic of Iran was the greatest that either superpower had faced from the oppressed world. Khomeini therefore expected a reaction from these two oppressors that almost certainly would be collaborative. The United States, as the oppressor power most seriously damaged by Iran's challenge, would surely take the lead in responding. But the Soviet hand would be apparent to the aware observer as well. The particular form of the response was not predictable; it could be direct action, such as a punishing bombing of Iran. But Iran's will to resist was too strong and hence such direct action was unlikely. More likely, the oppressors would engage Iran through the many puppet regimes the oppressors had imposed on the oppressed peoples.

Iraq's attack on Iran ten days after Khomeini's speech therefore must be viewed in the context of Khomeini's expectations. No major Iranian official, regardless of faction, doubted that the Iraqi attack was inspired by and orchestrated by the United States.[33] The case for them was only too clear. Having suffered a major blow to its credibility, the United States government mobilized its regional surrogates to restore the damaged power balance. King Hossein of Jordan, seen as a second among Middle Eastern leaders only to the late shah in terms of his servitude to the oppressors, took the lead in rallying the support of like leaders throughout the Arab world. Sadat of Egypt, now the United States' favorite in its stable of servant leaders, Hassan of Morocco, Fahd of Saudi Arabia, Borghiba of Tunisia, Numieri of the Sudan, and all the lesser leaders followed Hossein's lead. This is how the Iranian leadership interpreted the attack; they never had any doubt thereafter of the primacy of the American role. Iraq's Saddam Hossein had come out of the closet and revealed his agent relationship with the United States in 1975. His agreement with the shah at that time and their close relationship thereafter made clear Saddam Hossein's role. He of course had to give favorable lip service to the Islamic revolution in Iran, but it was never sincere, and it was only a question of time before his masters would order him to participate in a challenge to the Islamic Republic. This view in fact is held with such certainty by the regime today that anyone doubting it runs the risk of being considered part of the conspiracy.

The Iranian conviction that the Iraqi invasion was ordered by the

United States was deeply rooted in a view of reality that was a consequence of over a century of Iranian encounters with imperialism. The logic of the situation for them was utterly compelling. The fact (and it is a fact) that there is no overtly available evidence confirming this inference is of no interest to those who accept the conclusion. The operation would have been a top secret one and executed in the usual hidden-hand manner; confirmation would appear eventually, but only years after the fact.

Judging by American statements at the time regarding this period in U.S. diplomacy, and by now an impressive number of participant accounts by Carter administration officials, including Carter himself, one can find no basis for the Iranian view.[34] At the same time, there is no real indication that the United States was aware of the Iranian interpretation of events and of the intensity with which it was held.

Statements by Saddam Hossein and even more by his deputy Tariq Aziz prior to the attack and shortly afterward leave little doubt as to the motivation for and their expectations of the outcome of the attack.[35] Khomeini clearly saw Saddam Hossein as a tool of the oppressor powers—first of the Soviet Union and later, after 1975, of the United States. After the revolution he and his government stated quite openly that the Islamic revolution must soon embrace Iraq. Certainly there was a case to be made for Iranian provocation, but the statements of the Iraqi leaders indicate little or no perceived threat from Iran. Tariq Aziz, for example, in response to the Syrian argument that the Iranian revolution seriously altered the balance of power with Israel in the Arabs' favor, dismissed the argument as nonsense. He pictured Iran as literally entirely inconsequential, an overall liability rather than an asset in the larger Arab-Israeli picture.[36] Statements made at the time of the attack and afterward, but before the quality of Iranian resistance was recognized, are similarly revealing. Claims to the Iranian southwestern province of Khuzistan, called Arabistan by the Iraqis, were clearly explicated.[37] Also, from the beginning the conflict was described as one of Arab nationalism opposing Iranian hegemonic ambitions. Iranian exiles, including Shapur Bakhtiar, had been in close contact with the Iraqi government—and, indeed, had given them a reinforcing picture of a regime on the edge of collapse. Had Iraq seen a terrible threat from Iran, surely some effort to advance Bakhtiar's cause would have been made. But instead, by depicting the conflict as Arab versus Iranian, the Iranian collaborators were made to appear as traitors to their nation. Then finally Baghdad television and government pronouncements all depicted the Iraqi action as the vanguard of Arab resurgence with Saddam Hossein and his regime taking the lead.[38] The Syrian regime's persistence in a policy of friendship for Iran was depicted as treason to the Arab nation. Hafez Assad, Saddam Hossein's primary rival to the claim of spokesman for the Arab nation, was at first placed very much on the defensive.

The Iranian regime of course saw none of this picture. Their operating world view was simple and easily described. The Iraqi attack was a major effort on the part of the great oppressor, the American government, to restore its tarnished image of omnipotence. De facto collaboration by the other great oppressor government, the Soviet Union, was seen from the beginning, and expectations of a more overt participation were explicated.[39] Israel, as the primary oppressor power in the region, and as a usurper of the rights of Islam and the Palestinian people, was playing a central behind-the-scenes role.[40] It was certainly a full partner with Iraq in oppressor strategy. Then there were the lesser puppet leaders of Islamic states who followed unquestioningly American direction. Opposing this conspiracy were the true leaders of the oppressed peoples. Regionally these included Hafez Assad and his regime in Syria; Yasir Arafat and much of the PLO; Qaddafi and Libya; and, with some reservations, Algeria.

But there were in this picture the elements of apparently contradictory purposes in Khomeini's sense of divine mission. It was his task to guide the oppressed peoples out of the grasp of their oppressors. To accomplish this, he turned naturally to those regimes which became his allies. They had been in the forefront of the effort to destroy the influence of Western imperialism. But there were two problems with these allies. First, they all enjoyed good relations with the Soviet Union, in Khomeini's view one of the two great oppressors. Second, they were to varying degrees secular regimes. Indeed, in most respects, they resembled Khomeini's secular allies in the revolution, allies now purged from any position of political or social influence. Khomeini's second purpose, to guide Islam and ultimately all mankind toward an acceptance of the divine order, must make of these current allies future targets.

Khomeini—unconcerned as he tended to be with the details of strategy and convinced as he was that God would make evident, to one able to see divine patterns, the correct path to follow—seems to have ignored the policy dilemmas these contradictory purposes generated. He had aligned himself with allies of one great oppressor against the allies of the other great oppressor. But on occasion, and especially with regard to Afghanistan, he opposed the great oppressor ally of his allies. However, he did not ally Iran with the forces of resurgent Islam in Syria, his closest ally, when they opposed the secularist Assad regime. Indeed, his government went so far as to sanction the brutal suppression of the Moslem Brotherhood forces in Hamma, Syria, carried out by Assad in 1982.[41] In doing so, his policy appeared either a pragmatic response to a challenge to a desperately needed ally or, even worse, an alliance with the Syrian Alawi. The Alawi, an offshoot from Shia Islam and still regarded as part of the Shia world, were a minority in Syria of which Assad and an out-of-proportion number of Syrian officers were members. On the surface this gave the impression that Khomeini led a Shia as opposed to an Islamic movement, an impression Khomeini emphatically wished to avoid giving.

The Iran-Iraq war emerges, therefore, far more than most conflicts, as a war in which the combatants' views of reality had little in common. For the United States, the conflict immediately complicated the hostage crisis. Negotiations began very quickly after Khomeini's September 12 speech. They involved Khomeini's in-law relative Sadeq Tabatabai, and hence apparently had Khomeini's direct sanction.[42] But when Iraq attacked Iran, negotiations were frozen and remained frozen until it became apparent that Iraq's hopes for a quick Iranian collapse would not be realized. At that point, in November 1980, the Iranians entered into serious negotiations with the American government with the Algerians as intermediaries. The real purpose of the taking of the hostages, that is, the humiliation of the United States, having been served, negotiations now were concerned largely with technical matters such as the unfreezing of Iranian assets and agreeing on a formula for settling private claims of American corporations against the Iranian government.

## The Struggle for Power and Institutionalization of the Regime

Complicating this final phase of the hostage crisis, however, was the struggle for survival by the president of Iran, Abul Hassan Bani

Sadr. Sadeq Qotbzadeh, Bani Sadr's sometime ally, had left the foreign ministry after the parliamentary elections. He remained on the government payroll, however, as a member of Khomeini's office. But even before he left the foreign ministry, Qotbzadeh had embarked on a path that would lead to his execution. Nothing is more revealing of the strange quality of the Iranian political process than the opposition struggle of these two men, so recently at the top of the Iranian power structure. Neither had a substantial power base independent of Khomeini, although Bani Sadr, as mentioned, having won the presidency with the votes of three-quarters of the electorate, held onto the illusion of personal popularity. And the regime, having purged from any position of influence the large and once all-powerful secular community, was approaching in totalitarian repressiveness the China of the cultural revolution. Yet that regime tolerated clearly dangerous activities by two men who could have been eliminated without fear of serious repercussion. Qotbzadeh, in a manner fully congruent with his adventurous temperament, made contact with individuals prominent in the very sections of the society that the regime had relied on for its support but who were growing increasingly skeptical: clerical elements not associated with the Islamic Republic party, bazaar merchants, and officers who had remained in the armed forces.[43] Qotbzadeh went so far as to criticize the clerical leaders on television.[44] This led to his arrest in November 1980, but his influence with Khomeini's office was sufficient to gain a quick release that time. Bani Sadr used the occasion of the war with Iraq to spend much of his time with military officers at the front. His clerical opponents could not have avoided the conclusion that this activity was designed less to advance the war effort than to establish a support base within the military.

As late as November 1980, both Qotbzadeh and Bani Sadr were remarking publicly that the hostage crisis was seriously damaging to Iran. Fearful of some last-second maneuver to keep the hostages, Qotbzadeh continued to press for their release until the plane carrying them from Tehran was in the air. But Bani Sadr came to see the hostage issue as an instrument he could use against his tormentors. The tables had been turned by Khomeini's orders to engage in negotiations. Now the parliament, dominated by the men who had prevented success for Qotbzadeh's plans, had to conduct the negotiations. Bani Sadr, who had generally supported efforts to release the hostages, began to exploit the demagogic potential in their retention. His argument was that the terms being negotiated were close to being capitulatory for Iran.[45] Khomeini, presiding over the entire regime, appeared either unaware of or unconcerned with the political struggle taking place. All parties could reasonably claim to be close to him.

There was a serious danger, given this picture, that the hostage issue could not be resolved prior to the inauguration of Ronald Reagan. The most militant of Khomeini's supporters, the left, and Bani Sadr all were opposing release. Those negotiating a resolution of the conflict could only lose influence by succeeding in their endeavors and no one other than Khomeini could consider his political position as secure. Nevertheless, though obviously with great reluctance, the negotiations were successfully concluded. Qotbzadeh argued that this was possible only because Khomeini, at the urging of Beheshti who saw the hostage crisis as preventing a return to stability in Iran, reiterated his orders to the negotiators that they reach agreement.[46] Even if this is so, a serious misunderstanding or miscalculation on the part of the United States could have aborted the agreement.

By January 1981, when the hostages finally were released, the Khomeini regime was in the last stages of taking institutional form. There was in this a strange mix of absolute repression and freedom. Of course Khomeini could easily have assumed the role of absolute dictator and could have done so within the terms of the constitution. The institution of *vilayet e faqih* could have accommodated virtually any exercise of authority Khomeini might have considered. But as was inevitable, Khomeini gave definition to that most unique of institutions. In his hands the *vilayet e faqih* really did become an office of guidance, one that was distant from and only occasionally concerned with the world of daily policy decisions. When Khomeini did take a strong position, as with the taking of hostages or the conduct of war and diplomacy in the Iran-Iraq conflict, his stand was accepted without question. But even in most vitally important matters, such as the question of land reform, Khomeini more commonly took no position.

Since the other institutions established in the constitution were subordinate to that of the *vilayet e faqih,* the failure of Khomeini to utilize his office to give direction to government policy meant that other institutions would become more influential than the constitutional structure suggested. Inevitably, the early individual occupants of other major offices would play a primary role in the process of adjusting to the void in authority created by the largely advisory role played by the *vilayet e faqih*. Strong personalities would seek to augment the influence of the offices they occupied. The outcome of the power struggles taking place within the regime would therefore affect seriously the degree to which some institutions would be strengthened relative to others.

The major power struggle of the early period following the approval of the constitution involved the president, Bani Sadr, on one side and the Islamic Republic party, led by Ayatullah Beheshti, on the other. Having failed to win the presidency, the Islamic Republic party was determined to dominate the election for parliament. It did so, winning a clear majority of the seats. Thus the battle for control of the government was waged from the office of the president on one side, and parliament on the other. A standoff developed that prevented for some months the selection of a prime minister; hence the office of the prime minister was seriously diminished in importance. Beheshti was Bani Sadr's most powerful rival, but his official position, that of chief justice of the supreme court, could hardly be developed as an institutional rival of the presidency for the exercise of influence over appointments and policy. The most strategic position available to the IRP for this purpose was that of speaker of the Majlis. Hojatolislam Hashemi Rafsenjani was elected to that position. Rafsenjani emerged quickly in the revolutionary government, as a top contender for governmental authority. As speaker of the Majlis he was in the ideal position for bargaining with the president over appointments and policy. As a trusted former student, he enjoyed excellent access to Khomeini and his relations with Beheshti were cooperative. In his hands, the office of speaker of the Majlis has consistently rivaled that of the presidency in terms of influence exercised.

The struggle for ascendance between the IRP and Bani Sadr was surprisingly open and public. Bani Sadr, for example, wrote a daily column in his newspaper *Enqellab e Eslami* that attacked his rivals with an abandon usually only seen in open systems. The journals associated with the IRP answered in kind. This pattern of open conflict among regime competitors in fact was a characteristic of the Khomeini government from its first days. It was a reflection of Khomeini's decisional style. Khomeini from the time of his return had

called for unity among his domestic allies and had consistently resisted choosing among competing factions. On the contrary, he frequently responded favorably to the entreaties of a losing faction to
give them some show of support. In addition, he refused to compel
individuals responsible for the instruments of coercion such as the
local forces attached to the *komiteh*s or the revolutionary guard, to
accept strong and effective central control. The result was that terrorism tended to be decentralized and hence beyond the control of
the central government. Only rarely would coercion be applied
against high-level supporters of the government.

## Control of the Regime

Iran under Khomeini could thus be described as totalitarian but
without a dictator, either personal or collective. Khomeini for reasons of temperament, preferred style, and lack of interest or concern with detail, chose not to be an absolute dictator. And, whether
from conscious design or an unwillingness to choose among leaders
whom he saw as true and sincere Moslems, he did not allow the
triumph of any one faction that could have established tight control. The result was a brutal coercion of those outside of and unsympathetic to the Islamic Republic, but a coercion that emanated
usually from lower-level officials. For those who professed a true faith
in Islam, there was a surprising tolerance of free activity. This tolerance extended occasionally even to those who had finally lost in a
prolonged power struggle. For example, both Mehdi Bazargan and
Ibrahim Yazdi published articles and books and made public remarks
that were devastatingly critical of trends within the regime.

After the defeat of Bani Sadr in 1981, all the major institutions
of government were under the control of the Islamic Republic party.
The president was Mohammad Ali Rajai, who previously had been
forced on Bani Sadr as prime minister. The prime minister was Ayatullah Mohammad Javad Bahonar. Rafsenjani was speaker and Beheshti was chief justice. But in the course of the summer all were
killed by opposition bombings except for Rafsenjani. However, the
government showed a strength and resilience that shocked and dismayed its opponents. As it had when attacked by Iraq, the government proved to be capable of withstanding extraordinary blows. The
core public support was sufficiently broad and intense to provide a
base for the regime's survival. Still, following the bombings there

was a wave of arrests and executions sufficient to be described as a reign of terror that lasted some eighteen months. Then in December 1982 Khomeini signaled a major relaxation of coercion and a return to the relatively greater tolerance of the first two and a half years of the revolutionary government.

The challenge to the regime in this eighteen-month period had come from the left, in particular the Mujahaddin and the minority Fadayan in cooperation with the Kurdish Democratic party. The Mujahaddin had demonstrated on many occasions its continuing strong popular appeal. It could call into the streets huge crowds willing to demonstrate their disapproval of government policy even though in doing so they were risking some serious repression. But Khomeini's tolerance did not envelop them. He clearly saw the Mujahaddin, with its strong Islamic sentiments, as challenging his own image of a society conforming to God's intent. Dismissing them as "hypocrites," he obviously implicitly sanctioned their suppression.[47] When they adopted a strategy of violence, the regime responded with brutality, executing several thousand.[48] Even in this period, however, the coercive response lacked strong central control. Individuals such as Hojatolislam Mohammadi Gilani, revolutionary prosecutor-general of Tehran, and Hojatolislam Mohammad Mohammadi Reyshahri, chief judge of the military tribunal, appeared to be operating coercively beyond anyone's control.[49]

By the end of this period, the left which was fully independent of the Soviet Union had been defeated and, except for the peripheral areas where ethnic rebellion continued (especially in Kurdistan), regime control was complete. Masud Rajavi, the leader of the Mujahaddin, had allied himself with Bani Sadr when the latter was in hiding in Tehran. Then the two fled Iran together on the same plane and arrived in Paris proclaiming Bani Sadr as legal president of Iran and Rajavi his deputy. After the great challenge from the Mujahaddin had been defeated, Rajavi followed the same path that Bakhtiar had chosen earlier of cooperation with Saddam Hossein of Iraq. Symbolically he had chosen to gamble on a defeat of the regime by external forces. It was a dangerous gamble and one made after such a defeat administered by Iraq appeared extremely unlikely. The risk was a loss of nationalist legitimacy.

The relaxation of coercive control that Khomeini called for obviously did not apply to everyone. Two months after Khomeini's speech, the regime turned on the pro-Soviet left and, shortly there-after, against the Soviet Union directly. In February 1983, Kianuri was arrested and the suppression of the Tudeh quickly followed. In April 1983, eighteen Soviet diplomats were expelled from Iran. This marked the defeat of the Kianuri strategy and within days the Na-tional Voice of Iran was calling for a popular front to oppose the Khomeini dictatorship.[50] But even in this period, this outlet of the Tudeh organization inside the Soviet Union targeted the Islamic lib-erals, such as Bazargan and Yazdi, dead men, including Qotbzadeh (who had been executed a year earlier) and Chamran, and the Hoj-jatieh. The latter was a group of clergy best known for conservative interpretations of the Qoran and strong anti-Bahai sentiments, who had supported the revolution and provided some of its major fig-ures.[51] Apparently Tudeh and Soviet analysts saw the Hojjatieh as a major conservative, procapitalist, and anti-Soviet faction of the governing group in Iran. But evidence suggests that the group played a far less important role; in any case, the Hojjatieh had lost much influence in this same period.

Despite this assault on the pro-Soviet left, the relaxation of late 1982 that Khomeini called for was real. Politics in Iran settled into routine patterns. Factions tended to form and disintegrate. Rumors of a great rivalry between the president, Hojatolislam Ali Khamenei and Speaker Rafsenjani were sufficiently persistent to lead both pur-ported antagonists to deny publicly any important conflict. These problems continue to plague the regime. Given Khomeini's great age and sometimes fragile health, questions of political survival cannot be out of the minds of those prominent in the regime today. However, power is so broadly shared and central direction so weak that the political process resembles in ways the loose and constantly chang-ing coalitions of warlords. Many important clerics and officials in the government indeed have their own paramilitary detachments. However, the central authorities are aware of the problem and some significant progress has been made in centralizing control over local and coercive institutions. The *komiteh*s have been placed structur-ally within the Ministry of Interior and there is a cabinet officer heading a Department of Revolutionary Guard Affairs, but the con-trol actually exercised remains far from tight. In any struggle for power after Khomeini, in fact, revolutionary guard and *komiteh* leaders are likely to be found in competing factions and to play a major balancing role.

The question of succession to Khomeini as *faqih* is probably less interesting and important than might be thought because of the evolution of the office of *faqih* under Khomeini. Khomeini's great importance is a consequence of his charismatic appeal to the core support base of his regime. He is the master manipulator of appealing symbols. There is quite simply no one attached to the regime capable of succeeding him in this respect. Ayatullah Hossein Ali Montazeri, chairman of the Friday Mosque Prayer Leaders, has been officially designated as successor to Khomeini as *faqih*. But the office is unlikely to be focus of much authority. With Khomeini's passing there will be no one with a comparable ability to mobilize popular support for the regime. It follows therefore that coercive control must in the short term be sharply intensified. The struggle for power thus is likely to focus on gaining control of a coercive apparatus that can aptly be described as still hydra-headed.[52]

More important from the point of view of determining Iran's future fate than the question of succession to Khomeini is the question of the strength and survivability of revolutionary institutions. By 1979 the Iranian society and economy had become sufficiently complex as to require an elaborate technocratic and administrative structural base. Since much of the personnel who served the economy and society during the reign of the shah were secular-minded, the new regime viewed them with a mixture of skepticism and hostility. Much of the economic disruption of the first two years was a consequence of the purges and ill-treatment of these people, and, unhappily, a high percentage of them left Iran.[53] Recovery from this loss required the recruitment of replacements and, certainly in the short run, the return of many who had left their positions. As the formal institutionalization of the revolution proceeded, Iran's technocratic and administrative structure was reconstructed. Since there was no one voice at the top, the recruitment process was carried out in a series of increments rather than as part of a centralized plan. The result was that this administrative-technocratic structure was composed more of individuals who accommodated themselves to the regime than of individuals who accepted the norms of the revolution.

A decision made in 1987 to dissolve the Islamic Republic party (IRP) was startlingly symptomatic of the unique rhythm the institutionalization of the Iranian revolution was following. The formation of a single, authoritarian party was a natural step for the Iranian revolutionary regime. It should have served a number of useful purposes: recruiting and socializing a political and possibly a technocratic elite; serving as a base for constructing a broad range of supporting organizations; and providing a central locus for a broad educational and propaganda program. The IRP had in fact served a vital purpose for the clerical leadership in helping to defeat its rivals within the revolution. But once that victory had been achieved—and in particular following the death of its leader and inspired organizer, Ayatullah Beheshti—the IRP began to founder. It failed to pursue any of the purposes expected of a single, authoritarian party. Rather, it evolved into a large umbrella organization that reflected more than it influenced the pattern of factional formation and dissolution.

The elections held in Iran after 1982 followed the same pattern. By 1982 the polarization process was more or less complete. At one pole, those intransigently opposed to the regime were in effect totally removed from the political process. Unable to present a serious challenge to the regime, they could be and were largely disregarded. The atrophy of the IRP reflected the lack of a felt need for a major institution to mobilize the regime's supporters against a challenge from its opponents. For a regime that makes heavy use of brutal oppression, it was astonishingly free. To be sure, few secularists had the temerity to announce their candidacy and those who did attempt to run were denied official sanction. But the candidates represented a large range of social and economic positions, and the voters were offered a real choice of socioeconomic philosophies. There was little evidence of election-rigging, and contests were often close. Potential voters apparently felt there was little risk in not voting, despite the belief that a failure to vote could lead to a loss of ration cards. In 1984, 35 percent stayed home, as did 57 percent in the previous election. Furthermore, those elected acted with surprising independence in parliament, sometimes rejecting nominees for cabinet positions who were known to have Khomeini's approval. The electoral process was, in other words, far more meaningful than one would expect in an authoritarian system.

However, electoral behavior in Iran, given this degree of freedom, reveals another aspect of Iranian political life. In a situation in which elections are apt to be close and in which there is a large nonvoting public element, one would expect to see competing candidates attempting to reach out and appeal to nonvoters. In other such systems, such as Mubarak's Egypt during the same period, this expectation was fully realized. Opposition politicians allowed to run for office in Egypt often were successful in appealing to that portion of the electorate that was hostile to the regime but was not allowed to run its own candidates. In Egypt the most significant public element in this situation was a large group that looked to religious leaders for political direction. Opposition elements either ran candidates who were close to the clergy or who took positions that appealed to the religiously inclined. But in Iran no such pattern has appeared among antiregime secularists. Apparently, the hostility of the opposition pole was so intense that those occupying it could not see the differences among the regime's candidates and saw no strategic utility in attempting to play off competing factions against one another.

The Iranian political system in the era of the Islamic Republic hence has some easily identified strengths and vulnerabilities. But one overriding structural weakness must be remedied if long-term stability is to be achieved: the bitter polarization of society into secular and religious communities. For those at the religious pole, the regime is fully legitimate and deserves a support so intense that many are willing to make any sacrifice for its survival. For those at the secular pole, the intensely despised regime is so lacking in legitimacy that they are willing to make an alliance with its most hated external enemies: Iraq, the United States, and Israel. The vigorous support the regime enjoys from those at the religious pole is sufficient to grant it short-term stability, including the ability to survive a major internal assault and major aggression even from a well-equipped foe who could count on the assistance of much of the rest of the world. But the intensity of opposition from the secular pole makes it difficult to construct easily a stable institutional base that could oversee reconstruction following a war and foster economic and social progress.

Other vulnerabilities include, first, the heavy reliance for control purposes on the charismatic appeal of Ayatullah Khomeini. The problem of finding a successor to a political leader who appeals to the people with enormous symbolic force is always perplexing. In the case of Iran, the problem has not been solved. As a result, with Khomeini's death, the regime will suddenly be confronted with a need to attract support by means other than an individual's appeal.

In the short term, there really will be no alternative to increased co-ercion. But that means compelling compliance by internal security forces that so far have not been granted a sufficient role in the control process to give them the credibility essential for fulfilling that task.

A second vulnerability is closely related to the first. For whatever reason and whether by design or not, Khomeini has not allowed any individual or faction the kind of dominance and central direction of the government that could make for an easy transition. Instead, a plethora of unstable factions seem to be alliances based more on personal ambition than on issues. In a transition period, the maneuvering for a winning alliance will surely be intense. Individuals with established constituencies—in particular, politically ambitious officers in the security forces—should be in an excellent bargaining position. Since the intransigent opposition apparently pays little attention to the factional lay of the land, the maneuvering is unlikely to embrace them. Were it to do so, the possibility of radical change would be much greater.

Third, a major source of vulnerability is the regime's failure—symbolized by the abolition of the Islamic Republic party—to construct a strong institutional base designed to perpetuate its operating norms and to provide a base of operation for the governing elite which replaced that of the shah's regime. Such an institutional base seems to be developing, however, with a momentum of its own and without the benefit of any centralized plan. Most important of these institutions is the revolutionary guard, which now has its own ministry. The revolutionary guard appears to embrace many of the functions of the military, the internal and external intelligence services, internal security, covert operations abroad, and even foreign policy. In all areas it overlaps with existing institutions and the developing process involves virtually constant jurisdictional conflicts. The advantage of the revolutionary guard in such conflicts is that its personnel are thoroughly committed both ideologically and because of their own vested interests to the survival and vitality of the revolutionary regime. Other institutions with like commitment are the Ministry of Construction Jihad and the Ministry of Islamic Guidance. Sections of traditional ministries may be dominated by similarly motivated individuals and, as in the case of Behzad Nabavi and the Ministry of Heavy Industry, a minister may be a highly motivated proponent of revolutionary development.

A fourth problem, however, is that of the apparent inability of the regime to recruit and indoctrinate a new generation of technocrats. Whereas the above discussion indicates that there are areas of real success, interviews with bureaucrats suggest that their attachment to this regime is not significantly stronger than bureaucratic loyalty to the shah's regime had been. If this is indeed the case, the regime might well be abandoned, just as the shah's was, by the technocratic elements if it appeared to be highly vulnerable.

### Reagan Administration Policy

The Reagan administration came into office as Bani Sadr's position in Iran was becoming untenable. But U.S. policy showed no interest in internal developments in Iran. The nightmare of the hostage crisis had come to an end, and the next focus of Iranian-American relations would be a complex and tedious process of negotiating a resolution of the claims of individual Americans against the government of Iran. Conceivably these negotiations, to be conducted at the Hague, could evolve into a broader set of relations. But neither government appeared particularly interested in that prospect.

Iran's relations with the Soviet Union were hardly close. Iranian unhappiness with the Soviet occupation of Afghanistan was deep, and Afghan refugees in Iran, numbering perhaps a million and a half, were receiving some aid. Trade between the two countries was improving. But Soviet efforts to ingratiate themselves with Iran were not really successful. To be sure, the Tudeh party before 1983 was tolerated, but most government officials viewed it with profound suspicion. There was in short little cause for concern in Washington regarding Soviet inroads in Iran. That is not to say that penetration of the Iranian regime by Soviet-controlled agents was not suspected. Indeed, it was assumed. But there was little to indicate that, whatever their success in this area, Soviet agents were exercising a serious influence in the Iranian decisional process.

With regard to the region, the stalemate in the Iran-Iraq War reduced Iranian options very substantially. Halting and then reversing the momentum of Iraqi forces was an all-consuming task for the Iranian military. Iran's potential for influencing internal political developments within states in the Islamic Middle East was also substantial, because most of the sociopolitical factors that produced receptivity for Khomeini's appeal were present in other countries throughout the region. But an institutional base for constructing a strategy and a tactical scheme for its implementation had not been developed in Iran. The foreign ministry had been decimated and the recruitment and training of professional replacements would take much time. Revolutionary institutions such as the revolutionary guard or the Office of Islamic Guidance had not yet developed the capability for carrying out this function. Therefore, the efforts that were made to exploit opportunities in this area tended to be ad hoc and focused on particular individuals who recognized the potential. Here again the lack of a strong and attentive central leadership meant that institutional development to fulfill this need was likely to be unsystematic. Thus even though there was real vulnerability in those Arab regimes which the American government had described as "moderate and responsible," the wider threat from the Islamic movement in Iran was not yet serious.

In its first several months, the Reagan administration perceived little threat to American objectives in the Middle East from Iran. The Iranian impact on Reagan administration policies was instead symbolic. In his presidential campaign, Reagan had emphasized his determination to avoid the kind of humiliation suffered by his predecessor—first in watching helplessly as a loyal ally, the shah, collapsed internally and then enduring the taking of American diplomats hostage and holding them in terrible circumstances for 444 days. Following his election, Reagan sent his secretary of state–designate, Alexander Haig, to the area to assure friendly leaders that this administration would not desert them. But the incoming administration balanced this tough stance with an emphatic rejection of any proposal for developing a plan for reversing the situation in Iran. This was done in response to the pleas from a seemingly endless stream of Iranian exiles who believed that the only sure means for removing Khomeini was an American-sponsored and American-directed effort.

However, in September 1981 the stalemate in the war was broken; for the next nine months, the Iranians advanced against Iraqi-held positions inside Iran. When the city of Khorramshahr was recovered, the possibility of an Iraqi rout seemed momentarily very real. Iranian hopes and expectations that the large Shia majority among Arabic-speaking Iraqis would embrace resurgent Islam and establish an Islamic republic, and that indeed that the movement would embrace Sunni Arabs as well, had not been realized in earlier phases of the war. But Saddam Hossein's rule in Iraq was among the most repressive in the world. In addition, the Iraqi regime had made a major effort to satisfy the utilitarian demands of its populace. The quiescence among the Iraqi people therefore could be as misleading as had been the Iranians' quiescence under the shah prior to 1977. Now, perhaps sensing a vulnerability in the regime, Iraqi Moslems could rise much as their Iranian counterparts had done four years earlier. At this point, there was real concern in the international community not only that Iraq might be transformed into an Islamic republic but also that the movement would sweep into the Arabian peninsula and into Jordan, backed by triumphant Iranian arms and welcomed by an ecstatic populace.

The case could easily be made that the possibility of such a development should not be of much concern to the United States. Resurgent Islam was anitcommunist and anti-Soviet. Indeed, the Soviets would have every reason to be concerned about their own large Islamic population. And any regime controlling the great oil fields of the area would have no alternative to maintaining oil sales at or near the current level. Furthermore, the Israeli leadership seems not to have perceived a serious danger from the forces of resurgent Islam, as the sale of military supplies to Iran by arms merchants associated with the government of Israel earlier suggested. Thus pressure from Israel and its supporters was not a factor.

But a de facto alliance with "moderate" Arab regimes had long been a central characteristic of American Middle East policy. To be sure, that alliance had served an instrumental purpose in that these regimes were opposed to any Soviet advance in the area, were accommodating in their policies regarding oil sales and the investment of petrodollars, and limited their opposition to Israel largely to the level of rhetoric. By 1982, however, the United States' close relationship with such regimes appeared to be as much an end as an instrument for achieving an end. In any event, there was a serious concern apparent in Washington as to the consequences of an Iraqi defeat. A movement toward political reconciliation with Iraq had begun under Carter. Now it intensified. A drift toward (if not a policy of) opposition to resurgent Islam, at least in its Iranian expression, was setting in.

But the fall of Khorramshahr did not set the stage for a successful invasion of Iraq. On the contrary, Iraqi resistance stiffened as the battle moved toward and into Iraqi territory. The Iraqi military forces were far better equipped than the Iranian and suffered none of the difficulties produced by the Iranian bifurcation into competing military forces—the revolutionary guard and the regular military. But the Iraqi military seemed satisfied to use their superiority to establish and maintain a military stalemate. The unwillingness to accept the level of casualties absorbed by the Iranians suggested a lack of popular support for the war in Iraq. This suggested, in turn, that the Iranians' sense of a strong revolutionary potential in Iraq may have some basis. Whatever the explanation, the stalemate was clearly satisfying to the Reagan administration—as it also appeared to have been for the Soviet Union, Western Europe, and most regional actors. The options that observers feared were becoming available to the Iranians for spreading their revolution suddenly seemed to disappear.

Almost coincidentally with the turn of the fortunes of battle away from Iran, the Israelis in June 1982 invaded Lebanon. Israel's defense minister and chief architect of the Lebanon adventure, Ariel Sharon, expected the Israeli forces to be near Beirut and Syrian forces to be in full retreat forty-eight hours after the invasion. He expected as well that shortly thereafter Bashir Gamyel would be president/dictator of a Lebanon that would make its peace with Israel and, indeed, would become an Israeli ally.[54] But these expectations were not to be realized. Israel's military superiority over PLO forces was to be expected, and the destruction of the Syrian air force, if anything, surpassed expectations. However, Palestinian popular resistance, especially from religious-led forces in the Sidon area refugee camps, was more determined than anticipated. Syrian ground forces fought relatively well even without air cover, and Bashir Gamyel proved to be far less free to rule in an absolute manner than Sharon had assumed.

Briefly after Israeli forces reached Beirut, and U.S., French, and Italian forces arrived in the Beirut area, the defeat of the PLO, Moslem militias and the Syrians seemed almost total. Syria's acceptance of mediation from the United States, whose secretary of state, Alexander Haig, had given Israel the impression that the United States would not be displeased by an Israeli attack that eliminated two perceived Soviet allies in Lebanon—the PLO and Syria—gave testimony to the low state of Soviet prestige and the correspondingly high state of American influence. But in a remarkably short period of time, there was a major reversal of fortunes. By mid-1984 the United States' very presence in Lebanon was evaporating. This time under Ronald Reagan, the United States had suffered a humiliation that rivaled that of the Carter administration in Iran. Even more significantly, Israeli forces had begun a withdrawal from Lebanon that was to be complete by June 1985. Furthermore, indications were that Israel would have less control in Lebanon following that withdrawal than it had exercised prior to the invasion and before the PLO infrastructure had been destroyed. The regional balance of power was changing dramatically and rapidly. The image of an all-powerful United States capable of dictating the composition of local Arab regimes was seriously weakened.

What was becoming apparent was that the United States' ability to exercise influence in the eastern Mediterranean was more a product of its having projected an image of great power than of a direct application of force. The suspicion was developing that the United States was seriously overextended in the area. The Israeli withdrawal was also an implicit recognition of Israel's overextension. In an era of mass politics, Israel could not afford to occupy territory embracing a large and partially hostile population. Israel's weaponry and the quality of its military forces continued to make for a military asymmetry, in its favor, between Israel and its neighbors. Certainly Israel was in no danger of military defeat by any combination of its neighbors for many years to come. But Israel's ability to influence political developments within its neighbors' territories was in decline. Options were becoming available to Arab political leaders that previously had been denied them.

The United States' and Israel's relative decline in influence in the Middle East did not result in a corresponding increase in the USSR's and Syria's influence. As a Middle Eastern state as well as a major power, the Soviet Union suffered far fewer logistic difficulties than plagued the United States. But Soviet policymakers showed no signs of wishing to explore the possibilities of adding to their own influence position in the region. Nor could Syria rush in to fill the influence void simply because there was no void to be filled. The forces that persuaded the Americans and the Israelis to withdraw from Lebanon were indigenous, mainly associated with the Druze and Shia communities. The phenomenon redefining the area was the same as had redefined the situation in Iran: the sudden manifestation of mass politics in communities where it had not previously existed.

The one external government whose influence in the area had greatly expanded was in fact Iran. Within the Lebanese Shia community, a strong trend developed of looking to Ayatullah Khomeini and Iran as models and even guides. A relationship developed between Iranians and Lebanese Shia with many classic mentor/client features. Evidence of the actual process of interaction is scanty, and there is little to indicate an Iranian master plan or significant Iranian orchestration; the pattern rather appears to be that of Iran's responses to Lebanese solicitations. Iranians were seen supplying funds, logistic support, training, and advice. But how much control were they exercising over local Shia policies? The assumption on the part of victims of this collaboration, especially in this case the Americans, that the mentor does or could exercise control over the client is a central characteristic of this syndrome. This is true even though (as in this case) the victim may well be painfully aware of its own inability to control a client in such a relationship.

In any case, Lebanon became one of two major arenas in which a policy of the Reagan administration toward Iran seemed likely to crystallize. Lacking a formal military capability of any serious proportions, and working from a population base that was largely nonparticipant politically before 1982, the radical Shia leaders of Lebanon turned naturally to violence as a tactic, such as the car-bombing of the U.S. embassy and U.S. marines. Violence was effectively used against both the Americans and the Israelis. Neither the United States nor Israel had the intensity of commitment to remaining in the area that could have led to a really serious deployment of forces for that purpose. Thus both began to withdraw in the face of attacks, and this policy enhanced the prestige of the attackers. Furthermore, the response resorted to by the victims usually resulted in the destruction of villages and civilian deaths. This in turn pushed the indigenous population further toward direct political participation. But it had the effect as well of convincing American victims that the proper response to continuing acts of terrorism directed against Americans was to punish the mentor of the terrorists. Hence emphatic warnings were issued to Iran that persisting attacks on Americans or on U.S. property would necessitate a strong retaliation against Iran.[55]

The other arena of intense concern for the Reagan administration was the persisting one of the "moderate" Arab states, especially those of the Arabian peninsula. The rhythm there was constant. Whenever Iran's options began to expand, the concern for "moderate" regimes increased. The stalemate of the Iran-Iraq War in this context was too uncertain a factor. The conclusion appeared to be obvious that Iraq could not be allowed to lose that war. Iran had the advantage in its resource base and seemed to have the edge in depth of commitment and the ability to mobilize popular support behind the war. A relative improvement in weaponry by Iran, it follows, could produce dangerous consequences.

As of mid-1986, hostility toward Iran appeared to be crystallizing in Washington. Threats of violent retaliation against terroristic acts attributed to Iran were being made at the highest levels. A tilt toward Iraq, though denied officially, was unofficially admitted to be a definite policy. This tilt could be seen in improving relations with Iraq almost to the point of friendliness. But, more practically, it could be seen in a boycott of arms sales to Iran and a serious effort to persuade all arms producers of the wisdom of this course of action. The argument most consistently stressed was that some such prohibition was essential if Iran was to be induced to make peace.

Most strikingly absent from this policy was any serious targeting of internal developments in Iran. Though it is a safe assumption that Iranian exile groups continued to try to persuade the U.S. government to support their efforts, none apparently was successful. This suggests that government officials could not be persuaded that any exile group, even with full American assistance, could bring down the Iranian regime. Nor, apparently, as of mid-1986, was any consideration given to the impact of U.S. policy on factional rivalry within the Iranian regime.

However, at top levels of the Reagan administration, the stereotypical cold war view of the Soviet Union was held with a consistency unparalleled since the John Foster Dulles era. For those holding such a view, the tilt toward Iraq made little sense. Iran, not Iraq or the longtime friends of the United States in the Arab world—the so-called moderate, responsible Arab states—was the "stragetic prize" in the eyes of those perceiving an overweening Soviet threat in the area. Furthermore, the Baathist regime in Baghdad, seen as a Soviet satellite, was essentially the same regime that the United States, Iran, and Israel had attempted to destabilize through the Kurdish operation in 1974. Iraq continued to maintain close relations with the Soviet Union, even though friendship had been cooling since the USSR's failure to furnish any real assistance to Iraq during the Western-supported Kurdish rebellion. For an administration so dedicated to containing Soviet advance, a tilt toward a state friendly to the Soviet Union was a strange policy, to say the least.

How could rapprochement toward a close Arab friend of the Soviet Union be justified in the name of containing the Soviet Union? No serious effort has been made by U.S. government spokesmen to address this question. However, the tilt toward Iraq is probably best explained as a product of policy inertia grounded in the vested interests that developed with the framework of U.S. Middle East policy during the cold war era. The de facto alliance with the so-called moderate Arab states had been seen as instrumentally useful for achieving the three major purposes of U.S. policy in the area: containing the USSR, ensuring a free flow of oil to Western industry, and preserving the security of Israel.[56] By the 1980s, strong bureaucratic and industrial interests had embraced that policy. Longtime contingency plans for military cooperation in the Persian Gulf theater remained largely in effect, despite revolutionary change in the region and the integration of the economies of the oil-producing states with those of the advanced industrial nations. It may be true that, even should the worst case develop and the entire Arabian peninsula be incorporated in a great Islamic political movement, the development would not bring catastrophic results to the West. The new regimes, pursuing their own development programs, would surely continue to maintain close economic relations with the industrial West. However, the adjustment would be painful and the results unpredictable. U.S. industry in particular would run the risk of being punished for the United States' past sins in the region. The safest and easiest outcome would surely be a favorable status quo in the peninsula. Indeed, the notion that stability per se was a U.S. foreign policy objective came to be widely held and was rarely if ever questioned. The hold of that notion on the thinking of U.S. policymakers, in fact, became a major cause of deadly policy inertia.

But, as the American public would learn in 1986, those who looked longingly on the prospect of an alliance with a dedicated anticommunist Iran held important positions in the Central Intelligence Agency and on the National Security Council.[57] Gradually the fact emerged that simultaneously with the policy of moving toward Iraq, there was another policy, emanating from the White House itself, of moving toward an outright alliance with Iran. Just as administration policy was promoting a broad boycott of arms sales to Iran, that same administration was actively associated with selling Iran weapons that would reduce Iraq's technical edge over Iran. In his rationale for such a policy, Robert McFarlane, the former national security advisor, argued that he and the government were attempting to deal with Iranian "moderates," pragmatists who would move Iran back into a more easily recognizable anticommunist stance, one that would resemble the idealized image of the policy of the late shah. Friendly relations with Iran, he argued, would enhance the likelihood that such pragmatists would emerge victorious in the inevitable succession struggle following the death of Khomeini.[58] Vice-President George Bush soon after spelled out the case for moving toward an alliance with Iran in terms of classic cold war strategy.[59] But it was Colonel Oliver North who was to carry the policy to its logical conclusion. He went so far as to engage in discussion with Iranians as to how Saddam Hossein could be removed as president of Iraq.[60]

This policy shift was clearly not the result of a long struggle among diverse government factions for control of U.S. policy toward Iran. Rather, the policy evolved from a very specific and intense concern with gaining Iran's cooperation for the release of hostages held in Lebanon. Many of the hostages were believed to be held by groups toward which the Iranian government was in a strong bargaining position. As a consequence of these efforts, a policy of tilting toward Iran developed alongside a policy of tilting toward Iraq. The eventual confrontation between these two was avoided when the secret policy of selling arms to Iran and holding discussions with official Iranians was suddenly revealed. This policy was not defeated because a move toward Iran was considered illogical. To the contrary, early Reagan administration statements seemed to argue that the move toward Iran was in tune with an overall strategy of containing the Soviet Union. The defeat of the policy occurred as a consequence of further revelations that profits from the Iranian arms sales were to be transferred to the contra forces fighting the Sandinistas in Nicaragua — a policy that many in Congress considered extralegal if not illegal. Officials who had formulated and begun executing a rapprochement toward Iran were discredited and replaced. Policy direction regarding the Iran-Iraq War then returned to the State Department–based groups who favored a tilt toward Iraq as essential for the internal security of America's moderate allies among the Arab nations and for stability in the Middle East.

The critical problem for U.S. diplomatic strategists at this point was to regain control of the regional dynamics. Having pursued for several months utterly contradictory policies toward the area, regaining control required a clear definition of U.S. interests and of a strategic/tactical plan for their realization. But no such clarity was forthcoming. America's moderate Arab friends chose to depict the Iran-Iraq conflict as the Arabs' self-defense against unprovoked Iranian aggression. In a surprisingly effective Arab summit meeting held in Amman in November 1987, the overriding theme was that Iran had replaced Israel as the primary foe of the Arabs and as a basic obstacle to the achievement of Arab unity and dignity. Hafez al Assad, president of Syria, persisted in his claim that Iraq, not Iran, had been the early aggressor in the Iran-Iraq conflict. But he was clearly retreating from a position of support for the Islamic Republic. Virtually no one breathed the truth known to all: that the challenge emanated not from Iran's nationalistic ambitions but rather from Islamic political movements for which there was considerable receptivity in every Arab state. Nor was there any serious claim made that Soviet aggressive intentions lay behind the challenge from Islam.

U.S. policy in the area moved steadily toward implicit support for Iraq and explicit support for Iraq's moderate Arab allies. So strong were these dynamics, in fact, that when the U.S. frigate *Stark* was attacked by an Iraqi plane, no doubt as a result of mistaken identity, the incident added to rather than subtracting from the force of the momentum. The United States took the diplomatic lead in gaining approval for the UN Security Council's Resolution 598, calling for a return to prewar borders and a cease-fire. This would be for Iraq an optimal resolution of the conflict. Having given up any hope of victory and facing months or years of the waste of human and other resources in a now pointless war, the Iraqi government was fully prepared to accept the resolution. Iran did not reject the resolution. Rather, it called on the Security Council to recognize the fact publicly that the government of Iraq had been the aggressor in the war and that its individual perpetrators must be identified and punished.

Such an additional provision would strengthen Iran's claims for reparations and would place Iraq very much on the psychological defensive. Not surprisingly, Iraq disdained the Iranian addendum.

Iran's refusal to agree to the resolution without modifications made it possible to contend that Iran was now diplomatically isolated; such appeared to be the United States' primary objective in pushing so hard for the resolution. However, given Iran's definition of the situation, or world view, such isolation was meaningless. As described earlier, Iran saw the Islamic revolution as the most serious challenge to the hegemony of oppressor powers yet to emerge. To meet and defeat the challenge, the Iranians believed, the major powers had orchestrated an international conspiracy that included the USSR and the United States, some (but not all) lesser oppressors of Europe, the usurper Israel, and a plethora of the oppressors' regional lackeys. Foremost among the latter had been Iraq, Jordan, and Egypt. But following the rioting in Mecca and the massacre—as the Iranians viewed it—of several hundred pilgrims by Saudi security officials, Saudi Arabia was placed on the list of primary lackeys of the United States. The official Iranian view was that the Mecca massacre was planned and orchestrated by Washington.[61] Kuwait's name was also added to the list: by requesting Soviet and U.S. reflagging of Kuwaiti tankers and then giving the reflagged vessels naval protection, Kuwait was admitting its role in the great conspiracy. It could easily have avoided the loss of shipping and other punishment, Tehran repeatedly argued, simply by ceasing to give Iraq financial support and not serving as a relay station for weapons destined for Iraq. The events of 1987 indeed fully reinforced Iran's definition of the situation. Diplomatic isolation from the lackey governments of the oppressors, particularly the United States, was a mark of honor. It was the lackeys who were isolated—from their own people. The only crack in this reasoning concerned the Soviet Union. The USSR voted with the United States on UN Resolution 598, but refused to go along with the application of sanctions against Iran and even made some economic agreements with Iran that were most beneficial to Iran. Tehran's rhetoric began to take note of this apparent shift by referring to the U.S. policy alone as satanic.

But if Iran's world view was reinforced by events, that of the United States was badly shaken. Just how did increasing hostility toward Iran serve the anti-Soviet purpose, ensure the free flow of oil, or protect Israel? As the policy of selling arms to Iran and the vital role Iran could play in containing the Soviet Union indicated, there was a clear perception among the U.S. leaders that the Iranian revolution was anticommunist and the Iranian regime was potentially a critical ally in containing communist aggression. Also, the attack on shipping in the Gulf was inaugurated in 1984 by Iraq, not Iran; hence the Iranian response was reactive. Furthermore, as Israeli policy made clear well into 1987, Israel's leaders viewed Iraq as the greater of two evils. Israeli cooperation in the arms sales to Iran made this point indisputable. To be sure, U.S. statements regarding the naval presence in the Gulf argued that the United States was preventing Soviet domination of the area. But in fact the Americans and the Soviets were tilting in the same direction. The difference was that the USSR had seen the dangers in terms of loss of control in the reflagging operation, while U.S. policy was far less cautious. It granted Iraq the possibility of so provoking Iran by bombing ships carrying Iranian oil that Iran's inevitable retaliation would involve American shipping. This in turn could provoke a hostile response from the U.S. naval command and an escalation of the conflict that would be useful to Iraq in terms of broadening a war they could not win by themselves. The United States was being drawn unwittingly into conflict with the forces of Islamic resurgence. Increasingly, in fact, the Islamic Republic was being treated as if it, not the USSR, were the primary threat to American security.

The period of intense U.S. concern with Iran that followed World War II was characterized by deep involvement in Iran's domestic affairs. The central purpose of that involvement, this study has argued, was to ensure that Iran had a regime capable of resisting subversive inroads from the USSR. But a Reagan administration that saw an undiminished Soviet threat consciously avoided becoming involved in Iranian domestic affairs until 1986. Even then it appears to have stumbled onto a plan for influencing the succession of power in Iran rather than creating one. When the secret contacts with Iran were disclosed, U.S. government officials, including both President Ronald Reagan and Vice-President George Bush, argued publicly in defense of the overture that the purpose of the operation was to influence Iran's political succession in a moderate direction. Given the sensitivity in Iran to past U.S. interference, these remarks could hardly have been designed to achieve the desired direction of political succession in Iran. Indeed, the consequences, one might conclude, would be to discredit and politically destroy America's collaborators in Iran. But in fact this did not occur. Iranian contacts with Americans clearly had the support of Khomeini's office, if not of Khomeini personally, and the Iranians involved represented a broad spectrum of regime factions. The man most frequently mentioned as the primary supporter of the contacts, Speaker of Parliament Mohammad Hashemi Rafsanjani, may well have had some uncomfortable moments when an Israeli connection was disclosed. But he came through the episode relatively unscathed. The reason, quite simply, was that most regime supporters in Iran recognized that, given the importance of U.S. arms among the equipment inherited from the shah's regime, the purchase of spare parts and next-generation weaponry was critical for the regime's survival. In addition, the innocence and blatancy of the U.S. statements of purpose was a source almost of amusement in Tehran. This was hardly an example of the devious brilliance Iranians had come to expect from U.S. covert operations.

Nevertheless, U.S. policy toward Iran was of sufficient importance to have a major impact on internal political developments in Iran, whether or not the American government calculated such an impact. Iran's motivation in foreign policy was reflected in three critical and not easily reconciled directions. There was a strong religious and ideological messianism that was particularly important to the most revolutionary-minded of Iran's leaders. Just how the spread of Islamic ideology would be accomplished depended in large degree on available policy options, and the range of options in turn depended on Iran's capability. Buying critically needed weapons, it follows, gave Iranian policymakers a wider range of options and enhanced the bargaining position of those arguing for an activist spread of ideology. Since these individuals tended, like Khomeini, to identify the United States and the Soviet Union as the central actors in an oppressor world conspiracy to maintain global hegemony and hence as the primary negative targets of Iranian policy, they were a far cry from the anticommunist, pro-American allies the authors of the arms sales policy believed they were nurturing in Iran. To the contrary, they were precisely those most likely to favor policies that would disrupt the status quo.

Second, all of the regime's supporters were determined to defend Iran against attack. But the image of that external challenge varied broadly. As I have described, the view of Khomeini and the more revolutionary-minded was of a vast conspiracy, initiated and orchestrated by the United States and supported by the USSR, to snuff out the one great challenge to their hegemony from the oppressed world: the Islamic revolution in Iran. In this view, the oppressor conspirators' primary instrument was the joint lackey regime of Iraq. Its unprovoked attack on Iran in the waning days of the hostage crisis was sufficient evidence of that. As expected, the Iraqi attack had the full support of other lackey leaders, in particular King Hossein, King Hassan, and Anwar Sadat, as well as his successor, Husni Mubarak. Others, the less revolutionary, tended to see the Iraqi action as far more the personal responsibility of Iraq's president, Saddam Hossein. These individuals were far more receptive to the offers of a general peace settlement on behalf of Iraq and more willing to engage in more normal diplomatic activity. The United States' tilt toward Iraq and refusal to consider Iran's demands that Iraqi aggression be admitted and denounced, was what the more revolutionary-minded had expected. U.S. involvement in the Gulf, and especially in de facto collaboration with the USSR, fully satisfied the expectations of those intransigently opposed to a settlement. Ironically, the two contradictory U.S. policies—selling arms to Iran and then favoring Iran's enemy, Iraq—had the common feature of reinforcing the internal position of Iran's revolutionary-minded leaders. Those interested in a settlement would be reinforced by evidence that the Iraqi people themselves strongly supported Iraq's resistance to an Iranian invasion and by a serious effort of the U.S. government to recognize Iranian grievances and to see their redress.

Third, there was also a consensus among Khomeini's followers that the regime should survive. But here too there were substantial differences among leaders as to the best means to this end. The more revolutionary-minded sought to enhance the regime's support by exciting the population with evidence of great external successes or at least heroic resistance against overwhelmingly powerful enemies. Others were more interested in internal economic and social development. The relative bargaining positions of those representing these tendencies would be affected by U.S. policy. A nonhostile, essentially neutral relationship which included a good deal of economic interaction should encourage those who tended to look inward toward strengthening the regime. Conversely, a confrontational, hostile policy would offer a broad rallying point for those who came to see regime survival as impossible without major military victories.

U.S. policy toward Iran, following the denouement of the arms-for-hostages efforts, became increasingly hostile and confrontational. It was officially wrapped in anti-Soviet garb, preventing the USSR from taking advantage of a chaotic situation to enhance their presence in the Middle East. But in fact this involved what amounted to a de facto alliance with a Soviet protégé, Iraq. There was no serious effort to face directly the real nature of the Iranian "enemy." Like the Arabs at the November 1987 summit conference, the United States refused to state publicly that they were in fact confronting a politically resurgent Islam. Unlike the Arabs, who surely were fully aware of the real nature of the challenge from the Islamic Republic of Iran, U.S. policymakers may not have been aware of the nature of the challenge.

It may not be too far off the mark to conclude that U.S. policy reflected the disintegration of a world view. For a generation and a half, the U.S. world view was rooted in a basic image of a highly aggressive, monolithic, rational Soviet Union that would expand or not depending on whether American resolve was weak or strong. The United States' image of lesser actors was mainly a product of their relationship to the Soviet aggressor. Syria and Iraq, for example — small states dependent on the USSR for weapons and diplomatic support — were perceived as satellites of their mentor. Friendly regional states such as the shah's Iran, Jordan, Saudi Arabia, and Sadat's Egypt, were described as moderate, responsible, and pro-Western. The internal workings of the small states, for example, whether democratic or authoritarian, had little or nothing to do with the way they were perceived. Over time, a fairly stable and easily recognizable picture of the Middle East developed. Then came the Iranian revolution. How was one to understand a regime — the product of the overthrow of the pro-Western, moderate shah — that was fiercely anti-Soviet and yet a serious threat to the stable picture Americans saw? Tilting toward Iran under McFarlane and Poindexter made sense in one respect. It represented an alliance with an Islamic movement capable of attracting intense loyalties and adamant in its stand against any Soviet expansionism. Moving toward Iraq under Secretary of State Shultz made sense in a second respect. It represented a defense of those moderate and responsible friends in the Arab world against an Islamic movement that threatened to devour them and with them "stability" — a (once) favorable status quo. But both policies had the inadvertent effect of adding to the internal strength of Iran's most revolutionary-minded elements.

The period of intense American involvement in Iran that followed World War II was characterized by a deep American concern with Iran's internal affairs. The purpose of that involvement, this study has argued, was to insure that Iran had a regime capable of resisting Soviet subversive inroads. But the Reagan administration, which saw a Soviet threat of undiminished intensity, consciously avoided exploring the option of attempting to alter the Iranian regime. Since the same administration followed a policy of blatant interference in the internal affairs of Nicaragua with the declared intention of countering Soviet-inspired subversion, the explanation for U.S. restraint in Iran could not be a change in the American modus operandi.

There are two possible explanations for this striking change in U.S. behavior toward Iran during the 1980s, both of which suggest that the change is fundamental. The first is that, in spite of intense Iranian hostility toward the United States since the revolution, the argument that Iran is either directly or indirectly cooperating with the Soviet Union cannot be made convincingly. This has been true in spite of close Iranian relations with Syria, the People's Democratic Republic of Yemen, Cuba, and Nicaragua — all perceived as clients of the Soviet Union. Apparently both Iran and the forces of resurgent Islam generally are seen as strongly independent. As described above, the drift of American policy toward Iran by 1986 was clearly in a hostile direction. But at the same time there was apparently some sense of the value of associating with a movement, inchoate though it may be, that was capable of attracting enormous popular support and fiercely opposed to any external effort to establish control. There is in other words the beginning of a sense of major commonality of interest between the United States and the Islamic Republic. A generation earlier Americans such as Henry Grady saw a similar commonality of interest of the United States and the force of Iranian nationalism. That too was a popular movement that was fierce in its determination to throw off all external control. But Iran then was only beginning to enter the era of mass politics. Today it is fully a part of that era. Popular movements today are capable of attracting a support base so massive that even external states described as superpowers would find controlling them enormously expensive and difficult.

The other explanation is that there was a developing but still largely unrecognized acceptance of a fundamental shift in the balance of power and one not in America's favor. The Reagan administration advanced from its first days the proposition that the failures of the Carter administration were grounded in a failure of will. There was in this conceptualization no room for the contention that countries of the Middle East, now characterized by great advances in technology and an extraordinary growth in mass participation, had dramatically improved their relative power positions. Yet the Reagan administration's unwillingness to consider seriously interventionist options in Iran and the willingness to withdraw in defeat from Lebanon both suggest an acceptance of the United States' relative decline in the region.

Foreign policy tends to be an amalgam of ad hoc decisions. But viewed over time, these decisions do reflect patterns of change. The rhetoric of the Reagan administration had been vintage fifties, which has concealed to some considerable degree an appreciation of the change that is occurring in U.S. policy. However, the actual decisions of the Reagan administration appear to reflect an implicit acceptance of major change. The failure to write off the force of resurgent Islam as a phenomenon producing the kind of instability that serves Soviet subversive purposes and therefore one that should be a negative target for U.S. policy may well be explained by a still unconscious acceptance of the United States' inability to counter it. Strong verbal threats to retaliate against Iran for acts of terror committed by Lebanese or Iraqi Shia, seen as Iran's clients, reflect a sense of extreme frustration. But the disinclination to follow through with actual acts of retaliation suggests a recognition of the limited possibility and even the negative effect of such acts. Similarly, the tentative quality of the tilt toward Iraq as part of a policy of defending old regional friends suggests an implicit recognition that changed power relationships may necessitate a reconsideration of old alliance patterns. The argument that friendship with the forces of resurgent Islam could better serve the American national interest has considerable receptivity in Washington. The conclusion need not be that resurgent Islam is a major voice of the future. Indeed, its future is problematic at best. The conclusion is rather that Iran's capability, now that it has entered the era of mass politics, is substantial and that the costs, human and material, that would be required to control it are prohibitive for the American government. That conclusion holds as well for Western European governments. The proximity of the Soviet Union makes a Soviet effort to control Iran conceivable, but again the price would be exorbitantly high. Not only is the era of American involvement in Iran coming to an end, but also the much longer period of European involvement is ending as well.

# 7

## THE UNITED STATES AND IRAN:
## A COLD WAR CASE STUDY

When Iraqi planes flew over Tehran in April 1985 and dropped bombs on south Tehran (a core area of Khomeini support), mobs of Iranians appeared, shouting, "Death to America." Symbolically they were saying that six years after the collapse of the shah, Iran continued under siege from the United States, acting through its regional clients. Iranian exiles in the United States and Europe in 1985 were continuing their pleas that the United States act once again to oust an Iranian regime and replace it with one more compatible with Western values. Clearly in the minds of many Iranians, the American era in Iran was far from approaching its conclusion. The Iranian world view, regardless of one's opinion of the United States, persisted in accepting the image of a United States fully capable of exercising a major influence in Iran and in the region.

This tenacious rigidity of the Iranian world view with its image of American omnipotence gave testimony to the intensity of U.S. relations with Iran in a period covering only a generation and a half. But in terms of intensity, it was an asymmetrical relationship. For 444 days, the duration of the hostage crisis, the American public was preoccupied with Iran. However, throughout those days the anger and bitterness that Iranians were expressing toward the United States was simply bewildering to the American public. What possibly could explain this undeniable hatred projected on the television screens? The question was never really answered, and not long after the end of the crisis the question was no longer asked.

Yet the story of Iran-American relations after World War II is the story of a classic cold-war episode involving the United States and a so-called Third World country that happened to be of exceptional strategic importance. The patterns were not completely new. On the contrary, as the previous pages have shown, the United States, as part of its intense competition with the Soviet Union, be-

255

haved in Iran very much like Great Britain in its days of intense competition with tsarist Russia. In both cases, neither competitor wished to go to war to achieve preeminence in Iran, and yet both wished to gain that preeminence. In both cases, the battle between the two was fought in the Iranian domestic political arena, and both the British and the Americans tended to prefer conservative Iranians as their domestic allies. The difference was that in the prenuclear period the option of direct warfare between the competitors was always available as a last resort. In the nuclear period, however, the danger that direct violent confrontation would escalate and destroy both competitors was well understood. Hence, direct warfare between the competitors was no longer a rational option. Anglo-Russian competition in Iran prior to the Bolshevik Revolution followed an unusual pattern for that period, one that was taking place at the margins of both empires and was of central concern to neither. Soviet-American competition in the cold war era, by contrast, followed patterns that were replicated in parallel conflicts throughout the strategically important parts of the Third World.

## The Cold War Pattern of Interference

For Iranians, the legacy of external interference in their domestic political affairs is thus a century and a half old. They became familiar with a pattern of interference that was repeated with such regularity as to appear normal political behavior. The preferred political allies of both the British and later the Americans were members of Iran's traditional or conservative elite who were willing to accept some change but who could be relied on to control both the rate and the direction of that change. The elite combination that both nations in their periods of intense concern with Iran favored included, in addition to the conservative leaders, security force leaders, technocrats, and leaders of the commercial middle class. This formula was again and again, as with Mohammad Reza Pahlavi, able to produce the kind of controlled change that was best suited to avoiding chaos, a circumstance that both nations feared would be of benefit to their Russian competitor.

But two other types of regimes with different elite combinations appeared in Iran during the era of direct European-American involvement which the two external powers found less appealing. Far less desirable but still acceptable was the elite combination that characterized the regime of Reza Shah Pahlavi, a regime that encouraged rapid social and political change. Reza Shah established a military dictatorship with technocratic and commercial middle-class support. That combination could and did provide stability. But, as Reza Shah was to demonstrate, the resulting regime, once well established, would be extremely difficult for its one-time British mentor to control. Reza Shah's willingness to establish close and friendly relations with Adolf Hitler was a most disagreeable surprise for the British, who had played a significant role in his rise to power.

Still, a military dictatorship, especially one with a clearly supreme leader, was much to be preferred to the third political combination, one led by the liberal intelligentsia. This is the kind of regime that the Anglo-Americans seem most to dislike—at least, so it appears from the evidence, and not just in Iran. The Musaddiq regime, dominated by the liberal intelligentsia, became the target of a successful Anglo-American coup d'état. But long before the Musaddiq episode, in the 1920s, the British kept Zaghlul Pasha from consolidating power in Egypt; in 1940 they summarily removed Rashid Ali from Iraq. Both leaders and the movements they led paralleled Musaddiq and his movement in Iran. Then, following the Musaddiq case, the Americans played a role in eliminating Suleiman Nabulsi in Jordan and attempted to do the same with Shukri al-Quwatli in Syria. Such regimes appear to the Anglo-Americans as chaotic and beyond control. They therefore produce the kind of internal disruptions the two governments fear could result in an opportunity for their imperial competitor.

But now there is in Iran a fourth type of regime, one that is both populist and authoritarian. Change now is rapid and is following directions that resemble very little those the Anglo-Americans favored in pursuing their civilizing/modernizing strategies for Iran and the Third World. Furthermore, this new regime is utterly beyond Anglo-American control. The Musaddiq regime had had its populist element, but in Musaddiq's era the large majority of Iranians was politically nonparticipant and neither favored nor understood Mussadiq's purpose. Musaddiq's support was thin enough that a conservative domestic alliance with major directional, logistic, and financial assistance from Britain and the United States was able to overturn it in spite of the fervor and dedication of its supporters. Now the percentage of the population that is participant and mobilizable is very large. A repeat of the 1953 coup in Iran is no longer feasible. In 1979 the pattern had been broken; the likelihood that great-power competition would be fought in the internal Iranian political arena had become a distant one. Yet neither the Iranians nor the Americans understood how fundamentally power relationships had changed.

## American Policy and Ideology in Iran

The case of Iranian-American relations is instructive, especially with regard to the question of the importance of ideology as a factor in U.S. foreign policy. Hans Morgenthau believed that ideology as a factor in any government's foreign policy was little more than the basis for the symbolic wrappings of that policy.[1] The real determinant of the policy, he felt, was national interest defined in terms of power. The case of American policy in Iran argues that this judgment is too simple. There were times, as for example during the Woodrow Wilson presidency, when ideology seemed the most important determinant of U.S. policy in Iran. But such moments coincided with periods in which Americans and their government were little interested in Iran. The United States government became intensely interested in Iran when Iran was seen as a likely victim of an aggressive Soviet policy that had as its objective nothing less than world domination. At this point the American government not only did not sympathize with an Iranian regime that was philosophically close to its own; it did not even see the philosophical resemblance. When the perception of threat was intense, American behavior in Iran conformed closely to Morgenthau's political-realist expectations.

This point is perhaps best seen in terms of the manner in which the Iranian situation was defined by American diplomats in various periods of that relationship. Through the World War II years, when the intensity of American interest in Iran was still low, official political analysis of Iran painted a picture that was both complex and nonjudgmental. U.S. diplomats had no difficulty empathizing with Iranian attitudes toward external interference in their affairs. They often reported, with obvious sympathy, that many Iranians saw British and Russian policy as grounded in contempt and arrogance. (See chapter 3.) American interpretations rarely paralleled those of the British. Also, whereas there were no indications of ideological messianism on the Americans' part, there was at least some awareness that significant elements of the Iranian intelligentsia subscribed to the same Enlightenment values that provided the ideological foundation for the normative system that Americans saw as their own.

This same pattern held true for British diplomatic reporting during periods in which Britain's interest in Iran was of middle-to-low intensity. In fact, an important difference between the two is that Britain's official awareness of Iranians who shared the British ideology was somewhat sharper in these periods than was such awareness among Americans. This may be explained in part by the almost complete lack of interest in Iranian affairs among the U.S. academic and intellectual community in Iran. The only exception to this was a group of Christian missionaries, especially Presbyterians, who had long experience in Iran. But this interest was not shared by intellectuals and students in the United States. In England, by contrast, there was a sizable and influential community of scholars who were deeply interested in Iran. The intellectual historian Edward Browne was perhaps most noteworthy among Englishmen who recognized, described, and tried to encourage liberal, nationalist elements in Iran. They were so important that British diplomats could not avoid taking note of their analyses and their strongly anti-imperialist views.

The intensity of American policy concerns with Iran developed during World War II, the Azerbaijan crisis, and the early years of the cold war. Reporting during World War II was voluminous and detailed, and in this sense contrasted sharply with that of the prewar years. But the United States had not yet entered the war at the time of the Anglo-Soviet invasion of Iran, and when Americans joined the British and Soviets in occupying Iran, they were clearly the junior partners in political matters. Not surprisingly, American reporting continued to present a detached, complex, and nonjudgmental analysis of the Iranian scene.

As described in chapter 3, however, a change began to occur with the Azerbaijani crisis. Fear that the Soviet Union would be successful in subverting Iran or might even seize political control of Iran more directly began to worry American officials both in Washington and in Iran. Reporting began to reflect their fears, but it did so differentially. Ambassadors George Allen and Henry Grady continued to present complex pictures. Ambassador John Carroll Wiley, on the other hand, described the situation in simple stereotypical terms.

Increasingly, Iranian leaders were seen as polarized and were sharply judged. There were some, such as Razmara and later Zahedi, who were seen as tough, responsible, and courageous in their willingness to stand up to the Soviet Union and to resist Soviet subversion. There were others such as Musaddiq and his self-described "liberal" allies who were at best soft on communism. Iran needed the former as leaders if it was to avoid being drawn into the Soviet bloc. After Loy Henderson replaced Henry Grady as ambassador in 1951, a stereotypical cold war view would typify American reporting until the final great revolutionary crisis in Iran.

The cold war–induced definition of the situation paralleled closely the British definition of the situation in 1911. In both cases, the situation as defined made reasonable the argument for direct action to overturn the regime. Both governments saw a strong case for supporting conservative Iranian leaders, seen as fully "responsible" individuals, as alternatives to fanatical agitators who, they feared, would produce chaos and an uncontrolled situation, one easily exploited by the Russians.

## The Cold War Stereotype

This stereotypical imagery that characterized the American cold war view of Iran was typical of the American view of the entire strategically important Third World in that era. In its extreme form it appears as follows: The Soviet Union, a diabolical enemy seeking to impose its control over the world, is monolithic in decisional structure, highly rational in decisional style, and as such capable of orchestrating the most elaborate conspiracies.[2] It is overwhelmingly powerful whenever the free world, led by the United States, fails to recognize its evil purpose and to generate the will and determination to oppose it. If that purpose is understood, however, and a commitment to oppose it develops, the Soviet leaders, rational as they are, will retreat into their lair and wait for the inevitable appearance of less understanding and less determined leaders in the United States and the free world. There are in the Third World leaders who will cooperate in opposing this Soviet purpose. They are moderate in attitude and responsible in that they reject the temptations of demagoguery and have the courage to associate themselves with the free world alliance. But there is in this area as well an irresponsible and agitating leadership element that plays on the innocence and lack of understanding of their publics in order to achieve power. They are on occasion fanatics, but more typically they are irresponsible demagogues. In either case, they serve the Soviet purpose either directly or indirectly, and when they are in power they tend to allow their countries to become Soviet satellites. There are Americans and Englishmen who do not understand the Soviet purpose or pretend not to understand. These individuals, often well-meaning dupes deceived by Soviet agents, may take seriously the claims of the agitating leaders in the Third World that they are nationalists struggling to establish free and democratic systems in their countries. But this is a cruel hoax. There simply is no public opinion in these countries capable of understanding and supporting such a program.

It follows that those who see the Third World as anywhere close to this stereotypical image will argue for a policy of support for the "moderate and responsible" leadership. That may at times call for drastic action in the form of helping such leaders overturn a government controlled by "agitating elements" and in helping "moderate" governments suppress such elements internally.

## The United States' Impact on Iranian Politics

The impact of external intervention on Iranian sociopolitical development was far greater in 1953 than it had been in 1912. In the earlier period, only a thin veneer of the Iranian population was actively participant, or predisposed to become so, in the political process. But by 1953 the participating percentage was sufficiently large to make arguably plausible the contention that, without external action a liberal democratic system could have been established. As described in chapter 3, Musaddiq had by 1953 largely bested his rival for political control of Iran, Ayatullah Abol Qasem Kashani. Musaddiq's religious allies held a view of Islam that was far more compatible with that of Musaddiq and his liberal, secular nationalist associates than was Kashani's. The latter indeed had a view of a future Islamic society that was much closer to that of Ayatullah Khomeini.

The case can be made therefore that the decision to overturn Musaddiq was a truly historic one. Iran was at the point of change at which the percentage of the population entering the political process, or predisposed to do so, was increasing in geometric progression. These awakening individuals would look to leaders whom they recognized and trusted for the norms, values, and institutions that they could support. Had Musaddiq, the National Front, and the religious leaders who interpreted the Qoran more liberally remained in control of the Iranian government, they could have served as the socializing agents for this awakening mass. Instead, they were replaced by a royal dictatorship that stood aloof from the people. In the first great demonstrations focused on Ayatullah Khomeini in 1963, there were clear signs that much of the newly awakened mass was looking to an alienated and angry wing of the clergy as their leaders. In 1977 and 1978, as the revolutionary momentum gained force, this pattern was hard to deny.

The American moment of intense concern was brief in terms of years, but it occurred at a critical moment in Iranian social and political history, a moment of extraordinarily rapid change. The impact of American policy was substantial. It altered the direction of change away from those seeking to lead Iran toward liberal democracy and nationalist assertiveness. The Iranian leaders whom American policy directly assisted in 1953 were conservatives who hoped to maintain control in the hands of Iran's traditional elite and to slow the rate of change. A decade later the shah, with American acquiescence, shifted his domestic alliance away from traditional elements and toward a newly rich industrial and commercial class. This resulted in a period of rapid economic growth, but it also accelerated the growth in the percentage of the population that was ready to become politically participant. Neither the regime nor its American supporters manifested any particular concern with this rapidly awakening mass. A sense of relative deprivation—political, social, and economic—pervaded this element. When the Iranian economy suffered a growth in inflation, they grew increasingly receptive to the appeal of the oppositionist clergy. Liberals, nationalist and Islamic, dominated the revolutionary leadership, but their access to the awakening mass was limited. Their own natural support group was the professional and technocratic middle class. This element did join the revolution and played a decisive role in its success. But it joined late, long after a mosque bureaucracy–based organization had become the institutional heart of the revolution. In the struggle to control the direction of the revolution after the shah fell, the liberals were no match for the radical clergy.

Many Iranian exiles still hold the view that, given its overwhelming power, the United States government must have been directly involved in Khomeini's total triumph. There is in fact no evidence to support this contention. But the case is a strong one that American policy did indeed play a major but entirely inadvertent role in producing this outcome. U.S. policy did change Iran's history and in fundamental ways. It helped oust a liberal nationalist elite which had looked to the United States as its ideological ally and as its one reliable external supporter. In helping eliminate a government that symbolized Iran's search for national integrity and dignity, it helped deny the successor regime nationalist legitimacy. And in a generation and a half in power, neither that regime nor its American mentor made any major effort to establish legitimacy for it. Thus when it was faced with a serious but not catastrophic economic crisis, its vulnerability on grounds of legitimacy became only too apparent. The people turned to leaders with legitimacy — but this time the leaders were radical clerics, not the liberal nationalists.

Here too the case of Iran may be generalizable to that of the strategically important Third World. Seeing that world stereotypically, as described above, the U.S. government tended everywhere to oppose leaders their people saw as representing their nationalist aspirations. On occasion, as in Iran, Jordan, and Guatemala, they were ousted from power. More frequently conservative or traditional regimes were given the means to suppress them. The growth in the percentage of the population predisposed to political participation was, however, inexorable. And the consequence of American policy generally was to deny to a generation and a half of strong and educated nationalists the ability to provide leadership for and the normative guidance for the newly participant. Another consequence of blatant, virtually unconcealed, American intervention, applied as it was so often against leaders with nationalist legitimacy, was to deny such legitimacy to those leaders who were the beneficiaries of U.S. support. This produced a fundamental vulnerability in American-supported regimes. With nationalist leaders suppressed or discredited, the newly participant publics have tended to turn either to the left — or, as in so much of the Islamic world, to religious leaders.

## Iran in the Era of Mass Politics

The process of rapid change in Iran, the Middle East, and throughout the Third World may have in one vital respect reached its climax. In less than a century, Iran has changed from a society in which the vast majority of its people did not participate in politics and acquiesced in the political authority structure to one in which the vast majority is politically participant and nonacquiescent. A political process that yesterday directly concerned only a tiny elite must now be highly sensitive to the influence and material demands of a mass public. This change, astonishingly rapid as it has been, is yet to be comprehended by most Westerners who persist in seeing Iran, the Middle East, and the Third World through century-old Eurocentric lenses.

Possibly the most fundamental impact of this element of change in Iran and throughout the Third World in general is in the realm of relative state power. In the early stages of this change process, the power balance was skewed overwhelmingly in the favor of the Europeans. They confronted an Iran, a typical example, that had yet to enter the technological era, that had a security/coercive force adapted to traditional internal control needs but hopelessly inadequate for confronting a European power, and a governing elite that could not even consider the option of mobilizing its people to resist external threats. At this stage, resistance to intervention by a determined European power was ultimately hopeless. For Iran the only defense was to play the European competitors against one another. Because involvement by Europeans in Iran's domestic politics was impossible to deflect, individual Iranians seeking to improve their influence position would typically calculate how they could use the external presence to their personal advantage.

By the time of intense American involvement in Iran, the power equation was already altering. Reza Shah had built a military force that was more suitable for twentieth-century purposes. It was of course unable to halt an Anglo-Soviet invasion, but it could maintain internal order and unity and provide a means for resisting a regional challenge. More fundamentally, Iran now had a substantial section of its population that could be mobilized to confront the external threat. The British- and American-backed coup that overthrew the charismatic Mohammad Musaddiq came very close to failing. But traditional elements willing to cooperate with imperial forces were still sufficiently powerful to—with major external support—overturn even a very popular regime.

By the late 1970s and 1980s, a coup of the order that overturned

Musaddiq was unthinkable. The regime's ability to mobilize massive opposition from the military and public was only too apparent. As the Iran-Iraq War demonstrated, despite an extraordinary overbalance of external support for Iraq, a legitimate Iranian regime able and willing to mobilize its core support base could stand against a major external effort to overthrow it. Yet the rhetoric of both the Iranian and American governments seemed to persist in viewing U.S. power as virtually undiminished. Iranian spokesmen described the war against Iraq as American-orchestrated. And the Reagan administration continued to argue that the fall of the shah was a result of a lack of American will, not a reflection of a basic inadequacy in capability. But in policy both governments today appear to see a diminished American presence. Iran does not hesitate to take positions that implicitly carry the risk of a strong American response. And the U.S. government has not taken the option of using force against Iran even in the face of what have seemed to be strong provocations. A lag between rhetoric and policy of this order is a common pattern when change is rapid. It typically reflects differing perceptions on the part of political leaders and of the concerned bureaucracy—with the bureaucracy more sensitive to power realities. If, as suggested here, the case of Iran is consistent with change in the Middle East and the Third World more generally, the alteration in relative power standings must soon be reflected in some fundamental alterations in Western strategies relating to Iran and the Third World.

However, when the focus is shifted from Iran and the Middle East to the Third World at large, a clear pattern in American policy behavior is identifiable. Rhetoric may be the same universally, but practice differs sharply depending on the length of the logistic lines. In the Caribbean and Central America, the region of the United States' unchallengeable preeminence in capability, rhetoric and policy tend to be congruent. In the Eastern Hemisphere, the congruence is lacking, as in Iran; belligerent and assertive rhetoric is associated with a cautious and nonassertive policy. This suggests that when strategy is adpated to a rapidly changing power configuration, American policy will be increasingly focused on the Western Hemisphere.

As a close parallel, another element of major change in American policy toward Iran in the 1980s may be more generally applicable. The previous three chapters have argued that the United States' view of Iran, and in particular the extreme simplicity of that view, have been a function of the American preoccupation with the cold war. If so, it is possible to describe both the beginning and the near conclusion of that simplifying tendency. As mentioned above, some officials began to see Iran in simple and stereotypical terms during the Azerbaijan crisis, and by the late Musaddiq period this became the prevailing view. But when revolutionary forces began to gain strength, there were many, especially in the State Department, who recognized the great complexity of the situation. National Security Adviser Brzezinski persisted in the cold war view until the shah fell, but after the revolution succeeded, the tendency to describe the situation in cold war terms had largely vanished. Differing diagnoses were made especially regarding the prospects for the Bazargan forces in the new government. However, both sets of analyses reflected a complexity of view, and neither saw a clever Soviet orchestration at work. That view now was largely limited to Iranian royalists in exile.

Here again, official rhetoric and policy lacked congruence. President Reagan's "evil empire" image of the Soviet Union was an example of classic cold war imagery. Furthermore, the projection of that image in crisis areas in the Western Hemisphere, in particular Central America, was entirely consistent with the general view. A similar projection in Eastern Hemisphere crises occurred sporadically. Alexander Haig, for example, at the time of the June 1982 Israeli invasion of Lebanon, saw Israel's primary targets, the PLO and Syria, as essentially Soviet clients. Qaddafi too on occasion was seen as a virtual agent of the Kremlin. But this simplified view was not applied to other situations and, with regard to the Islamic Republic of Iran, only an occasional remark suggests a perception of Soviet control. Indeed, this inability to place Iran in a cold war frame had much to do with the United States' policy confusion relating to Iran. Strongly anticommunist religious leaders appeared to be natural allies. However, Iran's hostility to good American friends, such as Jordan and Egypt, the belief that Iran supported and even directed terrorist attacks against Americans, and lingering anger over the hostage case all stood in the path of rapprochement.

## Tendencies in American Policy Toward Revolutionary Iran

Is the United States likely to make a second historic mistake in Iran, one fully comparable to that made in the 1953 overturn of Musaddiq? The answer would be yes if the United States, confronted with another populist phenomenon, this time focused on the Islamic community, should place itself in opposition to a movement that reflects a basic sociopolitical trend in the region. But there are several reasons for concluding that this will not occur.

First, whether the United States could play a decisive role in a successful effort to replace the Islamic Republic is very much in question. The regime's ability to stand up to the attack from Iraq even though a seriously effective arms boycott had been imposed on Iran while Iraq had received a great deal of external assistance argues the negative. As long as the regime maintains its core support base, it is probably invulnerable to external actions short of a full-scale invasion by a great power. Punishing Iran for its alleged responsibility for terrorist attacks or an escalation of military support for Iraq would ensure long-term enmity from the regime's supporters. But such acts are unlikely to result in imposing a new ruling elite on the country and, in so doing, to alter Iranian development in unpredictable directions as was the case in 1953.

Second, as did not happen in 1953, there appears to be surprisingly little tendency to conclude that the regime is increasing the subversive potential for the Soviet Union in Iran. On the contrary, and as suggested above, there is a discernible tendency in the Reagan administration to accept the conclusion this time that a populist development such as this Islamic movement is a major impediment to the USSR's ability to make inroads internally in Iran. The United States' strong attachment to conservative Arab regimes is a consequence of a historical evolution of cold war policy in the Middle East. Since these regimes feel threatened by the Islamic revolution and have appealed successfully for U.S. security assistance, that cold war–induced alliance system is a major factor in American policy toward Iran. But U.S. officials seem more willing to understand the fears of these allies than to share them.

Third, there is strong reason to question that the Islamic movement focused on the person of Ayatullah Khomeini is comparable in historic importance to the nationalist movement focused on the person of Mohammad Musaddiq. Musaddiq was vulnerable to an externally supported coup despite his popularity because only a narrow element of the population was then politically participant. Thus a conservative elite was able to mobilize a large but uncomprehending mob to overthrow him. But among those who participated in politics, Musaddiq's popularity was overwhelming. Even among those who felt he should be forced from office, there was respect for his uncompromising nationalism. Because of his involvement in the coup, the shah was never able to recover his legitimacy as a leader of the Iranian nation; when his regime became vulnerable, the lack of any strong support base was only too apparent. In early 1979 Iranians were united as never before, and there was no reason to ask if the community they so strongly identified with was the Islamic community or the Iranian national community. For most Iranians, the two communities were one.

The Khomeini phenomenon, in contrast to the Musaddiq phenomenon, has appeared in an Iran that is thoroughly politicized. The day of the mercenary mob, mobilizable on occasion but incapable of sustained political attention, has passed. Indeed, Khomeini's core support base, willing to make any sacrifice for his movement, is disproportionately representative of the very social element that was mobilized to overturn Musaddiq. It is now both comprehending and fully capable of prolonged sustained interest. The strength of the regime and its very survival is a consequence of this support. But the impression this gives that the regime is popular is seriously misleading.

To begin with, the Iranian people under Khomeini have been seriously polarized. Paralleling the large and intensely supportive core group is another large and intensely antagonistic group. The latter lacks unity and any strong sense of efficacy for producing change, but it is irreconcilable to Khomeini's image of an all-embracing Islamic society. Its disaffection in fact is so severe that its response goes beyond simple anticlericalism; for many in the group, the response is anti-Islamic. For his part, Khomeini has succeeded with his core support in disparaging nationalism. For this group, the nationalistic Iranian is acculturated, a converted European without roots or dignity. As they see him, the nationalist has rejected his past and himself.

However, there may be far less here than meets the eye. The largely clerical group that has become the governing elite of Iran is far too thinly based to maintain long-term control of Iran's complex and highly diverse society and economy. It is able to remain in power thanks to the ability of the charismatic leader to maintain an intensely committed core support, plus the existence of a large and effective, if decentralized, coercive control system. For the moment, the regime is relatively stable, and the image it projects of an ideal Islamic society soon to be created cannot be dismissed lightly. But its underlying vulnerabilities could surface with sudden force. Most serious of these is the critical reliance on Khomeini's ability to mobilize support by the effectiveness with which he manipulates Islamic symbols. There is no one in his entourage with even remotely comparable abilities. Thus his death or loss of personal effectiveness would compel the regime in the short run to turn to enhanced coercion. However, there is here too a serious vulnerability. Khomeini, by not permitting the triumph of a strong political leader or faction from within his entourage, has inadvertently prevented the appearance of centralized control over the coercive instruments. The most important of them, the revolutionary guard, has a number of competing leaders who are available for alliances with competing factions that are certain to engage in a serious struggle for power with the passing of Khomeini's dominance.

A third vulnerability lies in the paucity of technocratic competence among members of the governing elite and their closest supporters. There has been an effort to recruit and to train young people who are supporters of the regime to fill this void. But the effort, again reflecting a lack of central leadership, has not been particularly effective. The fact is that a secular trend has been strong in Iran throughout the twentieth century and has been particularly manifest among the better educated, the very group from which competent technocrats must be recruited. To manage a complex of social and economic programs the regime really has no alternative to co-opting technocrats, many of whom will be secular, nationalistic, and apt to identify only lightly with Islam. With Khomeini's passing, the importance of this element is likely to strengthen.

The range of possible scenarios that could occur when the unavoidable leadership crisis develops is large. But a component feature of most of them will surely be a broadening of the governing elite to include individuals who look at least as much to the national as to the Islamic community. To assure stability in Iran over the long run, the polarization of the Khomeini era must be overcome. That will not be easy; in the short run, violent conflict between polarized elements is certainly possible. But the reconciliation process is likely to occur because most Iranians identify with a single community that is both Shia Islamic and national. Leaders who stress this commonality rather than the difference between secularism and sectarianism are ultimately likely to prevail. Secularism in Iran is far too pervasive to allow for the persistence of a ruling elite that seeks to purge the secular-minded from a role in Iranian politics and society.

If the basic contention of this study is valid—that the era of European political dominance in Iran has come to an end and that the same conclusion is possible for much of the non-Western world—then a fundamental change in the international system is now taking place. The change is most apparent in relative capability. The day in which the term *superpower* seemed to describe well the United States and the Soviet Union has passed. Now that mass politics characterizes most of the world, the relative ability of two or a few powers to impose their will on much of the world through participation in their domestic affairs has passed as well. Regional associations of middle-ranking states can now seriously think in terms of deterring any aggressive moves by states previously described in power terms as "great." Iran's ability to stand alone against an Iraq that is the beneficiary of assistance from much of the world does indeed tell a great deal about the massiveness of this change.

However, even if the thesis is valid, there is little awareness among the world's leaders and publics of the change and its momentous implications. Khomeini's contention to Qotbzadeh, that many powerful shocks, such as the fall of the shah and the long retention of hostages would be necessary before the United States realized its loss of relative capability, appears, in retrospect, remarkably prescient. Other shocks have followed, such as the dramatic American pullout from Lebanon. But still the old power imagery persists. Even Khomeini and his entourage, proud as they are of Iran's ability to stand up to a broad hostile alliance and explicitly asserting the change in power relationships, continue to exaggerate American power. The belief that the United States orchestrated the Iran-Iraq War illustrates that point.

There may well be, as I have suggested, an unconscious adjustment in U.S. policy to the new power realities in the Middle East. For an example, compare American policy in Central America, where allegations of Soviet orchestration of revolutionary change are accepted by the Reagan administration as beyond question, with the

Middle East, where there is considerable willingness to look at the force of revolutionary change as autonomous. But the cold war continues to give primary definition to Middle East policy for the Reagan administration. There is a real possibility that, if hostility continues to characterize Iranian-American relations, a U.S. administration could come to see the force of resurgent Islam as Iranian royalist exiles do—that is, as fully under Soviet control. This could mean a return to an interventionist policy in Iran. Given the risks of escalation of conflict in the nuclear era, this could be exceedingly dangerous. Confrontation and war, with the United States and Iran on opposing sides, are possible as long as the old imagery persists, but a return to the era of prolonged U.S. dominance in Iran is no longer feasible.

Notes

Index

# NOTES

## Chapter 1. Introduction

1. Two comprehensive but succinct histories of ancient Iran are A. T. Olmstead, *History of the Persian Empire* (Chicago: University of Chicago Press, 1948); and R. Ghirshman, *Iran: From the Earliest Times to the Islamic Conquest* (Baltimore, Md.: Penguin Books, 1954).

2. See Sir William Tarn, *Alexander the Great,* 2 vols. (Cambridge: Cambridge University Press, 1948).

3. On Parthia, see H.D.H. Bivar, "The Political History of Iran Under the Arascids," in *The Cambridge History of Iran,* vol. 3, ed. Ehsan Yarshater (Cambridge: Cambridge University Press, 1983).

4. Abd Al-Husain Zarrinkub, "The Arab Conquest of Iran and Its Aftermath," in *The Cambridge History of Iran,* vol. 4, ed. Richard N. Frye (Cambridge: Cambridge University Press, 1975).

5. J. A. Boyle, "Dynastic and Political History of the II Khans," in *The Cambridge History of Iran,* vol. 5, ed. J. A. Boyle (Cambridge: Cambridge University Press, 1968).

6. Still perhaps the richest picture of the motives for nineteenth-century imperialism is John A. Hobson, *Imperialism: A Study* (London: G. Unwin, 1902).

7. For an excellent critique of that literature, see Philip Green, *Deadly Logic: The Theory of Nuclear Deterrence* (New York: Schocken Books, 1966).

8. See, for example, Harry Eckstein, ed., *Internal War: Problems and Approaches* (New York: Free Press of Glencoe, 1964).

9. See Paul Blackstock, *The Strategy of Subversion* (Chicago: Quadrangle Books, 1964); Andrew Scott, *The Revolution in Statecraft: Internal Penetration* (New York: Random House, 1965); Richard Cottam, *Competitive Interference and Twentieth Century Diplomacy* (Pittsburgh, Pa.: University of Pittsburgh Press, 1967).

10. This notion is developed in Alexander George and Richard Smoke, *Deterrence in American Foreign Policy: Theory and Practice* (New York: Columbia University Press, 1974).

11. See Carl Deutsch, *Nationalism and Social Communication* (Cambridge, Mass.: MIT Press, 1966).

12. For example, see Samuel Huntington, "Political Development and Political Decay," *World Politics* 17 (1965): 386–430.

## Chapter 2. The Illusion of Sympathy

1. For a glimpse of traditional tribal life in Iran, see Frederick Barth, *Nomads of South Persia: The Basseri Tribe of the Khamseh Federation* (New York: Humanities Press, 1961).

2. On the role of the clergy in the preconstitutional period, see Hamid Algar, *Religion and State in Iran, 1785–1906* (Berkeley and Los Angeles: University of California Press, 1969).

3. George N. Curzon, *Persia and the Persian Question,* 2 vols. (London: Longmans, 1892).

4. For a revealing view of the outlook of one Iranian intellectual of this period, see Hamid Algar, *Mirza Malkum Khan* (Berkeley and Los Angeles: University of California Press, 1973).

5. Nikkie R. Keddie, *Sayyid Jamal ad-Din "al-Afghani": A Political Biography* (Berkeley and Los Angeles: University of California Press, 1972).

6. On the tobacco rebellion, see Nikkie R. Keddie, *Religion and Rebellion in Iran* (London: Frank Cass, 1966).

7. See Firuz Kazemazdeh, *Russia and Britain in Persia: 1864–1914; A Study in Imperialism* (New Haven, Conn.: Yale University Press, 1968).

8. The Foreign Office in London consistently instructed the legation in Tehran to coordinate their responses to the Iranian situation with their Russian colleagues. See, for example, *State Papers,* 1909, Persia No. 92, p. 93.

9. The diplomatic correspondence begins to reflect a social analysis only after the revolution is under way.

10. See, for example, *State Papers,* 1909, Persia No. 3, p. 1.

11. *State Papers,* 1909, Persia No. 91, p. 92.

12. See the book by an early U.S. minister, S.G.W. Benjamin, *Persia and the Persians* (Boston: Ticknor and Co., 1887).

13. *United States Foreign Relations,* 1889, p. 685.

14. *United States Foreign Relations,* 1904, p. 667.

15. Ibid., p. 492.

16. *United States Foreign Relations,* 1892, p. 30.

17. *United States Foreign Relations,* 1906, p. 1217.

18. Ibid.

19. Edward Browne, *A Brief Narrative of Recent Events in Persia* (London: Cambridge University Press, 1909).

20. Arthur J. Funk, "The Missionary Problem in Persia," *Moslem World,* April 1920.

21. See Edward Browne, *The Persian Revolution of 1905–1906* (Cambridge: Cambridge University Press, 1910), pp. 172–96.

22. *State Papers,* 1909, Persia No. 177, p. 90.

23. Morgan Shuster, *The Strangling of Persia* (New York: Century, 1912). See also Robert McDaniel, *The Shuster Mission and the Persian Constitutional Revolution* (Minneapolis: Biblioteca Islamica, 1974).

24. *United States Foreign Relations,* 1911, p. 683.

25. Ibid., p. 685.

26. This is reflected in the judgment of the editors of *United States Foreign Relations.* No dispatches of any importance from Tehran are included in these years.

27. *Documents on British Foreign Policy, 1919–1939,* 1st Serv., 4:1138–39.

28. Harold Nicolson, *Curzon: The Last Phase, 1919–1925* (New York: Houghton Mifflin, 1934), p. 133.

29. Ibid., p. 128.

30. *The Near East,* November 20, 1919, p. 599.

31. Abraham Yeselson, *United States–Persian Diplomatic Relations, 1883–1921.*

32. *United States Foreign Relations,* 1919, pp. 714–17.

33. Ibid., p. 708.

34. Ibid., p. 719.

35. On Kuchek Khan, see Suroosh Irfani, *Iran's Islamic Revolution: Popular Liberation or Religious Dictatorship?* (London: Zed Books, 1983).

36. *United States Foreign Relations,* 1921, 2:633–34.

37. On the actual British role, see Richard Ullman, *Anglo-Soviet Relations 1917–1921: The Anglo-Soviet Accord,* vol. 3 (Princeton, N.J.: Princeton University Press, 1972).

38. Regarding Modaress, see Shahrough Akhavi, *Religion and Politics in Contemporary Iran: Clergy-State Relations in the Pahlavi Period* (Albany: State University of New York Press, 1980).

39. For a sympathetic account of Reza Shah, see Donald Wilber, *Reza Shah Pahlavi 1878–1944: The Resurrection and Reconstruction of Iran* (Hicksville, N.Y.: Exposition Press, 1975).

40. Hossein Maki, *Tarikh Bist Saleh Iran,* 3 vols. (Tehran: Chapkhaneh Majlis, 1945–47). See esp. vol. 3, pp. 153–221.

41. On Reza Shah's impact on Iran, see Amin Banani, *The Modernization of Iran, 1921–41* (Stanford, Calif.: Stanford University Press, 1966).

42. On Teymurtash, see Niron Rezun, *The Soviet Union and Iran: Soviet Invasion in 1941* (Geneva: Sijthoff and Noordhoff, 1981).

43. See Alan W. Ford, *The Anglo-Iranian Oil Dispute of 1951–1952* (Berkeley and Los Angeles: University of California Press, 1954); and Ruhollah Ramazani, *The Foreign Policy of Iran 1500–1941* (Charlottesville: University Presses of Virginia, 1966).

44. See, for a good example of Iranian thinking, *Shahed,* January 29, 1952.

45. *United States Foreign Relations,* 1938, 2:346–47.

46. For example, *United States Foreign Relations,* 1939, vol. 4, Oct. 19 and 21.

47. Violet Conolly, *Soviet Economic Policy in the East* (London: Oxford University Press, 1933), pp. 53–75.

48. Ibid.

49. *United States Foreign Relations,* 1923, 2:711–13.

50. *United States Foreign Relations,* 1937, 2:742–61.

51. For an excellent discussion on this subject, see Rezun, *The Soviet Union in Iran.*

52. *United States Foreign Relations,* 1923, 2:711.

53. *United States Foreign Relations,* 1937, 2:742–61.

54. *United States Foreign Relations,* 1928, 3:722–28.

55. *United States Foreign Relations,* 1939, 4:527–28.

56. *United States Foreign Relations,* 1936, 3:372.

57. See Arthur Millspaugh, *The American Task in Persia* (New York: Century, 1925); *United States Foreign Relations,* 1927, vol. 3. The correspondence on Millspaugh is voluminous from January through September 1927.

58. *United States Foreign Relations,* 1940, 3:634.

## Chapter 3. The Cold War Takes Over

1. *United States Foreign Relations, 1940,* 3:634.

2. *United States Foreign Relations, 1941,* 3:419.

3. See *Great Britain and the East* 54 (February 22, 1940): 120.

4. See the issues of *Darya* newspaper for this period for a well-articulated picture.

5. See Hossein Maki, *Tarik Bist Saleh Iran,* 3 vols. (Tehran: Chapkhaneh Majlis, 1945–47).

6. *United States Foreign Relations, 1941,* 3:462.

7. *United States Foreign Relations, 1943,* 4:329.

8. For a fully developed discussion of the left, see Ervan Abrahamian, *Iran Between Two Revolutions* (Princeton, N.J.: Princeton University Press, 1982).

9. See Richard W. Cottam, *Nationalism in Iran* (Pittsburgh, Pa.: University of Pittsburgh Press, 1979), ch. 14.

10. See Shahrough Akhavi, *Religion and Politics in Contemporary Iran: Clergy-State Relations in the Pahlavi Period* (Albany: State University of New York Press, 1980).

11. For a U.S. picture of the British estimate, see *United States Foreign Relations, 1943,* 4:320–25.

12. *United States Foreign Relations, 1941,* 3:419–21.

13. *United States Foreign Relations, 1944,* 5:393–95.

14. Ibid., 5:425–26.

15. Ibid., 5:436–40.

16. Arthur Millspaugh, *Americans in Persia* (Washington, D.C.: Brookings, 1946).

17. See, for example, *United States Foreign Relations, 1945,* 8:381.

18. See, for example, *United States Foreign Relations, 1942,* 4:157.

19. See, for example, *United States Foreign Relations, 1941,* 3:463.

20. *United States Foreign Relations, 1943,* 4:330–31.

21. *United States Foreign Relations, 1944,* 5:397–99.

22. Ibid., 5:740–42.

23. *United States Foreign Relations, 1943,* 4:331–36.

24. See William Eagleton, Jr., *The Kurdish Republic of 1946* (London: Oxford University Press, 1963).

25. Nejafqoli Pesian, *Morg Bud Bazgasht Ham Bud* (Tehran: Sherkat Sahami Chap, 1949).

26. *United States Foreign Relations, 1945,* 4:331–36.

27. Ibid., 8:496–97.

28. Eagleton, *The Kurdish Republic of 1946.*

29. *United States Foreign Relations, 1946,* 7:362–64.

30. Ibid., 7:350–54, 733–34.

31. *United States Foreign Relations, 1947,* 5:927.

32. George Lenczowski, *Russia and the West in Iran* (Ithaca: Cornell University Press, 1949); *United States Foreign Relations, 1946,* 7:386.

33. *United States Foreign Relations, 1945,* 8:418–20.

34. Lenczowski, *Russia and the West in Iran; United States Foreign Relations, 1945,* 8:470.

35. *United States Foreign Relations,* 1945, 8:418–20.

36. Robert Rossow, "The Battle of Azerbaijan," *Middle East Journal,* Winter 1956, pp. 17–32.

37. *United States Foreign Relations,* 1946, 7:417.

38. *United States Foreign Relations,* 1945, 8:420–22.

39. Harold F. Grosnell, *Truman's Crises: A Political Biography of Harry S. Truman* (Westport, Conn.: Greenwood, 1980).

40. *United States Foreign Relations,* 1946, 6:460.

41. *United States Foreign Relations,* 1945, 8:497; 7:291.

42. *United States Foreign Relations,* 1946, 7:350–54.

43. Ibid., 7:400.

44. Ibid., 7:406, 460.

45. Ibid., 8:479.

46. Ibid., 7:423.

47. Ibid., 7:423–24.

48. Ibid., 7:449.

49. Ibid., 7:448–50, 495.

50. Ibid., 7:478.

51. Ibid., 7:490.

52. Ibid., 7:505.

53. Ibid., 7:478.

54. Ibid., 7:490–91.

55. Ibid.

56. Ibid., 7:497–98.

57. Ibid., 7:499, 503.

58. Ibid., 7:510.

59. Ibid.

60. Ibid., 7:516.

61. Ibid., 7:517.

62. Ibid., 7:522–23.

63. Ibid., 7:533–35.

64. Ibid., 7:536–37.

65. Ibid., 7:560–61.

66. Ibid., 7:561.

67. Ibid., 7:563.

68. Ibid., 7:566.

69. Ibid., 7:565.

70. *United States Foreign Relations,* 1947, 5:949.

71. Ibid., 5:913.

72. Ibid., 5:924.

73. Ibid., 5:951.

74. Ibid., 5:931–32.

75. Ibid., 5:934.

76. Ibid., 5:945–46.

77. Ibid., 5:960.

78. Ibid., 5:961–62.

79. See Bruce Kuniholm, *The Origins of the Cold War in the Middle East: Great Power Conflict and Diplomacy in Iran, Turkey, and Greece* (Princeton, N.J.: Princeton University Press, 1980).

80. Kuniholm's accounts on Iran and on Greece are entirely in tune with mainstream analysis and implicitly contradictory with regard to Soviet intentions.

81. *United States Foreign Relations, 1947,* 5:978.

82. Ibid., 5:972.

83. Ibid., 5:873–74.

84. Ibid., 5:990–93, 998.

85. *United States Foreign Relations, 1948,* 5:161.

86. Ibid., 5:156–57.

87. Ibid., 6:516–17.

88. Ibid., 5:155.

89. Ibid., 5:474–75.

90. *United States Foreign Relations, 1949,* 6:590.

91. Ibid., 6:545–51.

92. *United States Foreign Relations, 1950,* 5:479–80, 490–91.

93. *United States Foreign Relations, 1949,* 6:545.

94. *United States Foreign Relations, 1950,* 5:510.

95. Ibid., 5:549–50.

96. Ibid., 5:558.

97. Ibid., 5:610–11.

98. Ibid., 5:612–13.

99. Ibid., 5:613–15.

100. Ibid., 5:634.

101. For the British account of this, see: CAB 129/47 XCA 19766, C.P. (51) 257, September 26, 1951, "The Oil Dispute with Persia," pp. 3–5.

102. See Richard W. Cottam, "Iranian Political Parties," *Iranian Studies* 1, no. 3 (Summer 1968).

103. F.O. 371/98593, "Reports on Events in Persia in 1951."

104. CAB 129/46 XCA 19766, C.P. (51)200, July 11, 1951, "Persia," F.O. 371/98593.

105. For example, see the *New York Times,* October 18, 1952, 5:5.

106. C.P. (51)257, "The Oil Dispute with Persia."

107. Ibid.

108. Ibid.

109. Kermit Roosevelt, *Countercoup: The Struggle for the Control of Iran* (New York: McGraw-Hill, 1979). The first printing was withdrawn. The only changes made were to substitute "British intelligence" for "AIOC."

110. See Cottam, *Nationalism in Iran,* p. 219.

111. C.P. (51)60, CAB 128/20, pp. 231–34, CM (51)56.

112. F.O. 137/983, August 11, 1952, "Anglo-US Discussions."

113. For a summary British estimate, see C.P. (52)285, August 19, 1952, "Persia," pp. 114–19.

114. See Cottam, *Nationalism in Iran,* pp. 276–77.

115. Hassan Arsenjani, interviews with the author throughout 1957.

116. See CAB 129/55; C.P.(52)337, October 13, 1952, "Persia"; C.X. (52)341,

October 17, 1952, "Persia: Internal Situation"; F.O. 371/104574, December–January 1952–53, "Persia's Political Economy."

117. See C.P.(52)354, October 23, 1952, "Persia United States Ideas for Settlement of the Oil Dispute."

118. On Henderson's negotiations, see CAB 129/58: C.P.(53)1, January 1, 1953, "Persia"; C.P.(53)5, January 5, 1953, "Persia"; C.P.(53)15, January 10, 1953, "Persia"; C.P.(53)41, January 31, 1953, "Persia."

119. F.O., March 13, 1953, unnumbered.

120. Roosevelt, *Countercoup*.

121. F.O., May 7, 1953, and June 16, 1953, unnumbered.

122. British documents on the subject are not available. One account does discuss the shah's attitude toward the coup: see F.O. report by Sir Roger Makins, undated 1953, unnumbered.

123. See Kennett Love, "The American Role in the Pahlevi Restoration," unpublished.

124. Roosevelt, *Countercoup;* Roosevelt garbles the names in his book, but there is no question he means the Rashidians.

125. Mark J. Gasiorowski, "The 1953 Coup d'état in Iran," *International Journal of Middle East Studies,* August 1987, p. 274. Kashani published a letter he allegedly sent Mussadiq warning him of the Anglo-American coup plan. For the text, see *Keyhan Havai,* August 7, 1985. For further evidence of Kashani's involvement, see Suroosh Irfani, *Iran's Islamic Revolution: Popular Liberation or Religious Dictatorship?* (London: Zed Books, 1983), p. 78.

126. See the "confessions" of E. Tabari in *Keyhan Havai,* August 7, 1985, for a particularly bitter denunciation of the Tudeh in which he accepts the authenticity of Kashani's accusation of Mussadiq.

## *Chapter 4. Consolidating the Royal Dictatorship*

1. F.O. 371/104659, August 18, 1953.

2. These figures are based on the calculations of Mark J. Gasiorowski, "U.S. Foreign Policy and the Client State: Implications for Domestic Politics and Long Term U.S. Interests in Iran," Ph.D. diss., University of North Carolina, 1984.

3. Ibid.

4. For a good account of the details of the oil settlement, see George Lenczowski, *Middle East Oil in a Revolutionary Age* (Washington, D.C.: American Enterprise Institute, 1976).

5. Gasiorowski, "U.S. Foreign Policy and the Client State," p. 171.

6. F.O. report by Sir Roger Makins, undated 1953, unnumbered.

7. Richard W. Cottam, *Nationalism in Iran* (Pittsburgh, Pa.: University of Pittsburgh Press, 1979), p. 171.

8. Gasiorowski, "U.S. Foreign Policy and the Client State," p. 171.

9. For a discussion of Tudeh political activities in the military, see Sepehr Zabih, *The Communist Movement in Iran* (Berkeley and Los Angeles: University of California Press, 1966). Concerning the demographics of Tudeh membership in the military, see Ervan Abrahamian, *Iran: Between Two Revolutions* (Princeton, N.J.: Princeton University Press, 1982), pp. 337–38.

10. George Kennan, *Russia, the Atom and the West* (New York: Harper, 1958).

11. See Miles Copeland, *The Game of Nations: The Amorality of Power Politics* (London: Weidenfield and Nicolson, 1969).

12. For a development of this theme, see Richard Cottam, "The United States in Palestine," in *The Transformation of Palestine,* ed. Ibrahim Abu Lughod (Chicago: Northwestern University Press, 1971).

13. Among the few books even to discuss this important episode is Patrick Seale, *The Struggle for Syria* (London: Oxford University Press, 1965), pp. 289–96.

14. Cottam, *Nationalism in Iran.*

15. Ibid.

16. Cottam, "Political Party Development in Iran," *Iranian Studies* 1 (Summer 1968): 3.

17. See Foreign Service Despatch no. 698, May 3, 1960, for the U.S. embassy's summary of the political situation.

18. Mohammad Reza Pahlavi, *Answer to History* (New York: Stein and Day, 1980).

19. See Gasiorowski, "U.S. Foreign Policy and the Client State," p. 152.

20. Abrahamian, *Iran: Between Two Revolutions,* pp. 422–24.

21. Ibid.

22. Cottam, *Nationalism in Iran,* p. 305.

23. Interviews with Hassan Arsenjani, fall 1956, Tehran.

24. Eric Hooglund, *Reform and Revolution in Rural Iran* (Austin: University of Texas Press, 1982, p. 44.

25. *New York Times,* June 10, 1963.

26. For the U.S. embassy account, see Bureau of Intelligence and Research memorandum, RHA, June 26, 1963.

27. Ibid.

28. Mehdi Bazargan has described this in *Enqellab e Iran dar do Harekat* (Tehran, Sanduq Pesati, 1984).

29. For a discussion of the shah as decision maker, see Robert Graham, *Iran: The Illusion of Power* (New York: St. Martin's, 1979, ch. 4).

30. See Shahram Chubin and Sepehr Zabih, *The Foreign Relations of Iran* (Berkeley and Los Angeles: University of California Press, 1974). This is a central thesis of the book.

31. These are well developed in Graham, *Iran: The Illusion of Power,* ch. 7.

32. For a full description of economic achievements, see Jehangir Amuzegar, *Iran: An Economic Profile* (Washington, D.C.: Middle East Institute, 1977).

33. See the Bureau of Intelligence and Research memorandum, RHA June 26, 1963.

34. For a good summary of the overall security apparatus, see Graham, *Iran: The Illusion of Power,* ch. 8.

35. This picture emerged from an interview with Iranian students studying at the American University of Beirut, May 1971.

36. See Hooglund, *Reform and Revolution in Rural Iran;* and Farhad Kazemi, *Poverty and Revolution in Iran* (New York: New York University Press, 1980).

37. See the discussion in Abrahamian, *Iran: Between Two Revolutions,* pp. 439–46.

38. For the best articulation of the shah's mood, see Oriana Fallaci, "The Shah of Iran," *New Republic* 217 (September 1, 1973): 18.

39. Cottam, *Nationalism in Iran,* p. 347.

40. See Fallaci, "The Shah of Iran."

41. Michael Hillman, *Iranian Society: An Anthology of Writings by Jalal al Ahmad* (Dublin, Ohio: Mazda, 1982).

42. This is abundantly clear in the U.S. Department of State, "National Policy Paper: Iran," February 2, 1967.

43. See ibid.

44. For example, see the extravagant rhetoric during the Teng Ying Chao visit to Iran in December 1977 (Peking Radio, December 2, 1977, recorded in United States FBIS, China, December 2, 1977).

45. Pahlavi, *Answer to History.* pp. 131–33.

46. For Khrushchev's attitude, see *New York Times,* February 27, 1959, 7:5.

47. Fallaci, "The Shah of Iran."

48. The shah makes clear these aspirations in Mohammad Reza Pahlavi, *Toward the Great Civilization* (Tehran: Imperial Pahlavi Library, 1976).

49. Henry Kissinger, *The White House Years* (Boston: Little Brown, 1979), pp. 1258–65; Henry Kissinger, *Years of Upheaval* (Boston: Little Brown, 1982), pp. 667–76.

50. Henry Kissinger, *The White House Years,* p. 1262.

51. Chubin and Zabih, *Foreign Relations of Iran,* pp. 310–12.

52. *New York Times,* March 12, 1975, 47:2.

53. Nikki R. Keddie, "The Minorities Question in Iran," in *The Iran Iraq War: New Weapons, Old Conflicts* (New York: Praeger, 1983), p. 101; Gerrard de Velliers, *The Imperial Shah* (Boston: Little, Brown, 1976), pp. 245–47.

54. See U.S. Department of State, "National Policy Paper: Iran." For a summary analysis of reporting on Iran, see INR document no. 486, "Political Intelligence Issues," September 11, 1981.

55. U.S. Intelligence report no. 416, "Adequacy of Political Intelligence Contacts with Oppostion Elements," September 1981.

56. Kissinger, *Years of Upheaval,* p. 669.

57. See for example the *New York Times,* August 26, 1977, 8:2; and October 9, 1977, 1:1.

58. *Village Voice,* February 16, 1976, p. 85.

59. Ibid.

60. Richard Cottam, "The Case of the Kurds," presented at the annual meeting of the American Political Science Association, Washington, D.C., 1977, p. 34.

61. For a brief discussion of this episode, see Fred Halliday, *Arabia Without Sultans* (New York: Random House, 1974), pp. 316–73.

62. Kissinger, *The White House Years,* ch. 21.

63. Ibid., p. 911.

64. Kissinger, *Years of Upheaval,* p. 675.

65. Ibid., pp. 673–74.

66. Chubin and Zabih, *The Foreign Relations of Iran,* p. 245.

## Chapter 5. The Collapse of the Shah

1. Oriana Fallaci, "The Shah of Iran," *New Republic* 217 (September 1, 1973): 18.

2. Robert Graham, *Iran: The Illusion of Power* (New York: St. Martin's, 1979), ch. 3.

3. Zbigniew Brzezinski, *Power and Principle: Memoirs of the National Security Adviser, 1977–1981* (New York: Farrar, Straus, and Giroux, 1983), pp. 124–29.

4. Mohammad Reza Pahlavi, *Answer to History* (New York: Stein and Day, 1980), pp. 164–65, 170.

5. Richard W. Cottam, "Arms Sales and Human Rights: The Case of Iran," in *Human Rights and U.S. Foreign Policy,* ed. Peter G. Browne and Douglas MacLean (Lexington, Mass.: Heath, 1979), pp. 281–302.

6. For some texts of letters, see "Letters from the Great Prison: An Eyewitness Account of Human and Social Conditions in Iran," Washington, D.C.: n.p., 1978; and articles in *Nezhat,* the publication of the Radical Movement of Iran.

7. See for example *Iran Free Press,* published in Washington, D.C., in this period.

8. Mehdi Bazargan, *Enqellab e Iran dar do Harekat* (Tehran, 1984).

9. For a brief but pointed picture of Shariati, see Abduaziz Sachedina, "Ali Shariati: Ideologue of the Iranian Revolution," in *Voices of Resurgent Islam,* ed. John L. Esposito (New York: Oxford University Press, 1983).

10. William H. Sullivan, *Mission to Iran* (New York: Morton, 1981).

11. See the testimony of Charles Nass, "Human Rights in Iran," hearings of the Subcommittee on International Organizations, House International Relations Committee, October 16, 1977.

12. Neither Brzezinski nor Gary Sick mentions the letter in their accounts of their experiences: see Brzezinski, *Power and Principle;* Gary Sick, *All Fall Down: America's Tragic Encounter with Iran* (New York: Random House, 1985).

13. The common assumption in Tehran was that it had been written by Minister of Information Dariush Homayoun. See John D. Stempel, *Inside the Iranian Revolution* (Bloomington: Indiana University Press, 1981), p. 133.

14. Brzezinski, *Power and Principle,* p. 368.

15. See Imam Khomeini, *Islam and Revolution,* trans. and annotated by Hamid Algar (Berkeley, Calif.: Mizan Press, 1981). Much of this picture is based on my interview with Khomeini in France, December 1978.

16. Pahlavi, *Answer to History,* p. 165. For the U.S. Labor party view, see Robert Dryfuss, *Hostage to Khomeini* (New York: New Benjamin, 1981).

17. Anthony Parsons, *The Pride and the Fall: Iran 1974–1979* (London: Jonathan Cape, 1984), p. 68.

18. See Abuhassan Bani Sadr, *Khianat bar Amid* (Paris, 1983).

19. Parsons, *The Pride and the Fall,* p. 113.

20. The details of the plan were given me by one of its chief architects, Bahram Bahramian.

21. Sullivan, *Mission to Iran.*

22. INR report no. 704, "The Future of Iran: Implications for the US," January 28, 1977, p. 1.

23. INR document III E(2)-14, September 1, 1978. The dispatches published by

the Iranian captors of the U.S. embassy give a good picture of the embassy view. There was an awareness of a burgeoning opposition, but a poor understanding of it. No clear analysis of its appears. The embassy was also convinced that the shah could continue on his liberalizing path and had unreasonably high expectations for the Sherif-Imami government. See *Dakhalati Amrika dar Iran* (3, 4, 5), *Esnad Laneh Jasusi* (12, 13) [American Interference in Iran Documents of the Nest of Spies].

24. Stempel, *Inside the Iranian Revolution,* p. 129.

25. Bazargan describes the moment in *Enqellab e Iran dar do Harekat.*

26. Stempel, *Inside the Iranian Revolution,* p. 129. An important dispatch published later by the Iranians who captured the embassy throws much light on this point. Henry Precht, the Iran desk chief in Washington, indicated both his own preference for a transitional plan and his belief that Washington's policy was totally in Brzezinski's hands. Dispatch, December 19, 1978, *Dakhalati Amrika dar Iran* (5) *Esnad Lanen Jasusi* (13).

27. Brzezinski's view of the revolution as to some degree Soviet-orchestrated is somewhat played down in his book. But that was how it was described to me by his opponents in the Department of State. An editor of the *New Republic* told me that Brzezinski had telephoned saying that he agreed completely with the article by Robert Moss, "Who's meddling in Iran?" (*New Republic,* December 2, 1978, pp. 15–18), which does paint exactly such a picture. Brzezinski's attraction to the Moss article is confirmed in Sick, *All Fall Down,* p. 106.

28. Brzezinski, *Power and Principle,* pp. 359–61.

29. Ibid., pp. 371–82.

30. Ibid., p. 361.

31. Ibrahim Yazdi, interview, December 1978, Paris.

32. Parsons, *The Pride and the Fall,* p. 121.

33. Brzezinski, *Power and Principle,* p. 364.

34. Jimmy Carter, *Keeping Faith: Memoirs of a President* (New York: Barton, 1982).

35. Brzezinski, *Power and Principle,* p. 379.

36. Stempel, *Inside the Iranian Revolution,* p. 130.

37. Parsons, *The Pride and the Fall,* pp. 98–100.

38. This description is based on my visit with and interview of Beheshti, December 19, 1978, Tehran.

39. Parsons, *The Pride and the Fall,* pp. 113–17. Parsons favored this approach and gives a rationale for it.

40. See Alexander Bover, "Iran: Consequences and Reasons," *Literaturnaya Gazeta,* October 25, 1978, FBIS, November 1, 1978.

41. See for example the National Voice of Iran broadcast of January 6, 1979, FBIS, January 8, 1979.

42. Tass, November 23, 1978, has a discussion of the elements of the revolution. The clerical group is coupled as "rightist," the liberals as "bourgeois" (FBIS, November 19, 1978).

43. *Pravda,* November 19, 1978, FBIS, November 19, 1978.

44. Tehran Radio Domestic Service, February 9, 1979, FBIS, February 9, 1979.

45. I attended a meeting of the Iranian Committee on Human Rights and Liberty in late December 1978 and heard a full evaluation of the Bakhtiar proposal.

46. On the Huyser mission, see Sick, *All Fall Down;* Brzezinski, *Power and Principle.*

47. Sick, *All Fall Down,* p. 156.

## Chapter 6. The Rhythm of the Revolution

1. Mehdi Bazargan, *Surai Enqellab va Dolat Movaqat* (Tehran: Sanduq Pesati, 1984), pp. 35–40.

2. Ibid., pp. 18–24.

3. Mohammad Modir-Shanetchi, interview, May 1984, Paris.

4. For an excellent account of the dynamics of the revolution, see Shaul Bakhash, *The Reign of the Ayatullahs* (New York: Basic Books, 1984).

5. Imam Khomeini, *Islam and Revolution,* trans. and annotated by Hamid Algar (Berkeley, Calif.: Mizan Press, 1981).

6. Bazargan, *Enqellab e Iran dar do Harekat* (Tehran, 1984); Oriana Fallaci, "Everybody Wants to Be Boss," *New York Times Magazine,* October 28, 1979.

7. Bakhash, *The Reign of the Ayatullahs,* p. 75.

8. See the following interviews with Kianuri in this period: *Horizont* (East Berlin), no. 9 (1979): 11, FBIS, March 11, 1979; *L'Humanité* (Paris), April 4, 1979, FBIS, April 1, 1979; *Horizont* (East Berlin), no. 16 (1979): 14–15, FBIS, April 24, 1979; *Unsere Zeit* (East Germany), FBIS, April 23, 1979.

9. See *L'Unità* (Milan), September 20, 1979, FBIS, September 25, 1979.

10. National Voice of Iran, November 11, 1980, FBIS, November 13, 1980.

11. Interviews with a group of leading royalist exiles, May 1984, Nice, France.

12. "Brzezinski, the Ally of the So-called Struggling Moslems of Afghanistan," National Voice of Iran, February 5, 1980, FBIS, February 12, 1980.

13. Tehran Domestic Service, April 2, 1979, FBIS, April 3, 1979.

14. See for example Tehran Domestic Service, March 29, 1979, FBIS, March 30, 1979.

15. Ibrahim Yazdi, interview, September 1979, New York.

16. *New York Times,* May 19, 1979, 4:3.

17. On the shah's admission to the United States for treatment, see Gary Sick, *All Fall Down: America's Tragic Encounter with Iran* (New York: Random, 1985), pp. 176–86.

18. Unpublished letter to the editors by Rahmatollah Moqadam Maraghei'i.

19. In December 1979 I met in Tehran with Qotbzadeh, a friend of twenty years' standing, and had several long discussions with him. For the next twelve months of the hostage crisis I spoke with him by telephone often daily and at least weekly. The statements and interpretations attributed to him in this chapter are based on these extended discussions.

20. Mehdi Bazargan, interview, December 1979, Tehran.

21. Abuhassan Bani Sadr, *Khianat bar Amid* (Paris, 1983).

22. On the election, see Bakhash, *The Reign of the Ayatullahs,* p. 75.

23. Zbigniew Brzezinski, *Power and Principle: Memoirs of the National Security Adviser, 1977–1981* (New York: Farrar, Straus, and Giroux, 1983), pp. 477–84.

24. See Tehran International Service, February 12, 1980, FBIS, February 13, 1980.

25. This is particularly apparent in Jimmy Carter, *Keeping Faith: Memoirs of a President* (New York: Barton, 1982).

26. See "Qotbzadeh Addresses Islamic Conference," *Pars* (Tehran), May 20, 1980, FBIS, May 21, 1980.

27. Hal Saunders, "The Crisis Begins" and "Beginning of the End," in *American Hostages in Iran: The Conduct of a Crisis,* ed. Warren Christopher et al. (New Haven, Conn.: Yale University Press, 1985).

28. Qotbzadeh's view provides the main theses of Pierre Salinger, *America Held Hostage: The Secret Negotiations* (Garden City, N.Y.: Doubleday, 1981), and Hamilton Jordan, *Crisis: the Last Year of the Carter Presidency* (New York: G.P. Putnam's Sons, 1982). Sick's *All Fall Down,* on the other hand, reflects an opposing and skeptical view of Qotbzadeh's strategy.

29. Saunders, "The Crisis Begins" and "Beginning of the End."

30. Jordan, *Crisis,* p. 230.

31. Gary Sick, "Military Options and Constraints," in *American Hostages in Iran,* ed. Christopher et al.

32. FBIS, April 28, 1980.

33. See Khomeini's speech to the nation, February 11, 1983, FBIS, February 15, 1983.

34. Sick, *All Fall Down;* Carter, *Keeping Faith;* and Jordan, *Crisis,* all present the same view of a dismayed U.S. reaction to the invasion.

35. A most revealing speech by Tareq Aziz is reprinted in Tareq Y. Ismail, *Iraq and Iran: Roots of the Conflict* (Syracuse, N.Y.: Syracuse University Press, 1983), pp. 89–100.

36. Ibid.

37. In a Paris press conference, September 25, 1980, Tariq Aziz said the people of "Arabistan" would decide their own future (FBIS, September 26, 1980). But the line followed by Baghdad Radio made very clear the major play by the Iraqi regime on treating "Arabistan" as part of the Arab nation of which Saddam Hossein was, in the words of one citizen of Arabistan whom the radio quoted, "the great leader." See for this very strong propaganda line, for example, Baghdad Domestic Service, September 21, 1980, FBIS, September 22, 1980.

38. David B. Tinnin, "Iraq and the New Arab Alliance," *Fortune* 102 (November 3, 1980): 44–46.

39. The conspiracy thesis is fully developed in a speech by Speaker of the Majlis Hojatolislam Hashemi Rafsenjani, February 25, 1983.

40. Ibid.

41. See the statement of Foreign Minister Ali Akbar Velayeti, *Ettelaat,* March 4, 1982.

42. Jordan, *Crisis,* p. 341.

43. Qotbzadeh described these activities to me over open telephone lines in the summer and fall of 1980.

44. Tehran Domestic Service, "Supreme Defense Council Statement," November 7, 1980, FBIS, November 10, 1980.

45. For a good example, see Bani Sadr's reaction to the hostage release in *Enqellab Islam,* January 15, 1981.

46. Telephone conversation with Qotbzadeh, December 1980.

47. Tehran Domestic Service, December 17, 1983, FBIS, December 19, 1983.

48. See "List of Names and Particulars of 10,300 Victims of the Khomeini Re-

gime's Executions," compiled and published by the People's Mujahedin Organization of Iran, 1984.

49. One prominent Iranian exile told me of a message sent him by President Khamenei in Iran to the effect that he could not protect him from Reyshari and Mohammedi Gilani and thus implying that he should flee the country (interview, May 1984, Paris).

50. National Voice of Iran, October 12, 1983, FBIS, October 13, 1983; December 9, 1983, FBIS, December 13, 1983.

51. National Voice of Iran, September 20, 1983, FBIS, September 22, 1983.

52. For a brief picture of internal security officials in Iran, see Shahrough Akhavi, "The Power Structure in the Islamic Republic of Iran, in *Internal Development in Iran,* ed. Shireen Hunter, Significant Issues Series vol. 7, no. 3, Center for Strategic and International Studies, Georgetown University, 1985.

53. For a succinct but comprehensive summary of the economic situation in Iran, see Djavad Salehi-Isphahani, "The Iranian Economy Since the Revolution," in ibid.

54. For an excellent journalistic account of Sharon's thinking, see Ze'ev Schiff and Ehud Ya'ari, *Israel's Lebanon War* (New York: Simon and Schuster, 1984).

55. *New York Times,* April 2, 1985, 1:3.

56. For a good summary analysis of U.S. policy, see Seth P. Tillman, *The United States in the Middle East: Interests and Obstacles* (Bloomington: Indiana University Press, 1982).

57. *Report of the President's Special Review Board,* February 19, 1987 (Tower Commission).

58. *New York Times,* November 11, 1986, 1:6.

59. *New York Times,* December 4, 1986, 14:1.

60. See the statements of Hashemi-Rafsanjani and Ayatullah Khomeini, FBIS, Near East and South Asia, August 3, 1987. For North's statement regarding the necessity of removing Saddam Hossein, see *Report of the President's Special Review Board,* III-18.

61. Hashemi-Rafsanjani was asked in an interview if Iran would ask for Soviet help in the event of a U.S. invasion. He replied that no help would be necessary. FBIS, Near East and south Asia, September 9, 1987. Tehran commentaries throughout the fall of 1987 mentioned only U.S. culpability; see ibid., October 6, 1987.

## Chapter 7. A Cold War Case Study

1. Hans J. Morgenthau, *Politics Among Nations,* 5th ed. (New York: Knopf, 1972).

2. On the diabolical enemy stereotype, see Richard Cottam, *Foreign Policy Motivation* (Pittsburgh, Pa.: University of Pittsburgh Press, 1977).

# INDEX

## PITT SERIES IN POLICY AND INSTITUTIONAL STUDIES
*Bert A. Rockman, Editor*